A BRIGHT AND
BLINDING SUN

Also by Marcus Brotherton

Nonfiction

Blaze of Light

Shifty's War

A Company of Heroes

We Who Are Alive and Remain

Call of Duty (with Lt. Buck Compton)

Voices of the Pacific (with Adam Makos)

The Nightingale of Mosul (with Col. Susan Luz)

Tough As They Come (with SSG Travis Mills)

Grateful American (with Gary Sinise)

Fiction

Feast for Thieves

A BRIGHT AND BLINDING SUN

A WORLD WAR II STORY OF SURVIVAL, LOVE, AND REDEMPTION

MARCUS BROTHERTON

Little, Brown and Company

New York Boston London

Little, Brown and Company
Hachette Book Group
1290 Avenue of the Americas, New York, NY 10104
littlebrown.com

First Edition: May 2022

Little, Brown and Company is a division of Hachette Book Group, Inc. The Little, Brown name and logo are trademarks of Hachette Book Group, Inc.

The publisher is not responsible for websites (or their content) that are not owned by the publisher.

The Hachette Speakers Bureau provides a wide range of authors for speaking events. To find out more, go to hachettespeakersbureau.com or call (866) 376-6591.

Map by Pamela Fogle

ISBN 9780316318914
LCCN 2021947483

10 9 8 7 6 5 4 3 2 1

MRQ-T

Printed in Canada

Everything I understand, I understand because I love.

—Tolstoy

Contents

Contents

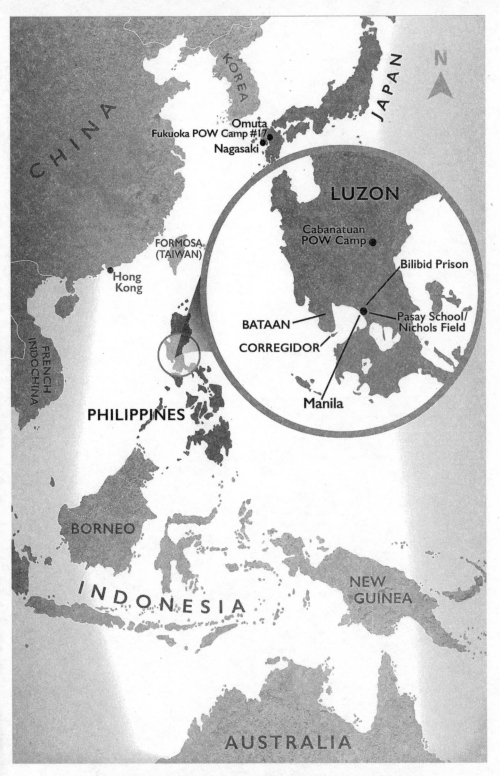

THE PHILIPPINES/EAST ASIA IN WORLD WAR II

PART I

I was in a whorehouse in Manila, trying to steal a prostitute, when I was fifteen years old.

It was a shit night, I remember. Rain's beating a steady rat-tat-tat on the roof. Last Saturday of September 1941. War ain't broke out yet for us. There I was, top of this old wooden staircase, peering down the dusky hallway into the gloom. Whole place smells like cheap perfume and an old Army boot.

I says to the lady, "She still here?"

Mama Rosa's her name—the madam—and she knows exactly which girl I'm talking about. Mama Rosa's a big heavy lady with huge bosoms who works all the girls at the joint. But she doesn't own the place, right? That's a thug named Manny Tang. I only met him once—him and his goons. You cross Manny Tang and he'll slit your throat. But anyways I says to Mama Rosa, "I'd like to take her out on the balcony first, for a bit, if that's fine by you." I give her my dollar.

"I'll go get her," Mama Rosa says, her voice all sugar. "Don't be outside for long. It's too cold for the girl tonight."

Couple minutes later, the girl comes out of one of the bedrooms, being led by the madam. Perpetua's her name, and damn if she ain't beautiful as always. Slender. Short. Wearing this thin gown with a ropey shawl across her shoulders. Whole face beams when she sees me. I hug her tight, and she hugs me right back.

Mama Rosa turns away so she can attend to another soldier, and I lead Perpetua by the hand toward the balcony. There I glance over my shoulder and see that Mama Rosa's disappeared into the dark again at the far end of the hall.

That's our chance.

Real gentle, I place my finger across Perpetua's lips and say,

"Follow me." Her eyes grow wide. I whisk her toward the back door, and before she can say a word we're climbing down the rickety steps that lead to the alley behind the brothel. An old Filipino driver is standing there, where my buddy Frisco had arranged for him to meet us. Driver has a calesa—one of those little one-horse-carriage things. I get Perpetua aboard, then climb in next to her. The driver gives the pony a click and a hiss and we're off. But Perpetua's shaking. Shivering. Wet from the rain.

"What's happening?" she whispers. "This isn't allowed."

"Don't be afraid," I say. "You want to go, right?"

She nods.

"Everything's set. You won't have to work there no more."

Her whole body's trembling, and I wrap my arms around her to keep her warm. The pony's clip-clopping down the street at a fast trot. At most, we have twenty minutes before Mama Rosa discovers she's gone.

"I can't leave," Perpetua says to me. "The streets have eyes."

"You'll be safe," I say. "Promise."

She starts to cry, and I hug her closer. Rain's pelting us now, hammering the canopy of the calesa. Water pouring in from front and sides. We're getting soaked. Hushed, our driver hurries us through the city to this tall, brick building near the base. It's got a big wrought-iron fence around it. I tap the driver on the shoulder, and the calesa stops. I help Perpetua out. Driver clucks his tongue again and hurries away.

My heart's beating like a jackhammer. Me and Perpetua are standing in front of the building's tall steel doors, and I bang against the door with the flat of my hand. Once. Twice. Three times, all in sequence. I pause. Then bang one more time. That was the knock, see? The one I'd arranged.

But no one's coming.

"C'mon, c'mon, c'mon," I mutter. "Answer the damn door."

I bang the sequence again. This dog starts barking—gonna wake the whole neighborhood. I see a porch light flicker on down the street. We're caught for sure, and I don't know what to do. I'm looking this way and that, tense as a steel rod, positive I'm gonna see Manny Tang spring at us with his knife. Bracing myself to fight back. Hell—

Perpetua was only fourteen.

No bullshit. The world can be a broken place, my friend, and it took me a while to understand that. She made some regrettable choices, and she had her reasons. Weren't many options back then for a young girl with no family, no support. Your stomach gets empty for long, and you get desperate. I made my share of regrettable choices too, and I made a few of them with Perpetua at the start. Every damn one of us needs redemption. It took me a while to come around, to wise up, to see that Perpetua was important. She might've been a teenage prostitute halfway around the world, but she was important. Besides, I wasn't saving her. She was saving me.

Now, I didn't know if I'd die that night in the rain with the door not opened to us. But if you're a soldier you got to be willing to die for the folks you're called to protect. Looking back on it all now, I can't say I was always willing. I ain't no hero. Neither then nor now. Scrapes I been in. No way I should've been in the Army at my age, and no way I should've been inside a whorehouse in the first place. No way any kid like me should've been standing up to what was coming next for all of us—civilians and soldiers alike—full invasion of the country by Imperial Japan. And after the Philippines fell, well...when a boy grows up in a prisoner-of-war camp—working as slave labor for one of the most vicious enemies the world has ever known—a lot changes for him on the road to becoming a man.

You ask: How had I gotten myself into this trouble?

How did I ever manage to survive?

Folks have told me my story is one for the ages. One that sounds so far-fetched you have trouble believing it's real. But it ain't fiction. Every damn bit of it happened. If you're gonna read about me, you should start at the beginning. It's a survival story and love story like no other.

CHAPTER 1

Little Bird Walking

Memphis, 1933

From the front of the classroom, the teacher calls his name in a firm, chirpy voice. The boy is seven years old and doesn't move, though he feels a sudden urge to pee. Parents, grandparents, and students shift in their seats and stare at the boy. Each child has written an original poem. His turn has come to recite for the audience, and he is proud of his poem, but his resolve has vanished, his legs locked as if in irons. His teacher calls his name again.

"Joseph Johnson. Joe?"

One drop. Two. His underwear dampens. The boy squeezes his thighs together while his eyes dart back and forth, searching for escape. The door to the hallway is shut tight. The chalk-dusted walls of the second-grade classroom at Christine Elementary School are wainscoted with hard yellow pine. Someone coughs. The boy's attention snaps back to his teacher. She is tapping her foot. He wills himself to stand, walks to the front, and faces the crowd.

At the back of the classroom, Joe's mother, Edna, leans forward in her hard-back chair and fidgets with her pocketbook.

Next to her sits Joe's aunt Ethel. His father has been gone from the family for three years. Edna lays her pocketbook flat on her knees, folds her hands on top, and beams toward her son.

Joe shifts his weight from one foot to another. His mouth stays frozen. The teacher's voice is cheerful yet urgent. "Tell us the name of your poem, dear." But stage fright has overtaken the boy. She prompts again. "The title, Joe. What's your poem called?"

For one long moment he stands speechless in front of the audience, his mouth gluey, his heart hammering, then he blurts: " 'The Little Bird.' " And begins to read, "Once there was a little bird...." And stops, because no more words will come. Seconds tick by like forever. Finally the teacher speaks again.

"And what was the little bird doing, dear?"

Joe tries to read beyond the first line of his poem, but his eyes blur and he cannot connect to the page's print. He knows he needs to say something. Anything. Finally he glances toward his teacher and without reading further answers her in a high, quavering voice, "He was walking down the road, just walking down the road!"

His classmates burst into laughter. So do some of the parents. Joe looks out into the sea of staring eyes and sees his mother and aunt burying their faces in their hands. Whether to keep from crying with embarrassment or laughing, he never knows.

Joe shakes his head, drops his chin, returns to his seat. His mother pats him on the shoulder but the damage is already done. In that flicker of a moment, a seed finds root in his heart, a vow he points toward himself and much later learns to identify as resolve. *Never again,* he thinks.

Never again give in to fear.

Joe's upbringing is shaped not only by the Depression, but by the hardships of an absent father—his dad went looking for work when Joe was four and never returned. By 1938, when Joe is in sixth grade, his mother has grown lonely. Sometimes at home Joe discovers her crying. She is tall and slim with long legs and beautiful golden plaited hair. Every morning she leaves the house at 6 a.m. and rides a streetcar across the city to her job with the Works Progress Administration. Rent is ten dollars a month, and she earns ten dollars a week at her job sewing flour sacks into dresses. Sometimes she can't make rent, and when the landlord comes around to collect, the family hides in the middle room of their three-room shotgun duplex until he leaves.

Each night after work Edna returns at 6 p.m., exhausted. By then Joe has returned from school, done his homework, chopped wood, carried coal, looked after his two younger siblings, put on a pot of beans, fried up a batch of hot-water corn bread, and made up the beds. They're a team. Joe's a responsible boy and a good student. His favorite subjects are history and geography. A music teacher encourages him to appreciate classical music and has him memorize the words to "La Marseillaise," the French national anthem. Joe sings it word for word with gusto. His favorite composers become Borodin and Rimsky-Korsakov. He devours books and dreams of great things ahead, but life's hardships are holding him down.

One family ritual is never overlooked, poignant in its display of austerity. On a blustery Saturday evening, Joe stokes the coal-oil stove in the duplex, heats water in pots and pans, and ladles it into a large washtub in the middle of the kitchen floor. The duplex has no designated bathroom, although a plumbed commode sits in a planked-off area on the back porch. Joe leaves the kitchen and shivers. The March wind blows cold outside, and the rest of the house is chilly. A few chunks of coal smolder in an open fireplace in the middle room, where the beds are kept. He moves closer to the fireplace, where his younger siblings linger in the warmth, and turns his back to his mother while waiting his turn. Edna steps out of her simple dress and underthings in the kitchen, stands with goose-pimpled skin in the radiant heat of the stove, then slides into the hot soapy washtub for her weekly bath.

She has borrowed a red dress from her neighbor, a black woman, because races mix without qualms in this part of Memphis's sooty slums. When Edna's bath is finished, she dons the borrowed dress, bundles into her old coat, gives her children a finger wave, and heads to a nearby beer joint, where she quickly sheds the poverty of her outer layer and smiles at the proprietor, a one-legged man named Mr. Jake.

Meanwhile at home, Joe heads into the kitchen and strips, dips himself into the same water, and sighs with anticipated pleasure. Joe is thin and bony, with brown eyes and a shock of dusky hair that hangs over his forehead. He can't afford hair oil, so each Monday morning he rubs lard on his palms, then smears it through his hair to keep it slicked in place. By Wednesday of each week, his hair smells. Kids at school wrinkle their noses when he walks down the hallway. Joe is embarrassed by the odor. Each week, he can't wait until his Saturday-night bath. When he is finished, his little brother, Charlie, jumps into the same water. The water is dirty and tepid by the time their little sister, Betty, takes her turn. Coal oil is required to heat fresh water, and coal oil costs money.

Joe's mother stays out late in the loud jukebox evening. Elegant on a barstool, she taps out a long cigarette from a pack of

Chesterfields, inserts the tip into her mouth, and leans across the counter so Mr. Jake can light it for her. He obliges with a smile. Anytime young Joe is out walking in the neighborhood, he searches for clean, discarded name-brand cigarette packages. Edna buys tobacco for a nickel a pouch at the grocery store. Joe rolls her cigarettes on the kitchen table using a hand-operated rolling machine. He trims the ends neatly with scissors and carefully places the cigarettes in whatever clean package he last found. He knows his mother likes to look stylish.

Mr. Jake takes care of Edna's hamburger and beers, even though he is married. His wife is not happy that her husband is offering free food and drinks to a divorced woman, and tonight's free meal is not the first Edna has received at the joint. Edna comes home half-tipsy, and Joe hears her stumble in the early hours of Sunday morning. Mr. Jake and his wife live on top of the beer joint with their three sons. On Sunday afternoon the husband and wife argue fiercely, and she kicks him out of the house. Mr. Jake tells himself he has nowhere to go. On Sunday night he knocks on the door of the Johnsons' duplex and asks to come in.

Edna has met other men at the beer joint. Most drink too much, and once in a while a fellow walks her home, and she needs to fight him off at the front door. But Edna likes Mr. Jake's look, so they start going together. Late that first Monday afternoon when Joe comes home from school, he discovers the new arrangement. He slips out the door into the backyard and throws rocks at the coal shed for hours, muttering under his breath until he can throw no more.

———

For the next several months Joe tries to live like nothing's changed, even though he knows it's a lie. Mr. Jake's wife has commandeered the beer joint, so he is now out of work. His three sons go to the same school that Joe attends now—Humes, a combination middle school and high school that later becomes famous for graduating a young warbler named Elvis Presley. Mr. Jake's sons harass Joe and spread playground rumors that his mother has broken up their once-happy home. Joe can't decide whether the boys are louts or if they're simply as despondent as he is.

For the time being, he shrugs off the allegations. He needs to focus on his work. School lets out, and the hot, sticky Tennessee summer begins. Every two weeks he pulls his wagon to the city auditorium to pick up surplus government food. Edna qualifies because of her low income. Refrigeration and storage are a problem at the auditorium, and the food's never anyone's first choice. Joe brings back rancid butter, wilted apples and cabbages, dried milk and flour crawling with weevils. Neighborhood kids taunt him on the walk home.

Fortunately, Edna finds a union job at RKO Pictures, inspecting movie reels for damage when they're returned to the studio from theaters around the mid-South. The new job comes with better pay, so Edna moves them a block up the street to a house with two bedrooms and a bath. She and Mr. Jake take one bedroom. The children sleep three to a bed in the other.

One Saturday morning, as usual, Joe stands outside the grocery store with his wagon along with other neighborhood kids, all hoping some kindhearted homemaker will take pity on them and choose a child to haul home her groceries. A good tip is a dime. A lousy tip is a nickel. An even worse tip is a cookie and half a glass of milk. Joe knows the best tippers and has high hopes. He makes two trips with his wagon and earns fifteen cents. When the day grows long, he talks to the grocer to see if he has a loaf of day-old bread to give away. Edna likes her work sandwiches made with bread. If there's no bread, Edna will make sandwiches with biscuits—but biscuit sandwiches get old, she complains to Joe more than once.

On the way home from the grocer with two stale loaves under his arm, Joe heads to the railroad yard and hunts for coal along the tracks. A worker yells at him for trespassing and chases him out of the yard. Joe waits in the shadows until the worker disappears. He slips back inside and keeps scrounging until his wagon is full.

He likes being the man of the family and doesn't like Mr. Jake lounging around. Often they argue, and the friction between the boy and the newcomer only grows. Mr. Jake looks for a job, but it's the Great Depression, and jobs are as scarce as hen's teeth.

Seventh grade begins for Joe in the fall of 1938, and Mr. Jake's three sons start up their needling again. Joe feels harassed from every side. His mother won't listen to him, if ever he tries to explain his feelings. Mr. Jake's no help. They're arguing nonstop now. Edna tells Joe to simmer down; Mr. Jake's not going anywhere. To top things off, little Charlie has begun to wet the shared bed nearly every night. A faraway thought begins to invade Joe's mind and take shape: *Surely my family would be better off without me.*

His Aunt Ethel has moved to San Antonio along with others from the extended Johnson family. Joe keeps Ethel's address stuffed deep in a pocket. The person he really wants to find is his father, a carefree wanderer who collects silver dollars to give away and works as an itinerant horse trainer and sometime commercial chef. He's been known to kill a fifth of whiskey like it was Coca-Cola, but Joe remembers him with fondness. The father has disappeared. Maybe Aunt Ethel will know his last location.

Early one morning in late fall 1938, without telling a soul, instead of heading for school, Joe makes a beeline for the railroad yard. He finds an empty boxcar heading toward southwest Texas, looks both ways, and jumps aboard.

Joe Johnson is twelve years old and venturing into the great unknown, as blind and unsuspecting about where the road will lead him as that little bird walking.

CHAPTER 2

Last Days of Boyhood

All that day and into the evening, the train moves in a headlong rush. Joe huddles in a corner of the boxcar, wondering how he will know he's arrived in Texas, watching his new world through a hole in the worn-wood slats. Memphis and the Mississippi River have vanished ages ago, replaced by the pine bluffs and chalky valleys of Arkansas. Every so often the train slows to a crawl as it eases into a siding. The boxcar door is flung open. Hobos jump off. Others jump on. Sometimes a wandering man will eye the boy, sizing him up, looking for hints of food or cash, before settling against the far side of the box. Other times the boy is paid no attention. All the men seem driven by private desperations; all are trying to survive unprecedented times.

Joe has read enough news to know the dangers of freight-hopping. Boxcars were never designed to hold people. A few weeks earlier, a young Tennessean named Hoyt Parker lost his grip while attempting to swing onto a southbound train. Shaken and badly bruised, Hoyt was fortunate to walk out of the Chattanooga hospital with only a broken arm. Another young Tennessean who hid on top of a boxcar as it passed through the low-hanging Missionary Ridge tunnel in East Chattanooga wasn't as lucky. His body was crushed too badly to identify.

Joe's stomach growls, and his throat is dry as dust. The slats rattle his back. He wishes he'd grabbed biscuits and a bottle of milk before leaving. He wonders what his mother will do when she discovers he's run away. Joe hates the thought of making her cry. He vows to write as soon as possible—though if he can't find his father, he doesn't know what he'll do. Joe has crafted no further plans. Perhaps he can make a new life for himself in Texas, he thinks—somewhere, somehow. Anywhere but Memphis.

After sundown the train slows again, and Joe's boxcar empties of men. It's time to sleep, and he hopes he will be left alone for the night's ride. The train leaves the station and begins to chug faster, slowly gathering speed. But just when it looks like the boy will get his wish, a man flings a walking stick and knotted kerchief into the car, then hauls himself aboard. He is tree-tall, slate black and rangy, with muscled shoulders, and wearing a coat with ripped sleeves. In the Deep South in 1938, it's not uncommon for whites to view blacks with suspicion, and any number of blacks have good reason to be wary around whites. Joe mixed freely with blacks in his neighborhood in Memphis, but the man is so large that the boy's courage evaporates, particularly as the big man scans the inside of the boxcar with a scowl. His stare drifts over to the boy and locks on. Joe considers his options. The train is running too fast for him to jump.

"Evening," Joe grunts with a nod, hoping a lead of sociability will prevent any violence. The man stays as silent as a sentry. He sits against the wall in the brooding darkness and watches Joe as the hours pass. The boy fears closing his eyes. It is chilly inside the boxcar, growing colder as night deepens, and Joe is shivering. The huge man never slumbers. When the train eases into another siding and slows, a shifty-eyed drifter jumps aboard.

By the glare of a railyard security light, Joe glimpses a knife stuck in his belt. The drifter eyes the large man, then backtracks, jumping from the boxcar into the night as if to wait for easier colleagues. Joe and the big man are alone again, and the train rolls on.

Another dark hour passes. Another. The train is still bearing forward when daylight begins to sift through the slats. Joe catches himself dozing and shakes himself awake. He studies the man more closely. He looks older than Joe first imagined. Flecks of gray wisp his temples. The man is still eyeing him, a sidelong stare from profile. Perhaps he is a predator. Or perhaps he has been standing guard.

Joe clears his throat. "Say…you know where we are, mister?"

All is quiet except for the *clickety-clack* of the wheels along the railway track. A minute runs by. Another. At last the man scratches, stretches, and speaks, his voice cavernous: "Hardships will make you stronger, son. But a boy like you best not ride the trains no more. Ain't safe—least, that's what I say. We're in Texas now. Soon in San Antone. You have kin there?"

"My father," Joe says. He grins, then adds, "Thanks." The boy checks through the hole in the slats and finds new landscapes passing by. Hardwoods and ponds, pastureland and black-eyed Susans. The information about his destination—as well as the unanticipated kindness—lifts the boy's spirits like a sunrise.

———

Joe walks from the San Antonio railyard into the city, stops at the first filling station he sees, and shows the attendant the crumpled paper with the address. The attendant unfolds a map and points. Joe's relatives live clear across town. Joe says thanks and starts to hoof it. He walks all the rest of the day. He has no suitcase to slow him. At suppertime, footsore and parched, he climbs the steps to the address in hand, his grandmother's house. He removes his torn cap and knocks on the front door.

"Lord have mercy!" his Aunt Ethel exclaims from behind the screen. She opens the door, rushes forward with a clatter, and squeezes him tight, hollering backward into the house: "Everybody come quick! Look who showed up."

His grandmother bustles onto the porch along with two aunts and an array of cousins. Fried chicken sizzles on the stove, and the aroma overwhelms the boy. The relatives shift into hospitality gear, rush him to the kitchen table with an order to sit, and plunk down a plateful of supper. Joe busies himself eating and fielding questions. Out of the corner of his eye, he glimpses an aunt head to the phone on the wall, wind the crank, and speak low to the operator. Joe wants to ask about his father's whereabouts, but he can't get a word in edgewise.

An hour passes in the noisy kitchen. Joe's on his third piece of apple pie when he hears the front door bang open. A familiar voice hollers his name. Unmistakable. The boy stands in a rush, then hesitates, the tight hold he's kept over himself the last few days suddenly slackened. His father bursts into the room and grabs the boy in an enormous hug. His father's crying, laughing, shouting. Joe cries too. All the aunts are crying. The whole household is an emotional mess. Joe breathes in the scent of his father's coat, allowing himself to be held like a small child. Then he finds his sturdiness again and hugs his father back.

His father is built like a boxer with a thick neck, big hands, and a broad nose that looks broken. A shingle of dark hair hangs across his forehead, and he wears his hat at a tilt. He asks Joe a few questions, wolfs a plateful of supper, gives his mom a hug goodbye, then drives the boy to Alamo Downs racetrack, about ten miles west of San Antonio.

"It ain't much to look at no more," his father says when they arrive. "C'mon, I'll show you where I live. Stay as long as you like."

In the moonlight, Joe can see the old concrete-and-wood grandstands, home to a thousand quivering bats. The seats are covered with droppings. At least the barns are intact. Joe's father explains the track is used mostly for training these days. Thirty broodmares and one stud are stabled at the track, along with an assemblage of two-year-olds and foals. A local gambler owns the horses, and Joe's dad works for him and stays in one of the tack rooms as part of his keep.

The father waves the boy into the room. He has a two-burner propane stove for cooking and a metal cot for sleeping. Bathing is done outside near a shed by hanging a running hose over a rafter. The father digs another metal cot from storage for Joe. It's late. Father and son are soon flopped on the cots, fast asleep.

Next morning, Joe awakes to the salty smell of frying bacon. His dad is busy at the stove. The father heaps potatoes and pinto beans onto a plate for his son, pours the boy a tin of coffee, plunks bacon on top of the feast. "Gotta put some meat on your bones," he says with a laugh.

The entire morning becomes delightful. Joe's dad shows him how to feed and water the horses, which the boy will do twice a day for chores, as well as muck out the stalls once. He takes him to the goats and shows him how to feed and care for them. He leads Joe over to where a mixed-breed dog is nursing her litter in the hay. Joe eyes the puppies with boyish longing. "Go ahead, pick one," his dad says. Joe's eyes widen. He looks closely, then carefully scoops up the one on the litter's edge. The pup is black and tawny, with floppy ears and a rough pink tongue. "She's all yours," his father adds. Joe nestles the puppy close, laughing with incredulity at the gift.

Father and son eat bread-and-butter sandwiches for lunch, fix fences in the afternoon, and dine on tamales for supper. So begins the best time of Joe's young life. He names his dog Mippy, and she becomes his constant companion. He adjusts quickly to the chore schedule and soon has his favorite foals and mares and pet goats. Before long his father has him up on horses, teaching him how to ride. One evening he remarks that the boy is a natural with animals. "You've got a true gift," the father says. "Someday you'll make a great trainer." The guidance, the manly praise—it's all new to the boy. Joe finds himself flourishing in his father's attention.

The autumn of 1938 passes, and it's not long until Christmas arrives. Joe's mother has been notified where her son is and she mails him a shirt as a present, but it's too small. She doesn't realize how much the boy has grown. In January 1939, Joe turns thirteen. In the spring, Joe's dad teaches him about foaling and breeding, and Joe becomes an old hand around the barn. By early summer the boy gallops horses up and down the back stretch of the old track, riding bareback to get a feel for balance. He befriends a Mexican boy named Chico, whose father works a cattle operation next to the racetrack. Chico keeps a rowdy Airedale named Loco, and in off-hours during the lazy summer, Joe and Chico wander the rolling scrub-oak hills, their dogs by their sides. They flush armadillos and hunt rattlesnakes. Joe has now missed a year of school, but his father hasn't forced the issue. He does mention that Joe will need to begin again in fall. Joe whines that he doesn't want to go.

"You'll do as you're told." His father's voice is surprisingly gruff.

In September, Joe and Chico trudge the two miles to the one-room schoolhouse where they both enroll in eighth grade, even though Joe has completed only a month or so of seventh. The schoolteacher tests Joe and finds him a quick mind and an excellent student when he wants to be—which isn't often. When the weather turns cold, Joe and Chico take turns stoking the old pot-bellied stove in the middle of the schoolroom. The fire gets to blazing, and whenever Joe walks near the stove, his teacher wrinkles her nose. Joe owns only one pair of cowboy boots. He never wears socks. Showering under the cold hose is fun in summertime but not in winter. One December afternoon when Joe sits near the stove, his teacher explodes.

"Joe! This class and I cannot tolerate the smell of your boots any longer. Go home immediately. Bathe. Tell your father to buy you a new pair of boots—and socks. You are not allowed to return until you have them."

Joe hasn't realized his feet are so ripe. He feels embarrassed and peeved. Back at the barn, Joe relates his teacher's message, word for word to his dad, who's busy soaping a halter and shank. The father doesn't answer. A few moments pass, then he mutters, "This weekend we'll go to town. I'll get you a new pair of cowboy boots and a dozen pair of socks. How about that?"

Joe nods, his eyes on his father's work.

His father pauses again, still focused on his task, then asks, "You learning much over there?"

"No," Joe answers. "Reckon I know as much as she does."

Without looking up, his dad snaps, "Then don't go back."

———

A second Christmas passes. In January 1940, Joe turns fourteen. When spring arrives, the balmy Texas winds whorl through the racetrack, fanning dust particles into circles and filling the air with pollen. Joe and his father stay busy with the hard work of breaking yearlings and training two-year-olds. Once again, mares are foaling and new life arrives in the stalls.

One Saturday afternoon, when Joe and his father have a rare hour to themselves, his dad drives the duo into San Antonio in his Chevy, the running boards rusty and dented. They head to the outdoor Mexican market, where the father treats the son to a late lunch cooked over charcoal at one of the stands.

Joe sits back after finishing his tamales and studies his father's visage as the man sips the last of his beer. The boy doesn't know much about the man or his story, other than his father's name is also Joseph, and he's a handsome man at whom women often steal second glances. He was already traveling by age eighteen, working as a section hand for the railroad when he met and married Joe's mom, who is three years older. She had her teacher's certificate from Louisiana Tech, one of only two of eleven children in her father's red-clay farming family who attended college. Her folks weren't pleased with the match to a "drifter," as they called him. Joe knows his parents' wedding date was June 12, 1925, that his own birthday is January 27, 1926, and that seven months and fifteen days didn't offer much time for licit baby-making.

His father never speaks of Joe's mother anymore. Before their baby had come, his father had quit the railroad and found work as a soda jerk to stay closer to home, but that hadn't lasted long. Joe's mom had had a good job teaching grade school in Bernice, Louisiana, where they'd lived then, but that job had ended too. Joe remembers an entry in his baby book: "I never saw my Daddy until I was two months old as he was working in Memphis."

At the lunch table, Joe screws up his courage and asks, "Why did you leave Mom anyhow?"

His father drains his beer, raises two fingers and beckons over the waitress, orders another cerveza. "Son, if you can't say something good about a person, don't say nothing at all."

"No, really," Joe says. "Why?"

His dad sucks in his breath, then exhales. "Your mother and I both made mistakes. That's part of life. Making them. Learning from them. I can't answer for your mother, but I'm always trying to answer for mine. My life ain't been easy, and I'm a restless man. I boxed some. Dealt cards. Cooked some. I'm a horse trainer now. Can't say my ship has come in. But I still have hopes for someday."

Joe gives his father a quizzical look and asks him to explain further.

"When your mama and I parted ways, I was in a rough place," the father says. "No job. Far from family. I'd forgotten what it felt like to live normal, and for a spell all I did was drink." He shakes his head, nods at the waitress who's brought his next beer, takes a sip. "But a life ain't ruined just because a man gets knocked down. You ice his hand. Close the cut. Put him in the ring again so he fights another round. God knows we all fail and fall, but every life can be lifted again."

Joe nods, toys with the straw in his empty soda glass. His father gives him a dime and motions up the street to the Joy Theater, where a double feature is showing. When Joe returns in the evening, his father is next to the stall at a cantina, fingering the braids of a young senorita. He slurs at Joe to go catch a few winks in the back seat of the Chevy while he finishes up some business with his new friend. Three hours later, the father stumbles to the car and wakes his son. Joe helps him lie down in the back seat, then slides behind the wheel.

The boy, age fourteen, drives his father home.

———

In early fall 1940, Joe's father decides to quit his job at Alamo Downs and open a public stable at Santa Anita in Arcadia, California. Opportunities are better on the West Coast, he insists, and he thinks he has enough connections to secure twenty stalls for the racing season.

Joe disagrees with his father about the move. He loves Alamo Downs. The boy will need to leave behind his grandmother, aunts, and cousins. He doesn't see them often, but the occasional Sunday dinner in a house full of noise and laughing has lodged within him as something to hold on to. The sharper, more immediate loss is leaving his only friend, Chico, his beloved mares and foals, and his dog, Mippy. Joe's father offers to let the boy stay behind and live with his grandmother, but Joe doesn't like that idea either. He wants things to stay the same. They leave by train on the *Sunset Limited* anyway, heading for California.

The boy's mood improves when they arrive a few days later. He inhales the sweet smell of orange blossoms. It feels like he can reach out and touch the mountains. The grounds and racetrack at Santa Anita are much newer than those at Alamo Downs. Right away, his father begins training horses for actors and producers in the movie business. He hires four grooms and two exercise boys, including Joe. For saddling, riding, and steadying thoroughbreds, and preparing them for the jockeys, Joe earns a dollar a day—flush wages for a Depression-era kid. Joe's father handles the horses for Barbara Stanwyck, Robert Taylor, George Raft, Lou Costello, and Max Factor. He travels to South America to pick up horses for Bing Crosby. The actress ZaSu Pitts buys a shirt for young Joe as a gift. A teenage Gloria Vanderbilt walks the shed rows, and Joe drums up the courage to say hello to her.

Stabled in the barn behind the quarters where Joe and his father stay is the famed thoroughbred Seabiscuit. Joe is exercising a horse one morning when he spies the legendary racehorse around the next turn. He gallops ahead to Seabiscuit and flies on past.

Despite the glamour and excitement of Santa Anita, Joe's not happy. He's been spending too much time at the track kitchen, putting on too much weight for an exercise boy, who needs to stay around 120 pounds. He's now five feet seven and 135 pounds—far too heavy for his job. His dad relegates him to walking hot, sweaty horses after their workouts. For less money. Joe and his father argue. His dad says he's grown too big for his britches—literally and figuratively. The same argument happens more than once. Joe smarts off to his dad. The boy grows dejected, his attitude surly.

Track officials notice the boy with the sour outlook and make inquiries. Joe is underage and is not supposed to be living or working at the track until he's sixteen. Also, he's not enrolled in school. They threaten to revoke his father's training license unless the boy shapes up.

Joe's father sits the boy down and gives him an ultimatum: "Either you go back to San Antonio and live with your grandmother, or you go back to your mother in Memphis. Whenever you finish your schooling and get your attitude straightened out, you're welcome to return. I'll make a trainer out of you. Sleep on it tonight, and the decision is yours. But no matter what, by this time tomorrow, you're on a train, leaving California." He reaches into his pocket and hands Joe two folded twenty-dollar bills. "This should be enough for whatever you decide. I'll get you to the station tomorrow and buy you a ticket."

"I ain't doing neither," Joe says. "I'm gonna join the Army."

It's a threat. A bluff. He hopes his dad will back down, keep him on. But his father says, "Hell. If they take you, you got my blessing."

That night Joe lies awake on his cot. He knows he has messed up, yet it's too late for apologies. No way is he going back to Memphis to be the breadwinner again for the freeloading Mr. Jake. Living with his grandmother wouldn't be bad, but he has already tasted the freedom of life on the wing. He fears his grand-mother would tie him down.

Before sunrise, Joe packs a small suitcase and steals out of the tack room. He leaves no note. He doesn't say goodbye. He catches a streetcar to the Post Office building in Pasadena, where he has seen a sign for a recruiting station inside. To join the Army, you need to be seventeen with a note from your parents, eighteen without. With as much vigor as he can manage, Joe climbs the steps and pushes through the front doors. He announces his intentions to the sergeant.

"Really." The man looks him up and down. "How old are you, kid?"

"Eighteen."

"Eighteen, my ass. You got a birth certificate?"

"Not with me. I'm not from California originally. It's back in my home state."

The recruiter rolls his eyes. "Well, let's send for your birth certificate. Where were you born?"

"Memphis."

"Memphis, huh? I'll tell ya what. You take this stack of papers and fill them out, stand over there and wait. We'll get this sorted."

Joe nods, receives the papers and a pencil, takes a step back, scribbles on the forms. His birthplace is not Memphis. It's Ruston, Louisiana. But that's a strategic part of his fib. He figures by the time the Army receives a copy of his birth certificate, he'll be long gone. Besides, the Army is eager for warm bodies. President Franklin Roosevelt has already hinted in the press that it's only a matter of time before the United States joins the Allies in the titanic struggle of World War II. A few months earlier, on September 16, 1940, Roosevelt signed into law the nation's first peacetime conscription bill. All men ages twenty-one through thirty-five are now required to register for military service. The

Army is hungrier for warm bodies than it has been at any time since World War I. He'll be doing the Army a favor, Joe thinks. And as far as Joe knows, America's not directly involved in the war yet. He's just a boy looking for adventure, and he's a good worker. He'll do his part.

The room grows busy as the morning grows long. After four hours, Joe and a cadre of men follow the recruiting sergeant up the street to a small office, where they're given a quick physical and ordered to eat lunch next door in a diner. Joe keeps his head down. He's lost in the shuffle.

Two hours later, Joe and the men are loaded into the back of a truck. Ahead is the long drive to Fort MacArthur and a grown-up world he knows nothing about.

CHAPTER 3

Where Sea and Sky Meet

The bumpy truck ride southward from the recruiting center in Pasadena through the city of Los Angeles to San Pedro on the coast takes an hour. It's early January 1941, and like many fourteen-year-olds, Joe is not a global thinker. As he climbs off the wooden seat and his feet hit the pavement at Fort MacArthur, just up the bay from the Long Beach pier, all he can think of is how much his butt aches.

He's certainly not thinking of world news. Not of how three principal partners in the Axis alliance have been running loose during these last few turbulent years. Not of how Nazi Germany has already invaded and conquered Poland, which had possessed one of the strongest and best-equipped armies in Europe, then done the same to Finland, Denmark, Norway, the Netherlands, Luxembourg, and Belgium. Not of how Great Britain and France are trying to fight back, and not of how France acquiesced and handed over the northern and eastern parts of its country to the Nazis. Not of how Fascist Italy had invaded and annexed Albania and conquered Ethiopia, then invaded southern France, Egypt, and Greece. Not of how the Soviet Union, supposedly on the right side of this conflict, is busy gobbling up countries of its

28

own. Not of how Imperial Japan had attacked China and intensi-
fied military activities throughout East Asia. And certainly not of
how Japan had decimated the city of Nanking, leaving more than
300,000 civilians of the Chinese capital robbed, raped, tortured,
and slaughtered.

None of this hostile action crosses his mind at the entryway
to Fort MacArthur, where Joe is ordered to fall in. He and two
dozen other enlistees are yelled at, bedamned, and marched up
the pavement to a single-story wooden barracks, which will act
as their quarters until they're sworn in. They unfurl their bed-
rolls, are marched outside in columns of two to the mess hall
(where they're fed supper), then marched back to the barracks
(where the "Lights out!" order is barked).

That night Joe lies awake on a top bunk, vigilant and watch-
ful, the snores of strange men surrounding him. He considers how
his life has changed so radically, so quickly. He knows there's no
one to blame but himself for running away from his problems and
getting into whatever this is. His mind teems with memories. He
misses the mares and their foals back at the stables. He thinks of
his grandmother, his mother, of little Betty and Charlie back in
Memphis. He regrets causing his father so much trouble. When he
thinks of his dog, Mippy, and how he needed to leave her back in
San Antonio, he buries his face in his pillow, stifling the sobs.

Early the next morning, the moonfaced corporal in charge of
the barracks shouts them awake. Joe trudges to the latrine,
washes his face, wets down his hair, stares into the mirror. It's
5 a.m. A man stands next to him, lathering his whiskers, preparing to shave. The man sets down his shaving brush and extends
his hand.

"I got the bunk underneath you," he says. "Raymond Rico.
Call me Ray."

The man is in his early twenties with high cheekbones, arched eyebrows, and a dark-hued complexion. Without thinking twice, Joe shakes the outstretched hand and says, "Joe Johnson." He wants to talk to the man more, to make a friend, even if he doesn't trust him fully. But another shout races down the hallway, and the enlistees are ordered to shut up and hustle. Soon they're outside in formation, yelled at again.

Joe wonders if they'll go for a run. If they'll be ordered to do push-ups. If they'll practice with their weapons on the rifle range. But there's not much to do yet. They are not assigned to a regiment, nor given uniforms, nor sworn in. They are nothing official yet except enlistees, waiting for the Army to figure out what to do with them.

The boy is tasked with kitchen duty a few times over the next few days. More new enlistees arrive, and the transitional barracks are soon at capacity. When he's not in the kitchen, Joe spends most of his time lying on his back on his bunk, listening to Ray spin stories from the bunk underneath him. Ray doesn't volunteer much personal information, but the stories flow from him like water through a sluice. He brags about working as a stuntman in the movies, giving a massage to an older, thrice-divorced actress named Kitty, drinking too much when gadding about town, and driving his car far too fast. Joe can't help liking the guy. Ray is full of panache. Or perhaps malarkey.

Days pass, and without a murmur of fanfare, Joe marks his fifteenth birthday while in the transitional barracks. In early February 1941, and without further question by military officials, he's officially sworn in with the rest of the enlistees and assigned to the 31st Infantry Regiment. On the morning before they're shipped north to Fort Ord in Monterey, a skinny captain informs the men in formation about a rare opportunity for raw recruits. A few openings are still available to join the 31st Infantry Regiment in the Philippines. It will mean travel, adventure, and seeing the world, the captain promises. If any man wants the assignment, he's to step forward.

Not a man moves. Joe has never been aboard a ship. He shrugs and finds his feet taking a bold step, as if on their own. Ray spots Joe out of the corner of his eye and steps forward with him. They are the only two volunteers.

"What were you thinking, anyway?" Ray hisses to Joe after the first sergeant has taken down their names and told them they're now heading to Fort McDowell, in San Francisco. "Didn't I tell ya to never volunteer for anything?"

"Girls in grass skirts," Joe says with feigned bravado. "Hammocks? Coconut juice?" He turns to face the older recruit. "What exactly were *you* thinking?"

Ray scoffs, "That you need somebody with you to keep you out of trouble."

———

The night after being sworn in, Private Raymond Rico takes Private Joe Johnson out to a bar to celebrate. The older soldier takes the lead on drinking. Joe follows suit. He drinks his first beer. Then another. Then one more. After that, Joe loses count. They tell jokes and laugh too loudly. The boy's head is so fuzzy he can hardly see straight. All he wants is to return to base to sleep.

The next morning Joe's head pounds. They leave by train for Fort McDowell; the chug of the locomotive's pistons beats a steady pattern of pain in Joe's inner ears. Once there, they will await their vessel to the Philippines. They still don't have uniforms and haven't even sweated through Basic Training yet, but in an extraordinarily rare move for the military, the boys are informed they will go through boot camp overseas. Joe hasn't notified either of his parents where he is yet. He has already second-guessed his decision to join the military, but he doesn't want to lose face and be forced to go home. He figures he'll write both of his parents after his adventure is well underway.

Off the train, shivering, Joe and Ray are put aboard a small Army boat and taken to Angel Island, just past Alcatraz. The dampness of the wintry San Francisco air cuts to their bones. After the boat docks at the pier, they are marched up a steep serpentine road to the barracks. Fort McDowell crawls with soldiers; it is even more crowded than Fort MacArthur. Most soldiers at McDowell are dressed in old World War I choke-collar blouses and sport wrap-legging trousers. The old-timers hoot and holler at the new recruits. Joe and Ray are issued blankets, linens, and towels, and told where to bunk. About 100 restless and bored men bunk in their barracks. Not all will go to the Philippines. Some will go to Alaska. Others to Hawaii.

Inside the barracks, they greet a lounging Michigan native named Dale Snyder, who rises on one elbow while lying on his bunk to introduce himself and shake their hands. He's been in the barracks two weeks, has a kind face and chiseled good looks, and is about Ray's age.

"There's gonna be a war," Dale says. "I figured I better get in and get it over with." He glances over his shoulder, whispers for the other two to huddle up, and adds, "Look. See that tall, eagle-beaked bastard that just walked in?"

Ray and Joe squint toward the door and nod. The soldier's nose is sharp and sizable. His eyes bulge as if too big for their sockets.

"Watch out for trouble," Dale says. "Sumpter's his last name. They call him Sump. He's from Alabama and has this little clique of rebs that follow him around. They got a nasty habit of baiting a loner into a fight."

"Humph," Joe says, trying to sound tough. Ray just glares.

"Here's another piece of advice," Dale offers. "You'll draw your uniforms soon. Before you do, slip a buck to the fella in charge of the clothing line. He'll see to it you get something that fits. Otherwise you're stuck with potato sacks."

The guys all guffaw.

Dinner that night is flopped into bowls and platters and rushed around the tables. Pork chops, mashed potatoes, green beans, white bread. The mess hall is a madhouse of flailing arms, shouts, and clangs. A thousand men all make noise at once. Joe manages to capture some mashed potatoes before everything's finished. His stomach growls.

"Most of these bums left their manners at home when they joined the Army," Dale shouts. He hands Joe an extra pork chop from his plate, along with two slices of bread. "Here. Make yourself a sandwich. It's dog eat dog when it comes to chow."

Dale's a good egg, Joe thinks, making a mental note to move faster at mealtimes.

The next morning, Joe and Ray each slip a dollar to the private on clothing duty. They're the only two recruits in formation who are given the new type of blouses, plus long trousers that fit. In the days that follow, Joe and Ray receive X-rays and blood tests, thorough physicals, and a tingling array of vaccinations. But mostly they just sit around. Dale naps. Ray smokes. They play cards. Joe wanders the grounds. He finds he's becoming fast friends with Dale and Ray. They walk the shores of Fort McDowell each afternoon, searching for shells and oddly shaped stones and driftwood. Afterward, they hike to the PX for Coca-Colas.

February passes. The first two weeks of March move slowly. One morning an order is tacked to the barracks bulletin board saying the men will receive partial pay and a weekend pass.

"Hey, see what I see?" Ray looks at the notice, then nudges

Dale in the ribs. They both turn and stare at Joe. He has wondered for a while now if they know he's underage, although he hasn't told anyone.

Dale chuckles and elbows Ray back.

"What are you guys gawking at?" Joe doesn't want to sound stupid. "It's just a pass."

Ray laughs again and points to Joe. "This weekend, little brother's gonna become a man."

————

The next day the Army pays them twenty bucks each. For the first time in their military careers the trio hits the city, all in uniform. Ray secures them a hotel suite with two adjoining rooms for two bucks each. They hop in a taxi and head to the downtown core for drinks. Joe begins to have reservations and says, "You know, guys, maybe I'll just head back to the room. I don't want to slow you down."

"What're you talking about?" Ray says. "We're gonna go crazy."

"Well...you know." Joe's voice turns flat.

"We don't," Ray says. "What?"

Joe scrunches up his face and wonders what he can say to remove himself from the quandary. He decides to come clean, at least to a degree. "I'm not much of a hard drinker," Joe admits. "A few beers here and there, but I've never had a real drink in my whole life. And..." His voice trails off. He decides to tell the truth. "Never been with a girl, neither."

Ray and Dale laugh. The cabdriver glances in his rearview mirror and smiles.

A moment passes and Dale says, "How the hell old are you, anyway?"

Joe doesn't hesitate. "Eighteen."

"Well, you look young for eighteen," Dale says. "But hey, if you want to head back, that's okay by us."

Joe looks out the window of the cab but doesn't say anything. The guys are cutting him some slack, giving him a way out, being true friends. Yet he's torn. He doesn't want to go along with them, but he doesn't want to let them down, either. He pauses before muttering, "What the hell."

The three drink whiskeys with beer chasers until they can stand no more, then wobble back to the hotel. Ray uses the bathroom, then migrates to the street again in search of some girls. An hour later he returns, bursting through the doorway with three young women on his arms. Ray holds a bottle in each hand. He introduces the women as Dottie, Marie, and Ginger. Joe can't quite tell if they're prostitutes or simply patriotic Americans, wanting to have drinks with some servicemen who are heading overseas.

The six hang around in the first room, all talking at the same time, laughing and swapping stories, drowning out the sounds of the old radiator's laborious hiss. The new bottles are passed around until they're empty. Joe's head swirls and his vision becomes cloudy, yet he notes that Ray has downed far more than he. Dale appears the most levelheaded of the gang and leaves the party early and alone, saying only that he needs to take care of some personal business. Ray's voice turns bombastic. He announces he's going to entertain Marie and Ginger in the other room. Joe is left alone with Dottie. He finds the woman attractive and wonders if he's falling in love or if it's simply the booze talking.

An hour passes, and when it's time for the women to say goodbye, Dottie kisses Joe on the cheek and says thanks for the fun time. Ray's still loaded. He closes the door behind the girls, flops onto the bed in the first room, and prods Joe for juicy details, but Joe doesn't want to talk about it. The youthful soldier plays along with Ray's questioning because he wants to be thought of as one of the guys. But Joe never does tell Ray any specifics about what happened—or didn't—between him and Dottie.

———

Late one morning toward the end of March at Fort McDowell, Ray and Dale are getting haircuts. Joe is reading by himself in the barracks. He spies a group of Sump's cronies against the far wall, yukking it up among themselves. Joe ignores the gang of rebs, sets down his book, and heads into the latrine just as Coot, one of Sump's cronies, is walking out. Without missing a beat, Coot shifts his step, thuds his shoulder against the boy, and saunters onward to join his buddies against the wall. They laugh like hyenas.

Joe turns around and glares. A mistake.

"Keep walking, boy," Coot calls over his shoulder.

"Maybe I don't feel like it," Joe answers.

"I know what you feel like." Coot addresses his buddies more than Joe, looking for another laugh. "Getting lucky again with that boyfriend of yours, Ray."

Joe clenches his fist. "What'd you say?"

"You heard me. He's humping you every night. And if I'm wrong, you and me can settle things down on the beach. Sump will referee."

Joe snorts at the insult. "Lead the way."

The gang pushes off the wall, heads out of the barracks, and hikes toward the rocky shore. Overbold and trying to think, Joe stands for a moment, all motion suspended, then shakes his head and follows. The fifteen-year-old has never been in a fight before, certainly never with a grown man, although his childhood vow propels him forward: *Never give in to fear.* They approach the high bank overlooking the beach, then half run, half slide down the embankment. Coot's on the beach now with his back toward Joe. Sump stands nearby, holding his flunky's jacket. A crowd from the barracks has followed and forms a ring. Joe approaches. The circle parts to let him in.

Without uttering so much as a grunt, Coot spins on his heel and slugs Joe square in the jaw. The boy stumbles backward, struggling to keep his feet. He feels blood on his lips. Coot smirks, lunges two steps forward, grabs Joe's shirt, and tries to throw the boy to the ground. Joe breaks free from his grasp and dips into a half crouch, shuffling his feet like a basketball player so he can circle Coot. The older man is sinewed and muscular, taller than Joe and cagier. Joe senses he's in trouble.

"C'mon, kid," Coot says, one eyebrow cocked. "That all you got?"

Joe ducks his head and charges the older soldier, hitting him mid-torso with his shoulder. They plunge to the ground, grappling and striking each other, both struggling for an advantage. Joe fights with frenzy. He's angry at himself for getting suckered into the fight, furious at his opponent for spouting off false accusations against Ray and himself. The boy slides out of Coot's grasp, slips to ascend the soldier's stomach, and clutches the man's neck with both hands, squeezing his throat. Joe pounds the man's head into the sand—again and again. The boy's winning the fight, killing the man, losing touch with reality, when he finds two hands yanking his shoulders upward and back. Joe stumbles off Coot and spins to see Dale breathless from having run from the barracks. Ray stands a few paces away next to Sump, staring down the gang's boss, telling him to back off.

"Relax! Just relax!" Dale yells to Joe. "You got him, kid. Don't kill him."

Joe pants, short-winded. He shakes off Dale's grasp and retorts, "I don't need your help."

Coot is helped up by one of his gang. His mouth is bloody and full of sand. His face looks as rattled as a pinball machine. He spits. The fight is over. The crowd disperses.

Ray and Dale help Joe back to the barracks. The boy is shaking so fiercely with adrenaline he can barely sit on his bed to gather his wits. Dale brings him a wet washcloth and helps him wipe his face.

"One thing I need to make clear," Joe says. "I don't need you two to rescue me every time I get into a scrape."

Ray puts both hands on Joe's shoulders and looks the boy in the eyes. "We just wanted to make sure you got a fair shake, that's all. It's actually the other guy we rescued." Ray grins, then turns serious. "Whether you like it or not, we're going to stand by you. We were told what Coot said, and I like that you fought our battle just as much as yours. But from now on, with Dale's help I'll do the fighting for us, okay?"

Joe slows his breathing. His shoulders sag. He nods.

Dale pats the boy on the back and gets him a fresh shirt.

That night Joe lies awake for a long time, imagining what might have happened if Dale hadn't held him back. He's still unnerved by the encounter, replaying each twist of the fight in his mind, imagining the bully's smirking face just before he beat his head against the sand. The boy senses a new and chilling feeling, and he isn't comfortable with it. He tries to erase the dark emotion from his mind, but it floats back like a phantom. It takes a while before the boy can name *hatred* for what it is—and he cannot help wondering, given his new profession, how much of it he might need to summon in the days to come.

———

Joe, Ray, and Dale have been told they're in the 31st Infantry Regiment, but while talking among themselves at a nearby beer parlor one evening, they realize they each could be assigned to a different company, even to different battalions. A corporal wanders by, overhears their talk, and offers a solution. For five bucks per man, he can guarantee they're assigned to the same company. The three pull out their wallets and pay up.

Later, lists are posted on the barracks bulletin boards. The corporal has delivered. Joe, Ray, and Dale are all assigned to D Company, 1st Battalion, and set to embark at 0800 on March 31, 1941, aboard the USAT *Republic* for duty stations in the Philippines.

On the morning of departure, tugboats ease the big white ship away from the dock at Fort Mason, the point of embarkation in San Francisco. The *Republic* is a sedate old passenger liner that's been pressed into service and outfitted to carry troops. The tugs cast off the lines, and the recruits feel the big ship's propellers start to churn the sea. She heads westward, venturing ever farther into the vast blue ocean, knifing through the choppy waves with determined purpose.

Joe, Ray, and Dale stand at the stern of the ship on the port side, watching the cheering crowd diminish in size as an Army band finishes a warm farewell. The recruits don't speak. They watch the hills and houses of the city grow smaller and smaller. Soon, the morning sun breaks through the clouds. A sailboat passes, its occupants waving goodbye to the ship. As the boys pass under the Golden Gate Bridge, Joe looks up, feeling the magnitude of the event is beyond words.

"Well, fellas," Ray says. "It's too late to change our minds now."

The next few days are spent gaining their sea legs. Joe, Ray, and Dale each take turns heaving their meals over the deck, noting that few empty spots are available at the railing. But soon their nausea subsides, and the recruits settle into life on the ocean. They play cards, read, and catnap. Joe thinks of his mother back in Memphis, and of how much he misses his little brother and sister. He wrote his mother a few quick lines just before leaving, and when he thinks of the words he penned to her in his sober, attentive cursive, a new wave of homesickness washes over him:

Don't worry, Mother, I'll be careful.

Joe often wanders alone topside, exploring as much of the ship as he's able, reflecting on the past and pondering his future. He has energy and he's curious. One morning as he watches seagulls follow the *Republic*'s wake, he meets a wizened merchant marine named Dewey Holzclaw who's been at sea for nearly thirty years. He's an oiler on the *Republic,* the worker who services machinery in the engine room. Joe finds him a fountain of information about the ship and the military.

"Joined in 1911 and sailed all through the Great War," Dewey says, puffing on a stubby cigarette. "So you're in the 31st, eh? Well, you couldn't send me to the infantry; you're just fodder for the artillery. So keep your head down when you hear them shells come a-whistling. Make sure you go home alive. Now, you consider my job. I do it right and nobody bothers me. That's how you live, son. Free and clear just like that."

For the next several weeks, Joe sees Dewey around the ship almost every day. Each time Dewey sees the boy, he offers some fatherly advice. "Don't ever take up tobacco like I did.... Don't gamble, the games are all fixed.... Don't re-up when the military comes calling again. Find yourself a nice girl instead, marry her, raise some kids, and have a family. A soldier's life is a lonely life, and you don't want that...."

Three days before the end of the voyage, Dewey confides to the boy, "Well, I got some hard news yesterday, son. This trip's my last. As soon as we get back to San Francisco, I'm to pick up my retirement papers. My life's work is finished." He lights a cigarette, blows smoke out his nose, and looks afar to the horizon, where sea and sky meet.

Joe eyes the man. "You got any family waiting for you stateside?"

"Nah. This beautiful ocean is family for me." Dewey flicks the remainder of his cigarette over the rail. "Hey, be sure you come up on deck at night, when the ocean's at its prettiest. The moon and stars glisten on the smooth Pacific, and you can see the flying fish racing alongside the ship. Promise me you'll do that at least once."

Joe thinks he hears the man's voice crack. He eyes him again. "I promise."

Dewey returns to his work, and Joe wanders the ship again. The *Republic* is set to arrive at Pier 7 in Manila on April 22, 1941.

The night passes, and with it the stars on the smooth Pacific. The next night passes and the next. But Joe has forgotten his promise.

On the final morning Joe looks for Dewey to tell him goodbye before they dock. He wants to thank him for his advice and wish him a safe trip home. As he approaches the hatch, he sees another crewman sitting in the spot where Dewey often sat. Joe walks closer and the crewman asks, "You lost, soldier?"

"I just hoped to see Dewey Holzclaw one last time."

"You knew Dewey?"

"Yeah. I talked with him quite a bit over the last few weeks."

The crewman's eyes narrow, as if trying to read Joe's face, then he mutters, "Dewey's no longer with us."

Joe pauses. "You mean he left the ship already? How could he do that? We're not even tied to the docks."

The crewman drops his gaze, stares at the sea. "I've known

Dewey a few years. Nice guy. Always did his job. Never left us a note as to why. I guess he couldn't handle the thought of all he loved being taken from him. Sorry to tell you this, son, but Dewey slipped over the side into the ocean three nights ago. Crew held a service for him yesterday evening. The captain and the chaplain both said a short eulogy."

Stunned, Joe turns away quickly so the crewman can't see his tears. He wanders the deck, not wanting Ray or Dale to see him with his eyes wet. He feels abandoned by a mentor, and his eagerness for seeing the world has lost its appeal.

The ship's horn sounds a plaintive blow.

The view of the harbor and the garrison city of Manila captures Joe's attention. He can see the rusting relics sunk during the Spanish-American War, still protruding from the bay.

Joe brings Dewey's face to mind one last time. He knows he has more letters to write as soon as he gets settled in Manila. He needs to write to his mother again, this time telling her how much he loves her. He needs to write to his father again, this time asking for his forgiveness. He needs to write to his little brother and sister, telling them they're the best thing that's ever happened to him.

The boy has arrived in the Philippines. He is more than 8,000 miles from home.

CHAPTER 4

Lost Babes in the Woods

A stifling heat covers the vast chain of docks at the Port of Manila. The rainy season has not yet begun. Two gangplanks are maneuvered into place at Pier 7, one at the *Republic*'s bow, the other amidships. Joe strides off the ship carrying his blue barracks bag slung over his shoulder, with a large brown envelope in his free hand that contains his company assignment. Dale and Ray are not far behind, although once on the docks Ray is directed to a different waiting truck than Joe and Dale. Joe is concerned. He wants all three friends to stay together.

Although he was a good student of history in school, Joe has little idea of what he's doing in Manila. He doesn't know that the Philippines, with its 7,100 islands and prewar population of more than eight million people, has been an American protectorate for the past forty-three years.

Joe remembers vaguely something about Spain's earlier influence. But he doesn't recall that the American presence in the Philippines began shortly after Spain had repressed Cuba's struggle for independence and the United States didn't like it, resulting in the Spanish-American War of 1898. Spain was defeated, and with the loss came the ceding to the United States of the Philippines, which had also been a colony of Spain's. Some Filipinos feared they'd merely swapped colonial rule by Spain for colonial rule by the United States, and an armed conflict erupted between America and the Philippines that lasted for nearly three years. By the end of 1902, America had established a firm possession of the islands, and a closer cooperation was eventually achieved. New roads, hospitals, ports, and airfields were built, and in 1934 a law was passed to lead the Philippines toward independence within the next decade.

Now, as the date for independence slowly approaches, the United States is gradually lessening its presence in the Philippines while still keeping a wary eye on Japan's aggression in East Asia. Roosevelt has sent aid and extended credit to China to help their defense. The US president slowed the export of steel, rubber, and iron to Imperial Japan, materials used in war production, and ultimately placed a full oil embargo on the country in 1940. That same year, in case any question of allegiances remained, Japan signed the Tripartite Pact, formally creating a military alliance with Nazi Germany and Fascist Italy. Yet even with tensions increasing, on the morning of April 22, 1941, when Joe walks down the gangplank, the United States Army's main goal in the Philippines is still peacetime defense, not troop buildup. During the Philippine-American War, more than 175,000 US troops were in the country. Now, fewer than 20,000 US troops remain.

Joe hops aboard a truck with the other soldiers. The convoy of military trucks starts off, shifting and grinding gears through the crowded streets.

Despite the intense heat, an agreeable tropical breeze hangs over Manila, and one of the first things Joe notices is color everywhere. Crimson flowers trail from hanging baskets. Bright lemon taxis dart here and there. Filipina mothers stroll along the sidewalks in pink sunlit dresses. Their children tag beside them, resplendent in orange, raspberry, and plum. Joe can't help marking the contrast with the excess of blues and olive drabs he's seen for the last few months.

The convoy moves east out of the city, heads through the gates of sprawling Fort McKinley and into a broad expanse of open field, kicking up a heavy cloud of dust. Joe lowers his head and covers his eyes. The trucks stop in front of rows of GI tents, and the order to unload is shouted. The recruits are told little about their location or the military's plans for them except that they are at "B Range," they are to hurry, and Basic Training will last for six weeks.

Joe and Dale are both placed in D Company, a heavy weapons unit—1st Squad, 1st Platoon, 1st Battalion, 31st Infantry. Ray is in the same company but a different platoon. He finds them and promises he'll try to get transferred so they're all together. Corporals march the recruits to large tents, where each man draws gear including fatigues, blankets, and a .45 caliber automatic pistol. They are fed dry bologna-and-cheese sandwiches for lunch along with a spoonful of cold pork and beans from a can. They will be housed in smaller tents. No running water is found at B Range. It's all carried in.

Over the next weeks, the enlistees are subjected to close-order drills, forced marches with full gear, endless calisthenics, morning and evening runs, and cold hose showers from barrels perched on supports. Joe and Dale are taught how to strip, reassemble, load, and operate a .30 caliber machine gun. They practice firing their pistols and throwing hand grenades. Since Joe and Dale operate a machine gun, they will not carry rifles, although they're taught to use them. Ray is unable to get transferred. Joe sends a telegram home. It reads simply:

Manila, Pi.
Dear Mother, from your son on the other side of the world, but with his heart still with his mother.
Love, your son, Joe.

At the start of the fifth week, Joe's machine-gun platoon is marched out to the firing range. Targets are placed 1,000 inches away (about twenty-eight yards), and each man must fire at two-inch squares arranged in patterns. A burst of exactly six rounds must be fired into each square as the gunner navigates the pattern up, down, and diagonally, all while being timed. Initially, the men trade boasts of how well each will do, ribbing each other in their competitiveness. Joe stays silent, his pulse racing. When it's his turn, he squeezes the trigger in short bursts, wondering if he's got what it takes. When the scores are tallied, the targets do not lie. Out of the twenty-eight men in his platoon, only Joe has qualified as "expert marksman."

The guys razz him afterward, and many of their taunts are lewd. He's only a boy, they jeer in ribald vernacular, his eyesight surely eroded by excessive self-pleasuring. That childish behavior makes a boy go blind, they insist. It makes no sense that Joe scored so high on a test requiring good eyesight. Maybe he cheated?

Joe shakes off the teasing. He is proud of his achievement at the shooting range, and several guys drop their jealousy and clap him on the back. In spare moments on the hike back to the tents, however, the boy finds himself analyzing their displays of crude masculinity, and gradually internalizing their outlook. Still impressionable, he senses a need to measure up if he wants to gain the older guys' respect. Joe has seen few models of grown-up masculinity other than his father the vagabond, the freeloading Mr. Jake, and the coarse subculture he's now in. He concludes that maturity means being able to boast about sexual exploits. He wonders when he will ever get the chance to have one.

———

When boot camp is over, the soldiers in Joe's heavy weapons company are trucked west to their quarters at Fort Santiago in an area of Manila known as Intramuros, the old walled city next to the port. Fort Santiago serves as the headquarters for the US Army, and the compound Joe is placed in is known as the *Cuartel de España*. Its cobblestoned streets are narrow and musty, shaded with palm and mimosa trees, and the architecture harks back to the days of Magellan and the early Spanish explorers. Across the street from Joe's barracks sits a convent. Two tall, squiggly trees grow in front of the barracks, as if for comic relief.

Through a large open dayroom, the men follow the squad leaders up the stairs to the second floor. Joe's squad is housed in a long, open room, with rows of bunks lining the walls on both sides. The men are all given mosquito nets for use at night. Overall, the barracks are big, airy, and clean. Dale is assigned a bunk three down from Joe's. Ray is assigned to headquarters squad in a different building. Joe feels disappointed at that news as he stows his gear and settles in.

From out on the street, the sound of footsteps in cadence can be heard. Orders are given, and soon the wooden steps of Joe's barracks shake. The regulars from the weapons company are returning from their drills. The regulars head to their bunks to change. These men are older, many with a hardened set to their jaws. It's obvious to Joe that the old-timers will be difficult to befriend. Some throw looks of disdain at the new recruits and mutter about what the Army has come to. The chow bell interrupts the sizing-up and starts a steady clanging. The men all head for the mess hall. Joe and Dale are two of the last to be seated.

The mess hall at Fort Santiago is orderly and mostly quiet. Filipino mess boys do the serving and refilling. Tables are set with porcelain dishes and loaded with roast beef, meatloaf, mashed potatoes, gravy with rolls, peas, beans, and relish trays. Joe can't believe his eyes. This is the best chow he's seen in years.

An old-timer at their table schools Joe and Dale about how to act in the mess hall. The main rule for new guys is to shut up. Old-timers don't like things to be disturbed, and whenever new guys arrive, it means more drills and exercises, which the old-timers hate. He explains that the ranks of the 31st consist of mostly Regular Army soldiers: hardened brawlers, boozers, and adventurers, many of whom haven't been stateside in years. They're referred to as "Asiatics," and they typically re-up only for the choicest two-year tours in Hawaii, Panama, or Manila—places where duty is a four-hour day, temperatures are hot and balmy, and ice-cold booze can be had for fifteen cents a slug.

"Oh, they'll know their business as soldiers when need be," the old-timer says. "But morally, a whole bunch of 'em are corrupt. Watch your wallets, boys. Some will do anything for extra booze money."

Joe tries not to look startled. He's about to ask a few questions, but the meal finishes and an announcement is given: tomorrow morning the men will be paid and allowed a weekend pass. The room erupts in loud, bawdy cheers.

Early the next morning, Ray finds Joe and Dale. The three collect their money, then show their passes to the Corporal of the Guard, who signs them out. They pick their way through a group of small Filipino waifs near the gate, all begging for money. Merchants ply them with pearls and cloths to send to their girlfriends back home. A gauntlet of Filipina women tug at the soldiers' arms, trying to entice the soldiers to go with them. Joe, Ray, and Dale make it past the crowd out to the busy main streets, where Ray hails a cab and tells the driver to take them to a cabaret.

It's not yet lunchtime, but the driver chuckles to himself and promises to take the boys to the best place in town. He swerves through traffic at breakneck speed, honking his horn and shaking his fist at other drivers. Ray is egging his two friends on, regaling them with stories of booze and women, insisting they're all bound to score soon.

The driver takes them to a noisy, windowless cabaret filled with slender Filipinas with hinting eyes. Joe and Dale nurse beers while Ray hits the harder booze. Three girls wander up to their table, bend low, and speak to the boys in beckoning whispers. Joe looks at one of the girls. She's perspiring and cheerless, her lips sketched with gaudy red lipstick. *Maybe now's the time,* Joe thinks, but Ray laughs and speaks for the group, saying not until after lunch at the earliest. The boys order cheeseburgers and more beers. Ray gets up to dance with one of the girls. He returns to the table sweaty, his collar curled and open. He drinks a jigger of gin and shouts over the jukebox music, "What a couple of duds you guys are! Get off your seats and grab some. It's here for the taking."

Dale furrows his brow, waves him off. The afternoon is wearing thin, the cabaret is filling up, and there's a puzzling lack of old-timers in the joint. Ray wanders off to dance again.

Two more hours pass before Dale mutters to Joe, "I don't know about you, but I'm ready to get out of this place. We got to do something better than sit around all day." Two more girls walk to their table, but Dale shakes his head.

"Yeah, let's ditch," Joe says. "It's almost dinnertime anyway."

On their way to the door they catch Ray and haul him outside and through the crowd that's waiting to get in. By now Ray is slurring and unable to walk a straight line. Dale hails a cab. They push Ray inside. He closes his eyes as the cab picks up speed. In one block, Ray's asleep.

The driver keeps his eyes on the heavy traffic and asks into the rearview mirror, "You men are from that batch of new recruits that just came from B Range, yes?" He speaks perfect English and looks more Caucasian than Filipino.

"How come you know so much?" Dale asks.

"It's no problem," he says. "I make it a point to know what's happening in my city. It helps me survive. But since you ask, I can see that you three don't have your uniforms tailor-cut yet. Plus, look at that place you were just in. Only greenhorns get suckered into there. You better get a place for the night to let your friend sleep it off. You can't take him back to the post in his condition, or he'll get a couple days in the guardhouse."

Joe glances at Dale and murmurs, "They won't lock him up just for getting drunk, will they?"

Dale shrugs. The driver has overheard and answers for him: "They'll lock him up for sure. Listen, fellows, I have no reason to lie to you. You're lucky the MPs didn't grab him outside the bar you just left. They patrol that area all the time. Get a hotel room. I know one for a reasonable price. The owner is honest. She'll keep her mouth shut."

Joe and Dale sit a moment, not knowing whether to believe the driver's advice. Ray is now snoring, a sprawling mess of gin and sweat.

Joe speaks up: "You said *reasonable price,* right?"

The driver offers a bemused smile. "Always."

———

The ride lasts perhaps thirty minutes, although Joe loses track of time through the maze of city streets. Darkness falls. The air is humid. The driver stops before a wooden two-story storefront and helps the friends lug Ray up to the second floor. The room smells clean and has three single beds, each with its own mosquito netting. They flop their friend on a bed, and Joe removes Ray's shoes.

"What's the name of this joint, anyway?" Dale asks.

"No name." The driver smiles. "This is where I live. My

mother owns the building. It'll be six pesos, plus cab fare, plus the fare when I take you back to your post."

Joe squints. "Why are you helping us like this? We just met you."

"Too many questions," the driver says. "Learn to accept kindness when it's offered. Now, if you'd like a place to eat, I know several places nearby. Good food. Cheap."

Dale motions toward Ray. "What if he wakes up while we're gone?"

"Nah, they slipped him a mickey back there," the driver says. "I could smell it on his breath. He won't be waking up anytime soon. Oh—one more thing." He looks at Joe and Dale. "Check your wallets. Those cabaret girls know all the tricks."

Joe and Dale pat themselves down. They both still have their money. They check Ray. His wallet's gone.

The driver laughs. "The place next door is good for seafood. Fresh lobster. Oysters. Very tasty. Lots to eat. If you want a girl, a far better place is Manny Tang's across from the restaurant. One of the best in town, and the lady who runs it is a friend of mine. Mama Rosa's her name, although they call her the Big Rotunda. Tell her Frisco Smith sent you. When it's time for your ride back, just tell the Big Rotunda. She'll know how to reach me."

"Frisco Smith?" Dale asks. "That's your name?" The driver nods, but Joe is still thinking about what Frisco said. His offer was so nonchalant. So commonplace, as if that's what everyone does. *Eat dinner. Get a girl.* Joe doesn't know what to think. Frisco laughs again. He pats Joe on the shoulder and leaves.

Dale and Joe head to Frisco's recommended restaurant. Dale orders first: lobster tail, quartered lettuce with Roquefort dressing, a double martini. Joe glances at the menu, shrugs, and orders the same. The waiter asks no questions and hurries away to place their order. Dale looks uncharacteristically upset, and Joe asks him what's wrong.

"I dunno," Dale says. "Here we are in a strange city in an unfamiliar country. We left our best friend passed out and broke in a stranger's house. You just ordered a double martini, and I doubt you can handle one, much less a double. Think, man. If you pass out, I can't babysit you both."

Joe sits back in his chair to think just as the waiter sets down the drinks. He resolves to sip his drink slowly. He can't help noting he's a long way from Memphis. With a mock smile, the boy lifts his martini. "Here's to Ray, our drunken bum of a best friend. Here's to Frisco Smith, who we've just trusted with our lives. And here's to us, two lost babes in the woods. May the good Lord watch over our two dumb asses." Joe takes a sip of his martini. "Humph. Not dry enough."

Dale cracks up laughing.

———

After supper, Joe and Dale linger on the street. The two soldiers are bathed in the warm light of the brothel across the way. Soft music emerges from inside its walls, songs that lure sailors to shipwrecks, and Joe wonders why Dale isn't immediately heading up to their hotel room so they can check on Ray.

"At four pesos a crack, I don't think you should develop any cravings for lobster tail," Dale says to the boy. "But I'm glad to see you managed the double martini without falling off your chair. That's another craving you should avoid."

Joe glances toward the brothel, then turns to face Dale. "It's been a long, crazy day, huh?"

"It sure has, buddy. I'm plowed. We should hit the hay. If and when I ever get you back to the barracks, I'm making you stay put for a month."

But Dale isn't moving.

And neither is Joe.

"What do you think?" Joe says at last.

"It's what Asiatics do, that's what I think." Dale's brow is furrowed again.

Joe scuffs his shoe on the sidewalk. Looks down. "Maybe we should go up to our room."

"Yeah," the older soldier says. "Although it probably wouldn't hurt to introduce ourselves to the Big Rotunda. Frisco said to contact her when it's time for our ride back. Remember?"

"I was just thinking the same," Joe says, then waits a long moment before speaking again. "We wouldn't want to risk not being able to get a ride back to base."

Dale grins.

As they reach the top of the stairs to the brothel, they're greeted from the far end of a long hallway by a large Filipina woman in a flowing red gown. She extends her arms and walks toward them. A wide smile shows several gold teeth.

"My American soldier boys! Welcome to Mama Rosa's house. Make this your home." Her voice carries loudly. With a flick of her wrist, two Filipina girls get up from a row of chairs along one side of the hallway and approach. Mama Rosa takes Joe by the arm, examines him more closely, and adds, "Oh! You are a young one. I have just the girl for you." She takes the hand of one of the girls and clamps it in Joe's. "Now, there's a match made in heaven."

Dale and the other girl disappear into a room. Joe feels his hands go clammy. The girl looks at Joe and smiles. She leads him by the hand to another room and closes the door. Now that he's here, he feels uncomfortable—all bravado vanished.

"What's your name?" the girl asks.

"Joe." His mouth is dry.

"I am Perpetua. Now I must take two pesos to Mama Rosa. Give me the money and take your clothes off. I will be back soon."

Joe slides a dollar out of his billfold and hands it to the girl. She squeezes his hand, gives him a smile. His eyes follow her toward the door. Her steps are as graceful as a ballet dancer's, and she gives him another smile as she heads outside. Joe rubs the back of his neck and takes off his pants but leaves on his shirt, jacket, and skivvies. He can't quite believe where he is. His mind does a double take, and he reaches for his pants to put them back on. But swiftly the girl returns. She closes the door behind her and says, "Your friend is with Deolinda. She is a nice girl and very pretty."

Perpetua moves closer to Joe and presses him toward the edge of the bed. They both sit. She removes his jacket and begins to unbutton his shirt. He stops her by clasping her hands. In the sullied light of the room he sees her lift her chin and look straight into his face. She has deep brown eyes. A perfect strawberry mouth. Her lips are trembling. She is just as scared as he.

"We don't have to do this," Joe says.

"No," the girl answers. "We must. Please. I must make you happy."

He shakes his head. "You're just a girl. How old are you, anyway?"

"Old enough." She goes quiet for a moment. "Fourteen."

He gives a little start. They compare birthdays, although Joe does not reveal his birth year. He realizes the girl is just a few months younger than he is. He has not seen a girl his age nor talked with a female peer for a long time. His hands grow slack. She removes one of her hands from his grasp and brushes her fingers along his sleeve. He asks the girl to tell him about her family. The girl looks surprised at the question but tells him simply that she lives here now and that she has no family anymore. He asks how long she has lived at the brothel.

"Not long," she says. "I have only started. You are my first American."

She asks him a few questions in return—where he comes from, what life is like at home. They both relax. Their conversation progresses freely, innocently. Joe feels like he could talk to this girl forever, but suddenly she changes the subject. "We must hurry. Mama Rosa won't like it if I don't make you happy."

Joe starts to explain that it's okay, he won't tell. But she is leaning closer to him now. He smells her perfume, balsamic and fresh. She lets go of his hand, stands, slides her dress from her shoulders, and lets him look at her body. She steps closer and presses her hand firmly against his chest so he lies flat on the bed.

It doesn't take long.

Afterward, she brings him a towel and washbasin. She puts on her gown again, gives him a warm kiss on the lips, and murmurs, "If I have made you happy, please tell Mama Rosa."

Joe gathers her in his arms, holds her close for a moment, kisses her on the lips in return. She wriggles out of his embrace and shakes her head. Their time is up.

———

Frisco Smith drives the three soldiers back to Intramuros in the daylight. Ray has sobered up but has a terrible headache and can't remember much about their weekend away. He grouses about his lost money, cursing them all for being such greenhorns in the city.

Joe says nothing. He can't stop thinking about Perpetua. Complex feelings swirl inside his mind. The idea of visiting a brothel makes him feel muted and low. Yet his time spent with Perpetua, especially their conversation, has filled a small corner of his lonely soul. He doesn't know any other girls in the Philippines, and certainly none his age. He wants to visit her again— not for intimacy. Not really. But for companionship.

The soldiers don't talk further about their weekend. The next few days at the base are a learning experience of daily routines. Each morning the soldiers march. Each afternoon they study manuals and clean their weapons.

Three days pass, and in the evening an old-timer corporal sidles up to Joe's bunk. Dale is there, and Joe and Dale are stamping the last four digits of their serial numbers on their clothes, as ordered.

"Hey," says the old-timer. "Y'all hear we're up for a short-arm inspection next week? How you boys doing down south?"

"The Army inspects us there?" Joe's eyes widen.

"Mandatory, once a month. There's always a couple fellas who don't make it. That's an automatic thirty days in the guardhouse, plus you lose a stripe. Look around some evening and you'll spot some guy trying to cure his chancres. He'll be pounding sulfur pills into powder, sprinkling it on his sores, smearing his whole thingamabob with ointment, wrapping it in toilet paper. I tell ya, always use a rubber when you hit them brothels. You can get 'em free from the company clerk. VD is a way of life over here. Gotta watch out."

The corporal slips away as quickly as he arrived.

Joe and Dale sit for a moment, lost in thought.

"That other night," Dale asks. "Did you use a condom?"

Joe winces. "Didn't even think about it."

CHAPTER 5

The Girl Named Perpetua

Joe thinks about her all the time. His encounter with the girl has seared its way into his psyche, as is the nature of intense experiences, and when he closes his eyes on his bunk at night, he can see the silhouette of her body, feel the filaments of her long cottony hair flow through his fingers, recall the touch of her thigh.

A week passes in barracks life, and Joe considers going to see her again, but something holds him back. The girl captivates his attention, yet he can't shake the reality of what she does for a living. He longs to see her again, yet he feels troubled about making another visit to a brothel.

Early one morning in the third week of June 1941, Joe rises from his bunk and stands looking at the bulletin boards in the barracks. He enjoys reading those boards. He feels informed, as if he's an insider. Newspapers from the States take a month to reach the Philippines, so they are never current at the barracks. But broadsheets from wire services and two newspapers, the *Manila Tribune* and *Manila Times,* are tacked up along with briefs from radio news. Joe reads that the Nazis have declared war on Russia and attacked that behemoth of a country by land, sea, and air. Some three million German troops have invaded the Soviet giant, pushing hard across the wide-open frontier with nineteen panzer divisions, 3,000 tanks, 2,500 aircraft, and 7,000 artillery pieces. Joseph Stalin, who had signed a pact of non-aggression with Hitler just two years earlier, was caught completely by surprise.

Bewildered, Joe scratches his head, tries to relate the news to himself. War still seems far away even with two Axis powers now fighting in Asia, at least for him and the rest of the soldiers of D Company, 1st Battalion, 31st Infantry. The top news around base seems much more relevant, if unimportant. Two more Filipino bunk boys have been hired. For that intrepid service, two dollars per month will be deducted from each soldier's pay.

Positioned next to the headlines, he reads the guard roster and spots his name on it. He's to be a "prison chaser" for his first time, and that bit of information fills him with both excitement and nervousness about the new duty, which starts this morning. He showers, changes into uniform, eats breakfast, then heads over to the guardhouse. He's handed a shotgun and ordered to double-time three burly prisoners from one location to the next. Soldiers could be confined, and demoted, for many reasons— drunkenness, theft, insubordination, dereliction of duty—but in Manila, one of the most common reasons was for contracting a sexually transmitted disease.

The four hurry out of the yard, and the duty seems simple enough until Joe and the three have cleared the line of sight from the guardhouse. Then all three prisoners slow to a crawl. Joe fingers the shotgun and tells the men to pick up the pace, but they laugh and tell him to eat dirt.

"How old are you, anyway?" growls a thick-necked American sergeant with a shaved head. He's in the guardhouse for a month for getting the clap.

"Eighteen." Joe is familiar with the question by now.

"You look twelve. Tell me to hurry again, and I'll yank that shotgun out of your hands and shove it up your ass."

Joe gulps and doesn't know how to answer. He walks at a slower pace behind the prisoners until they reach the destination. He's not afraid of hard work or confrontation, but he hopes he'll pull a different duty soon.

A day later, he catches a break. As Joe heads out of the barracks for breakfast, a young soldier sits on a nearby bunk polishing a bugle. Joe stops and admires the shiny horn.

"You play?" The bugler hands the instrument and polishing cloth to the boy to examine.

Joe gives an admiring whistle and holds the horn gingerly, using the cloth so he doesn't leave fingerprints. "Man, you've really got that thing glistening. I bet it sounds as good as it looks. No, I don't play anything. Never had the chance to learn. But I love music. A long time ago in seventh grade, I had a teacher who got me interested in music. Mostly classical stuff." He examines the bugle one more time, then hands it back.

"I'm shipping out in a couple weeks, heading home." The soldier holds his horn lightly, running his eyes fondly over its curls and angles. "I just hope whoever gets her will treat her kindly."

"You can't take her with you?"

"Nah, she's Army property. But you should put in for my job. Playing the bugle ain't easy at first. You need to develop a lip, and it takes about six weeks to learn. But you don't have to read music, and once you get the hang of it, it's a snap. I'll mention you to the corporal if you'd like. They might have somebody already lined up, though."

Joe says thanks, and the two part ways. Joe's not positive he wants to become the company bugler. He's seen how a bugler needs to make at least four—and as many as ten—different calls each day, from early in the morning until late at night. The duty seems like a lot of responsibility, and usually a bugler is reassigned to headquarters staff. But he thinks again about his stint as a prison chaser and reminds himself anything's better than that.

———

Next weekend Joe is up for a pass. His vacillation is finished. He wants to see Perpetua again. Business on Saturday night at Manny Tang's is booming, and the late-June rain beats a steady patter on the brothel roof. Ray has been assigned driver duty for a lieutenant and is unable to secure leave, but Dale and Joe stand at the top of the stairs in the dank wooden hallway behind a crowd of drunken sailors. No free girls are visible. They scurry in and out of the rooms, always stopping to press bills into Mama Rosa's hands. The sailors ahead are paired off with girls, and Mama Rosa beckons Dale and Joe closer. Their heads, shoulders, and feet are wet.

"Very busy tonight," she says. "The fleet just arrived in town, and they like to spend their money on Mama Rosa's pretty girls. I will have two ready for you in a few minutes."

"No—" Joe says. "I only want to see..."

Mama Rosa is already three steps away, palming more soldiers' money from girls. She pivots and attempts to pair Joe with someone else, but Joe shakes his head. A door opens and out steps Perpetua, her cheeks flushed. She rushes over, seizes Joe by the hand, and says to the madam, "This one for me, please? He was my first American boy." Mama Rosa nods and motions with her chin to a side room.

Perpetua leads Joe inside. The sheets are wrinkled and sour smelling. Perpetua wastes no time unbuckling his belt. "I must have four pesos this time. Then I will be back. You be ready then. Take clothes off, please." She holds out her hand.

"Four pesos?" Joe hands her the money. "Last time it was two."

"Last time was not payday." Perpetua rushes out the door. He buckles his belt again and sits on the side of the bed, fully clothed. She hurries back and sees him dressed.

"You not ready yet? We must hurry tonight. Very busy."

Joe reaches forward and clasps her hand, motions for her to sit next to him. She hesitates before taking a seat.

"Why you wasting your life like this anyway?" Joe asks, all in a rush. She shakes her head, tries to let go of his hand, but he holds tight. "I paid my four pesos, so I have the right to some time with you. If you want to make me happy, answer my question."

The girl wrinkles her nose. "You make trouble for me. Please. I cannot talk to you. You get undressed now. We have much fun." But her voice winds down from a rush, and tears well up in her eyes.

Joe releases his grasp, but Perpetua does not stand to leave. She sniffles once, twice, then buries her head in the crook of his neck. Her back heaves with sobs.

Joe is baffled. No words have accompanied her movements. He's never been the emotional type, but he does the most sensible thing he can think of doing: he wraps his arms around the girl and holds her close.

She cries for five minutes. Six. Seven. Abruptly she sits upright, stands, takes a step backward and away from him, hiccups, dries her eyes. Tries to smile.

Joe stands and the two stare at each other, both in unknown territory.

Perpetua is slender, diminutive in stature. She steps forward, tiptoes, kisses him on the lips. Joe kisses her back. He wants to hold her again. To take her to a movie. To have dinner together. Afterward to dance. If they were both in the United States and things were different, he would have a corsage in his hand. He would ask to escort her to his ninth-grade junior prom.

Instead she whispers, "Thank you for being kind. Nobody is kind here. Mama Rosa is waiting. . . . I must go." The girl slips out the doorway to entertain another paying customer.

———

At the start of July, payday arrives for the Army. It's the first full payday Joe has had since enlisting. Thanks to some back pay that also comes to him, he is allotted thirty dollars. Ray is driving the lieutenant around again and unable to leave base, but Dale and Joe secure passes and head past the gates into the city. An old-timer has informed them where to get their uniforms cut to size so they won't look like walking barracks bags anymore.

They stop at the tailor's shop first, then head to a bar for cheeseburgers and beer, then mosey back to base. Dale has talked Joe into returning early this time but hasn't articulated a reason. Joe's mind wanders to Manny Tang's and Perpetua, but he is okay with not visiting her this weekend. He continues to think of her often but is more perplexed than ever. In some ways he regrets ever meeting her. Their encounter was supposed to mark his passage to adulthood, but he is not sure he feels anything like a man since it happened. Instead, he feels a shift beginning. Perhaps it's not so smart to visit brothels after all, he thinks. Perhaps Dale has been thinking the same thing, for when they arrive back at the barracks he announces to the boy, "Get your GI swim trunks out. Let's head over to the pool and laze around. No one ever uses that thing. We'll have it all to ourselves."

The base pool is old and small and seldom used. Serious swimmers use the big indoor pool at the Y a few blocks away. The boys change in the locker room and emerge onto the sunlit patio near the water. It's a rare cloudless day at the start of the monsoon season, and the air smells lively from yesterday's rain.

Joe and Dale dive in, splash around, and swim a few strokes. Dale announces he's going to swim laps. Joe nods and treads water by the deep end. He glances up and sees the burly bald-headed sergeant who had given him so much trouble when Joe was a prison chaser. The former prisoner is sacked out on a lounge chair. He catches Joe's eye and waves him closer. Joe hesitates.

"C'mere," he barks. "I ain't going to bite you."

Joe strokes over, crawls out of the pool, and stands in front of the bigger man, who sits up and sticks out his hand.

"Just wanted to say I'm sorry," the sergeant says. "Let me give you an official welcome to Weapons Company."

Bewildered, Joe shakes his hand.

"I musta scared the shit out of you the other day," the sergeant says, "but you held up damn well for a kid. That's good. Do your job, and do it well—that's how you develop a good reputation around here. You're on the right track." He motions for Joe to scram, sits back on his lounge chair, and closes his eyes.

For a moment Joe holds his chin up higher. Then he dives back into the pool, treads water some more, and watches Dale finish his laps.

That evening Joe lies on his bunk in the dark. He thinks about who he is becoming. On one hand, he likes the swagger of being a soldier, of having money in his pocket, of heading downtown for lobster tail and martinis. But he's begun to see the darker side of the high life. He remembers Ray being passed out in a hotel room, penniless and drugged. He thinks of the sergeant he just talked to at the pool, apologetic and appreciative now. Yet Joe had learned that the sergeant had been jailed for thirty days and demoted from staff sergeant, all because he caught the clap from a prostitute.

Not for me, Joe thinks. He turns his mind's eye to a picture of becoming proficient at something purposeful. Learning a skill. Perhaps that should be the art of playing the bugle. Developing a steady character. He remembers what the sergeant told him: *Do your job, and do it well—that's how you develop a good reputation around here.*

His mind wanders to Perpetua. The first time he visited the brothel, he slept with her. The next time, he didn't. The first time, he stole something from her—a piece of her innocence, if ever so small. The next time, he gave something back—a shoulder to cry on. The girl seems so young. He wonders who looks out for her. He thinks of Betty and Charlie back in Memphis. When his little sister and brother needed someone to step up for them, Joe stood tall. A similar responsibility has begun to beckon to him here.

———

Dale pulls guard duty over the third weekend of July and can't leave base. It's more than six weeks since Joe first met Perpetua, and he can get a pass if he wants to see her again, but he isn't keen about heading into Manila's downtown core by himself. He wanders over toward the headquarters building to see if he can find Ray. Sure enough, Ray's on duty, waiting to drive the lieutenant around. Joe hasn't seen much of Ray lately, and he misses his friend. Ray has been an older-brother figure to him since back in Fort MacArthur. Ray is smoking a cigarette by himself, standing by the lieutenant's car, tapping his foot.

"This bum's never on time," Ray mutters when Joe's in earshot.

"And you're always working when we're off," Joe says.

"Not my fault," Ray snaps. "Look, if you're so bored, why don't you go get laid? At least that will get you off my ass."

Ray's outburst doesn't sit well with Joe. The boy stomps back to the barracks but doesn't know what to do. He considers going swimming again, but concludes that's no fun by himself. It's already late in the afternoon. Maybe he'll write a letter. *Who am I kidding?* he thinks and checks his billfold. Twenty dollars are left. Still in a huff, Joe hikes over to the orderly room, picks up a pass and a prophylactic kit. He heads off base, hails a one-pony carriage called a *calesa,* and yawps to the driver: "Tang's. Placido Street."

The calesa is slow and the driver wanders from street to street, taking his time before finding the joint. It's not yet five o'clock and Joe decides to eat first. He walks alone into the restaurant with the lobster tail and martinis, is seated by the hostess at a corner table, and orders all he knows how to order in a fancy place. He feels lonely and blue, angry at himself because he knows he's already made the decision. He's heading toward a place he genuinely doesn't want to go.

Out of the kitchen and over to the table walks Frisco Smith. "Private Johnson, what a pleasant surprise. Where are your friends?"

Joe smiles at the company. He explains the three are having a hard time all getting time off together, invites Frisco to sit, and offers to buy the cabdriver a drink.

Frisco laughs. "Thanks, but don't worry about the drink. It's on me. Didn't I tell you I'm the owner here?"

Now it's Joe's turn to laugh. "Two jobs. Wow. How do you ever find time to sleep?"

Frisco calls over a waitress, orders a cup of coffee for himself, then explains: "My father was an American sailor. My mother a Filipina girl. After she became pregnant with me, my father sailed away and never returned. Not because he didn't want to. He was a Navy diver. One day he went down but never came up.

Fortunately he left my mother with some life insurance. A thousand bucks, which is big money for these parts. Mom bought the building you stayed in the other night. She took in roomers and opened the little market in front. When I was old enough, she sent me to school."

The waitress brings his coffee. Frisco pauses, takes a sip, continues. "Ever since I was old enough, I've worked to help out my mother. I love her deeply and would do anything for her. That's why I still drive the taxi too. I opened this restaurant last year, and it's my dream for my mother to quit work someday. Whenever I see soldiers out on the streets who look like they need a meal or a room for the night, I help them find their way here."

"And also to Manny Tang's?" Joe asks.

Frisco shoots the boy a knowing look. "That's part of the draw around these parts." He slaps the table. "Dinner is on me tonight, okay? Gotta get back to work. Next time you're here, bring your friends."

Joe smiles, shakes Frisco's hand, takes another sip of the martini. He concludes that Frisco Smith is all right. He's a businessman and always looking to make a buck, but he's honest about hustling soldiers, doing it for a good cause.

The waitress brings Joe's lobster tail. The boy settles in and eats slowly. The buttered seafood tastes every bit as delectable as before, but somehow part of the glisten has gone out of eating a fancy meal. He considers what Frisco is doing for his mother, how love and duty are closely related. *People have a responsibility to help others,* Joe thinks. *Particularly those they love.* He finishes his meal, wipes the corners of his mouth with a linen napkin, then sits for a long time, thinking. Finally he pushes back his chair, rises, and heads across the street. It is nearly nine o'clock.

The hallway is quiet when he reaches the top of the stairs. A few girls are lounging in the chairs toward the back wall. No other soldiers or sailors are around. Mama Rosa spots Joe and greets him with a faint smile. She doesn't seem as light on her feet as times before.

"Mmm, the little American soldier boy," she says, when he walks closer. "You must try another girl tonight. We have some very good ones."

"I'd like to see Perpetua."

"No, not tonight. She is resting. You will have another young girl." Mama Rosa gives a slight hand wave. A delicate young Filipina stands and walks toward them.

Joe shakes his head, turns to leave. "Thanks, but no thanks. I'll come back when Perpetua is rested."

"Wait." Mama Rosa directs the other girl to sit. "I will see if she is awake. You stay here." She ambles down the hallway and enters a room. Two minutes pass, and Perpetua appears at the end of the hallway. Mama Rosa is with her and calls out to Joe, "You were lucky she is awake. Take your time. We are not busy tonight."

Perpetua gives Joe a weak smile, takes his hand, and leads him into a room. Her face is as beautiful as ever but pallid and drawn. Her breath smells galvanized, like she vomited recently. She tries to unbuckle Joe's belt, but he stops her and whispers, "Sit. You don't look well. You want me to call a doctor?"

She shakes her head and sits but doesn't say anything. He sits next to her and holds her hand. She leans her head on his shoulder, nestling into his side and shoulder with a somber sigh.

"Stay like this as long as you want," Joe says. From the corners of his eyes, he studies her. She lifts her hand to his chest in a half hug and brushes the front of his uniform.

"No, wait." Her voice sounds grieved. "I must take Mama Rosa the money."

Joe fishes out his billfold and presses two pesos into her hand. She walks slowly from the room, and Joe sits on the side of the bed for what seems like a long time. He thinks: *She's just a little girl in a cruel and noncaring world.*

Finally she returns. "Mama Rosa says it's okay if we walk on the balcony tonight. She thanks you. The air is fresh. It will do me some good."

Joe thinks the directive from the madam sounds unusual, but Perpetua is already leading him by the arm out the door, through the hallway, past curtained French doors to a wide balcony. A flight of stairs descends to a small backyard patio that opens onto a narrow alley.

The boy and the girl stand side by side. Joe takes her hand in his. They look out over the patio and inhale the warm, rain-washed night breeze. Perpetua looks up into his face and murmurs, "I will make you happy again. Tonight I am not well, but I will be better soon. You must take another girl tonight. I will understand."

Joe shakes his head. Kisses her forehead. Strokes her shoulders and back. Enfolds her in an embrace. They hold each other for ten minutes, twenty, lingering as long as they dare. Then, without a word, she lets go and leads him back into the hallway. Mama Rosa is sitting on a chair in the hallway with the other girls. They all look worn.

"I think she needs a doctor," Joe says. "Put her to bed, please, and I will pay for her again."

Mama Rosa nudges the girl next to her, who stands and leads Perpetua into a back room. "Walk with me," the madam says to Joe. She stands with some effort, plucks Joe by the elbow, and ushers him to the top of the stairway that leads to the front door. "Sweet boy, you are always welcome here. She will be okay, and don't you worry. You go home now."

Joe plants his feet. "What about Perpetua? What's wrong with her?"

Mama Rosa sighs. "It happens. The sickness. Comes and goes. Tonight it comes. Often in the mornings it is here, but tonight she has it too."

"What kind of sickness? You sure you shouldn't call a doctor?"

Mama Rosa brushes a bit of lint from Joe's lapel, turns his shoulders, heads him toward the staircase. "You are fine American soldier boy, and we all love you. No doctor for Perpetua. Not yet. You go now. Come back soon. She is pregnant. That is all."

———

Joe is jolted by the disclosure. He moves in a fog back to base and for days afterward ponders the implications of his actions. Others have been with the girl. Plenty of others. Still, could he be the one? It's a question he can't shake. And an even more urgent one: what will happen to Perpetua?

Early one morning in late July 1941, Joe stands before the barracks bulletin board, reading the news of the world. Japanese military officials have announced they will move their planes and warships into bases in French Indochina. In retaliation, Great Britain, Canada, and the United States have labeled the move as *aggression* and frozen all Japanese assets within their countries.

President Roosevelt appears alarmed. He has recalled for active duty the famed American general Douglas MacArthur, and named him commander of all US Army Forces in the Far East. General MacArthur will be in charge of all Filipino and American troops in the Philippines now. Joe scans midway through the article from the wire and reads: "U.S. military strategists long have planned to integrate the islands fully into the defense setup in the event of an emergency in the far east."

Joe can't imagine what kind of "emergency" they're envision-ing. Maybe they can't either. He scans farther down the page and reads the baseball scores. Memphis has no home team, but he's a big fan of the St. Louis Cardinals. They tied last night against the Washington Senators in the American League, 0–0. Joe sighs. He wishes he could see a baseball game. He's never seen a major-league game in his young life, but he hopes to someday. Some-how. Lately he hasn't enjoyed his time in the Army much. At first it seemed exciting and different, but now it seems weighted. He worries about Perpetua, and he wonders if the war will somehow engulf his new world.

The boy shakes off the thought, notices the company bugler sitting several bunks away, and wanders over to say hi. Joe has showered already, and they have a few minutes before breakfast.

"Glad you stopped by," the bugler says. "I forgot to tell you I talked to the corporal, who talked to the first sergeant. He asked me about you. You're supposed to go see the corporal. He'll send you over to the bandmaster at the gymnasium. You'll get on a practice schedule and be on your way. Looks like it's going to happen."

"That sounds swell," Joe says. "Thanks. Probably the best thing that could happen to me here." A twinge of the forlorn lies deep in his voice.

The bugler frowns. "What's wrong?"

Joe begins to say something, then stops. He decides not to spill his guts to the bugler, someone he doesn't know as well as Dale or Ray. Instead he says, "You've been here for a while, yeah?"

"Two years."

"Can I ask you an odd question?"

"Okay."

"What happens to a pregnant prostitute?"

The bugler laughs. "Is that the setup for a joke? I dunno. What?"

"Nope. I'm being serious."

The bugler looks at the horn, loses his laugh. "Well, I don't have much experience in that area, but I've heard it's sure not an egg in your beer. If she's pregnant, she'll get sent down to the port area—to the lower-class whorehouses. Some of the scum down there are turned on by young pregnant girls. She'll have it rough. Once she has her baby, she won't be able to work anymore. Not even to do that. She'll be out on the streets, begging with her baby." He shivers, looks away.

Joe's jaw strikes a hard line, but he doesn't explain anything further except to say thanks for the information and that he'll check in with the corporal. The boy heads over for breakfast. Each day he grows older, he thinks, he discovers the world is not a pleasant place for everybody.

When the food is served, the table is loaded with bacon and scrambled eggs, platters of hotcakes. Syrup, butter, and strawberry jam. Hot coffee. Joe sits, piles his plate the same as usual, then stares at his food, finding his appetite strangely vanished. He thinks again of duty and love, of responsibility and caring for people, and a question begins to race through his mind, one for which no answer follows.

What hope does she have now?

CHAPTER 6

She'll Make You a Star

The lukewarm tropical rain spits and fizzles one morning in early September 1941, and Joe sidesteps mud puddles as he heads toward the base gymnasium where he's been sent. He needs to meet the bandmaster to get set up on a practice schedule so he can become the new bugler for Weapons Company.

Joe's movement is languid as he tries to keep his feet as dry as possible. He's concerned about a cold he caught and kicked that's left a residue. He still coughs at night, and his chest is sore. Twice, he's run a fever that's abated.

The misty base is quiet and feels uninhabited, and as Joe moves he thinks of how he hasn't been reading the news much lately. Whenever he reads of life back in America, he thinks of home and a lump forms in his throat. He wrote his mother recently, saying he feels like he's aged ten years since arriving in the Philippines.

The boy heads inside the echoey gymnasium. Bleachers line the walls. A raised boxing ring sits in the middle. The entire room smells of dust and sweat. The bandmaster's office is fixed in the far corner of the gym, and when the man meets Joe, he grumbles and gripes and points a weathered finger toward a small cardboard box on the floor, replete with old mouthpieces. Joe is instructed to find one he likes, then practice blowing into it until a thick callus develops on his upper lip. The man offers no further instructions.

Joe tests a few and picks out the mouthpiece that feels easiest to blow into. But back in the barracks, when he shows the mouthpiece to the other bugler, he advises Joe to return to the gym and find one that's harder to blow into. The trick is for Joe to blow into it until his lip swells, then blow into it some more. He needs to blow to the point of discomfort, then push past the pain and keep going.

"Don't look for the easy way out," the bugler says. "If becoming a bugler was simple, everybody would do it. Until you develop a good callus, you aren't going to be able to do anything."

Joe finds a quiet spot on base and practices blowing into the harder mouthpiece, but he begins to have second thoughts about the whole matter. His lip soon aches, and if all the musicians are as crotchety as the bandmaster, he's not sure he wants to be associated with them.

———

When Saturday arrives after a long and demanding week, Joe has only one thought on his mind: Perpetua. Even though it's not always easy for the boy to talk with her, and they never seem to get enough time together, she's become the brightest spot in Joe's life. He has several more questions he wants to ask her, too.

Dale doesn't want to accompany Joe to the brothel this time, so Joe heads out alone and hails a calesa for the ride over. He proudly wears his newly tailored uniform so Perpetua can see him in it. The calesa pony clip-clops at an ambling pace, and it's already early evening by the time Joe reaches Manny Tang's.

It's a busy night, and Joe's at the end of the line. The men in front of the door clamor like a crowd at a bazaar, and by the time Joe gets inside and reaches the top of the stairs, the first girl he catches sight of is Perpetua, but she's leading another soldier into a room. Joe makes a slight growl in his throat. He turns and starts heading back down the stairs when a familiar voice rings out, "My American soldier boy, don't leave! Come say hello to your Mama Rosa."

Joe hesitates. Fuming, he turns around and slowly walks up the stairs toward the Big Rotunda. She smiles broadly, opens her arms, and pulls him into the mammoth folds of her bosom.

"Don't worry about Perpetua and her work," she murmurs. "She loves you—and only you. She will be sad if you leave without seeing her. Here, sit a bit and relax. She will be finished soon."

"I'm not jealous," Joe mutters. He tries to straighten up, but Mama Rosa clutches him in a tight mash against her breasts. He feels flustered and grows red in the face. She releases him and points toward a chair. Joe sits.

In no time, Perpetua emerges from the room and hands Mama Rosa a dollar. She spots Joe, runs over, and gives him a big hug. "Please wait for me. I really want to see you tonight. It won't take long."

Joe hugs her back. He can feel a small bump near her stomach, and he doesn't want her returning to that room. But he feels Mama Rosa's eyes burrowing into him, so he lets Perpetua go. The girl hurries into the room and closes the door.

"I told you she loves you," Mama Rosa says with a blanket smile. "You were her first American soldier boy."

"How far along is she?" Joe asks. "She's already showing."

Mama Rosa leans closer, lowers her voice. "Three months. Maybe a little more. She will not have to work here much longer. Don't worry. Many of our girls have babies. Things will be okay for her, I am sure."

Joe doesn't believe the madam, but he decides not to ask any further questions of her. He crosses his arms and waits. In a few minutes Perpetua returns from the room. She whispers something into Mama Rosa's ear, and the madam nods her acquiescence.

"Pay her your dollar now," Perpetua says to Joe. "She says we can go out on the balcony for a while." Joe hands his money to the madam. Perpetua seizes Joe's hand and leads him outside onto the porch overlooking the patio. Joe is happy to be outside with her.

The girl begins to hum a Filipino song. She faces the boy and fastens her arms around his neck. Her tune is heroic yet melancholic. Clumsily, he grasps her waist, just as if they were at a school dance, and begins to sway along with her to her song. Joe likes the way she feels in his arms. She is soft everywhere important, and her hair smells warm and woodsy, like a campfire on a beach.

"Know the melody?" Perpetua asks.

Joe shakes his head, secures her closer in his arms.

"It's 'The Kundiman,' an old Filipino love song." Softly, she sings a few lyrics in Tagalog, the first language of many Filipinos, then translates for Joe:

In the dark of night,
I stay up thinking.
Only your image
Will be my light.

"It's beautiful," Joe says. "Just like you."

He wants to ask Perpetua if she has made any plans for the future, if there's anyone in her life who can help with her pregnancy. But abruptly she stops dancing, pulls his face closer, and kisses him on the mouth. They stay like that, lips against lips, for ten seconds, fifteen, until he notices her tears. He tucks her head down onto his chest and strokes her hair. She keeps crying.

"What's wrong?" Joe asks. "Let me help."

The girl raises her head and wipes her tears with the sleeve of her gown. "I am sorry to cry. It's just that you are so kind to me all the time. I think of you every day and night. You are my special soldier boy."

Joe traces the contour of her cheek with two fingers. He wants to tell her many things, about the feelings he has for her that he can't yet articulate. But instead he murmurs simply, "You bring out all the good in me."

They embrace for another long moment, then she wipes her eyes a final time. Without another word, the girl leads the boy back to the hallway and releases his hand. Before she disappears inside the girls' quarters, she offers him one last lingering glance.

Tension rises inside Joe. Alone, he walks to where Mama Rosa sits. "How much longer will she work here?"

The madam glances around the hallway, as if searching for the right answer. This time she does not smile. "You wish to say goodbye to her before she goes?"

"Yes."

"You must come before the first of next month. No later."

Joe nods. A million questions race through his mind, but he considers the folly of talking more with the woman tasked with sending the girl away. Instead, he thanks her for the information and slowly walks down the stairs to the street. Outside on the sidewalk, he tries to inhale the fresh rain-washed air. Each time he has stood on this sidewalk over the past three months, his heart has felt like a rock. Now, he feels like a clock on a bomb that's ticking down before an explosion. He knows something must be done to help the girl. But what?

———

Early the next morning on base, Joe tries to clear his head. He hikes over to the locker room and practices blowing into his mouthpiece until his lip aches. He's not sure he'll ever get the hang of the bugle. In the afternoon he has some free time and tries to lounge at the pool with Dale, but nothing of substance is said between them. All day Joe feels uneasy. That night Joe pulls guard duty and is assigned to watch the finance office in the port area. His shift lasts from midnight until 4 a.m.

The office is in a building on a street near the docks. Joe enters the building by climbing a long flight of wooden stairs. At the top of the staircase is a heavy locked chain-link door that leads into the building's entryway. Joe unlocks the door, ventures inside, and patrols the hallways. Only a few dim lights shine within. They cast shadows over the walls, and as Joe tiptoes around the empty building he swears he sees the shadows move. The place gives him the creeps. Army life is losing its luster. All he can think about is Perpetua and the nagging questions about what the girl will do once she is sent to the docks to work. The silent shadowy hours only agitate his fears, and Joe hopes he never pulls this kind of duty again, but the next night he's assigned the same. He passes the time on duty by blowing into his mouthpiece, practicing, while trying to think up a way to help Perpetua. No solutions emerge.

In daylight hours, the bandmaster examines the boy's lip and sees that a good callus is starting to form. He gives Joe an old, tarnished bugle, teaches him how to make some sounds, and sends him away with an order to go someplace nobody can hear him, stick a handkerchief into the end of the horn, and keep toughening up his callus. Joe obeys the order but finds the bugle difficult to blow into. The sounds that emerge are amateurish and uncontrolled. The bugle groans in distress. Back in the barracks, he tracks down the other bugler.

"I don't know what I'm doing," Joe mutters. "I keep pulling these late guard duties that give me the willies, and my mouth looks like a mule's ass."

The other bugler laughs. "Keep working on it, kid. You'll get the hang of it soon. Your mouth looks exactly like mine when I first started."

The bugler gives Joe some tips about the best places around base to practice without being heard. The locker room at the swimming pool works well, especially during a hard rain. He shows Joe how to play "Reveille," and instructs him how to check out a Victrola from the bandmaster's office so he can listen to the calls and imitate them.

Joe thanks him, then pauses before saying, "Can I ask you something else?"

"Sure."

"That convent across the street. What kind of place is it?"

"With the nuns and stuff?"

"Yeah. Sometimes I've seen girls over there. They're not wearing the nuns' getup. What's that about?"

"Oh, they run some kind of home for Filipina girls who don't have any families. Some of the girls are pregnant, I think. Why? You sweet on one of them?" The bugler shakes his head. "Good luck with that. It's a fortress. Those nuns keep the place locked tighter than a drum."

———

Two weeks pass. It's nearing the end of September, and on Saturday Joe secures a pass and hails a calesa, but he doesn't head to the brothel to see Perpetua. Instead, he hopes to find Frisco Smith. The boy has considered talking over his idea with Dale and Ray, but in the end has decided against it. If something goes wrong, Joe doesn't want his friends to be involved.

It's pouring, and Joe is soaked by the time he reaches Frisco's restaurant. The hostess smiles and prepares to seat him, but Joe waves her off and asks to speak to the owner. She says Frisco is driving his cab tonight. Dejected, Joe heads outside and stands under the canopy in front of the restaurant, mulling various ideas.

The rain falls harder, as if made of lead. Joe stands on the sidewalk for more than an hour before he spots a familiar set of headlights. Frisco's cab pulls up in front. Joe opens the back door before Frisco can get out.

"Drive down the street a ways," Joe says. "We need to talk."

Without a word, Frisco heads down the street a few blocks and pulls into a filling station that's closed for the night. He shuts off the engine and headlights, turns around in his seat, and gives Joe a puzzled look. "What's with all this cloak-and-dagger stuff? You in some kind of trouble?"

"Can I trust you?" Joe asks.

Frisco nods. Joe tells him about his friendship with Perpetua and her pregnancy, what he's heard becomes of pregnant prostitutes, and that he wants to help.

Frisco sucks in his breath a long moment before answering. "It's true. She'll get beat to a pulp down at the port. But look, you can't be so naïve. Thousands of girls are just like her in Manila. You're not in the States anymore, and things are different here. If you mess around with one of Manny Tang's girls, you'll regret it. Understand?"

"Yeah. But—"

"I'm not shitting you, kid. You're in way over your head. Cross Manny Tang and he'll slit your throat—and hers, too. Just let it go. Promise me."

Joe sits but says nothing.

"Promise," Frisco says again, louder.

"The girls in the convent across the street—" Joe asks. "How do they end up there?"

Frisco slams his hand on the back of the bench seat. He

narrows his eyes, then slams his hand again. "You don't listen, do you?"

Joe shakes his head. It's his lifelong vow asserting itself: he doesn't give in to fear.

Rain pelts the taxicab. Frisco's face tightens. He begins to talk. The two huddle in the parking lot for another ten minutes, with Frisco whispering a minefield of information to the boy.

The cab starts up again in the darkness. Its headlights switch on, and Frisco drives the boy back to the entrance of the base. But Joe doesn't go inside the barracks. Instead, he looks both ways, jogs across the street in the dark, opens the gate in a wrought-iron fence, and heads through a small courtyard. He taps on the iron door.

The convent is a tall, brick building. No one answers. Joe waits and knocks again, this time a little harder. Nothing. He looks both ways again, then pounds with his fist. Finally a small iron window in the door slides open. An eye blinks, stares at him. Joe stares back. He hears chains rattle, a dead bolt being slid to one side. The door slowly opens and a nun hisses through the crack: "Go away, young man. This building is off-limits to servicemen."

"No, wait," Joe says. "Is this where the girls go?"

The nun nods and starts to close the door. Joe tries to stick his fingers inside but misses. The door shuts, and the dead bolt is rammed back into place. He pounds on the door again, but no one answers. He pounds until his hand grows sore. Finally, after a long while, the door opens again. This time an older nun stares into his face with stern, unblinking eyes.

"Have you been drinking?" she says. "What is your purpose?"

"No, Sister. I know a young girl who desperately needs your help. She's pregnant and works at Manny Tang's. She's only fourteen. Please."

The nun stares at Joe again. "You are stationed across the street?"

"Yes, ma'am."

She stares at him another long moment. Nothing can be heard except the steady beating of the rain. At last she says, "Come inside. It's wet."

Joe exhales. She opens the door and leads him into a small entryway, but will take him no farther. A tall wooden door looms ahead of them, shut tight. Two nuns stand in front of this inner door, as if to block entry. "Space is very limited here," the older nun says. "Our Lord and Savior appreciates your concern for the girl, but we have only so many beds and only so much space. You must understand. There is nothing we can do."

Joe's face falls. "Maybe you know of someplace else. I have money. If I gave you five dollars a month to take care of her, would that be enough to keep her, at least till she could find another place?"

The nun looks at Joe another long moment. "She has no relatives who can take her?"

"No, ma'am. Not a soul."

For a moment, Joe thinks the matter is finished, that nothing can be done. He reaches into his wallet and holds out a ten-dollar bill, if only to communicate the seriousness of his intent. The nun takes a step toward him, accepts the money, and lowers her voice to where Joe can barely hear.

"Come at night. Only at night. Knock hard three times. Then once. Bring the girl."

───────

It's the last Saturday of September 1941, and Joe is out of cash. Without explaining why, he asks Dale if he can borrow eleven dollars. He also confirms that Dale will be working the back gate later that evening. Dale has only two dollars, but he loans the boy his cash and confirms the duty. Joe says thanks and secures a

pass. He borrows nine additional dollars from a shark of a soldier who charges 20 percent interest, signs out with the Corporal
of the Guard, and grabs the first calesa he sees.

On the other side of the city, Joe pauses for a moment on the
top stair of the brothel's old wooden landing, then peers down
the dusky hallway into the gloom. A heavy rain beats on the roof.

"She's still here?" he asks, when the madam approaches. "I'd
like to take her out on the balcony again, if that's okay."

"Ah, my little soldier boy. I'll get her for you."

Perpetua emerges from one of the rooms, led by the madam.
The bump in her middle is larger than before. Her face beams
when she sees Joe.

The trip to the brothel, the escape with Perpetua, and the
arrival outside the convent take less than an hour. Now, as they
shiver in the rain with fear in their hearts, Joe repeats his knock
sequence on the door.

It seems to take forever. Finally the door opens. Two nuns glance
at the boy and the girl, then whisk Perpetua inside and through the
wooden door. They give them no chance to say goodbye. Before Joe
can move again, the older nun appears. Joe hands her his money.

"You will never see her again," she says. "If you try to knock,
no one will acknowledge you. When it is time to pay more, use the
alms box—it is the slot in the iron door." She glances more closely
into Joe's face and adds, more softly, "Thank you for this act of
kindness. The world needs more people like you. You may call me
Sister Carmella. If ever the time comes when you are in trouble,
remember me, and know that prayers for you are being said."

———

Joe's standing inside the locker room the next morning, practicing with his horn muted, when a sergeant sticks his head inside
and barks for him to double-time it over to the provost marshal,

the head of the base's military police. Joe's in deep trouble, but the sergeant won't explain why.

The boy hurries over, jogs inside the building, and immediately is ushered into the major's office. Joe snaps to attention in front of a large desk. The major is thickly built, no-nonsense, sitting behind the desk and slapping his palm lightly with a riding crop, as if waiting for the boy to arrive. To the left stands a short Chinese man dressed in a white sharkskin suit. Behind him stand two muscular Filipinos, also dressed in suits.

"That's him!" The short man points at Joe. "He did it!"

Joe stays frozen.

The major sets down his riding crop and says to Joe, "At ease, soldier. Where were you last night?"

Joe clears his throat. "In bed, sir." His voice is a tone too high.

"He lies!" the short man says. "I have a witness. He stole one of my best girls! I tell you—"

"Mr. Tang, this is my office and my inquiry. You will allow me to get to the facts. Understood?" The short man bites his lip, as if unaccustomed to being ordered to shut up. The major looks directly at Joe. "Were you at one of Mr. Tang's brothels last night around 2030?"

Joe collects himself and says in a lower tone, "No, sir, I was returning from the Ideal Theater and nowhere near any of Mr. Tang's brothels."

"Have you ever been to one of Mr. Tang's brothels?"

"Yes, sir. But not last night. It was raining and I was almost broke, so I went to a movie and came home early."

Manny Tang lets loose again. "He lies! He stole my best young girl. She was only fourteen. I pay much money for that girl. He must be punished and return her. I am very important person in Manila. I have many friends in the government—" He stops abruptly, sensing he's crossed the line.

The major picks up his riding crop again just as the Sergeant of the Guard appears in the doorway. He waves the man over. The sergeant places last night's pass book on the major's desk, points to a certain entry, and leaves. The major examines the entry, shifts his gaze to Manny Tang, and stares long and hard at the pimp and his two bodyguards. When he speaks again, the major's voice is firm as flint: "You admit buying underage girls for your bordellos. The Philippine authorities may look the other way, but the US Army will not. How would you like it if all your places are declared off-limits to every American soldier and sailor in the Philippines?"

"I wish to apologize, sir." Manny Tang's words rush out in a jumble. "I have received wrong information. Perhaps this is not the soldier after all."

The major swivels the open pass book so Manny Tang can see it. "This soldier checked in at 2045 from his pass. How could he steal one of your girls and get back here in such a short time? Where is he going to hide this girl, and for what reason? He's only a private, with very little money. This whole thing stinks to high heaven."

Manny Tang edges toward the door, his voice an ingratiating whine: "Major. I am so sorry to have taken your valuable time with this mistake. Please accept my apology. We shall forget this matter and stay friends. Sometimes these girls run away to the province. Perhaps this girl did that."

The major glowers at the pimp and points toward the door with his riding crop. Manny Tang and his thugs slither away. Joe stands in front of the desk. He doesn't blink. The major scowls at the boy.

"How long have you been over here, soldier?"

"Came over on the *Republic,* sir."

"Well, son, for such a young man with so little time in the

Army, you do get around. I strongly recommend you keep your pecker in your pants and your fly zipped. It will get you into trouble if you're not careful. Dismissed."

Joe snaps a salute, does a smart about-face, and heads for the barracks.

For the next several days, Joe spends any free moments practicing his bugle in the empty locker room. He has almost mastered the instrument, and he plays it with the brightness of someone from whom a heavy load has been lifted. He's conquered "Sick Call," "Drill Call," "Tattoo," and "To the Color." He can rip through "Reveille," "Assembly," and "Mess Call."

Music pours out of him with assurance and clarity, even when he hears that rumors about him are flying around base. Some say the boy's got his own gal stashed somewhere in Manila. Others say the boy bested one of the most dangerous thugs in all the Philippines. Some listen to Joe's newfound confidence through the pool-house walls and insist he's well on his way to becoming the best damn bugler in the whole regiment. Joe will neither confirm nor deny a thing.

Early in October 1941, a number of soldiers whose enlistments are nearly up are shipped back to the States. Joe's pal, the original bugler, is among them. No formal goodbyes are said, and Joe doesn't even know his friend is gone until he enters the barracks and finds that the man has left his shiny instrument on the pillow of Joe's bunk. It was the bugler's pride and joy. A note is attached:

KEEP MAKING US PROUD. SHE'LL MAKE YOU A STAR.

PART II

Was she the love of my life? Nah, I never married Perpetua, if that's what you're asking. Sorry to disappoint you. Hell, I disappoint myself—plenty of times. That's a good question, though, because she wasn't out of my life yet.

Heh. I tell ya, you don't meet a girl like that twice. Wish I could say I got myself straightened out when I came home after the war, flipped a quick U-turn, and headed straight back to the Philippines to look for her. But no, I came home to the States and married some Memphis gal I'd known for thirty minutes. I was nineteen, almost twenty. You do dumb stuff at that age. My first wife, Betty Jean, was seventeen, still in eleventh grade at Humes. We got hitched in the backyard of her mama's house. That was a riot.

You got to realize how banged up I was back then. 1945. Still got my hospital records around in a box. Here, see for yourself:

"Awardee of the Purple Heart.

"Wound, lacerating, posterior aspect right lower leg— severe.

"Malnutrition—severe."

What they don't say but may as well is "messed in the head— severe." These days, they'd call what I had severe PTSD. You don't go through what I'm gonna tell you about next and come out otherwise.

So, I married that gal, then bounced around a bit. Always searching, never finding. I reenlisted in the US Army Air Forces, precursor of the USAF. I wasn't looking to fight, but I needed a job. My head was so rattled. Not trying to make excuses, but PTSD plays a part in my story too. The gal and me broke up. I played minor-league ball but threw out my arm. It healed, but not enough for the majors. I joined the Marine Corps reserve when they promised I could play baseball for their team. Then in '50, Korea breaks out, and they call me up to active duty—this time as a Marine.

Shit. After all I'd been through in World War II, I didn't want to be anywhere near that fight. I only wanted to play ball. But I got my orders. Couple days later, a guy comes to my door, says I need to go. They sent me overseas a second time, and first day of battle I'm shot in the stomach. Done. Finished. My fifteen-minute tour of Korea was up.

Took several months to recover. It was particularly bad for me in the hospital, and being shot didn't help my memories from World War II neither. My wound healed, though, because I stayed in the Marines and served another enlistment before getting out in '53. Toward the end I was a drill instructor mostly. Medically retired is what they called it, 'cause I couldn't shake my nightmares. That, plus I'd been exposed to ionizing radiation, probably from being too close to Nagasaki. I don't know. Nothing felt the same for me.

I'd gotten married a second time—this pretty gal, Emma Lea. Her older brother had been killed on Mindanao in the war. I met her in San Antonio before I went to Korea. Me and the wife had two sons, Floyd Charles in 1949 and Jerry in 1951, but that marriage ended, sorry to say. I was always so angry. Times I'd wake up 2 a.m. and leave. Not tell a soul where I was going—or, after I came home, what I'd done. Once I woke us both up and we moved, just like that. Left behind everything we owned. Middle of the night.

Man, the things I'd shout at Emma Lea sometimes. Horrible things. Sometimes I'd be dreaming. Sometimes I'd be awake. I remember a buddy getting in my face then, telling me I was real messed up. I didn't disagree.

Did I love Emma Lea? Yeah. She was a better person than me. We divorced once, then got back together, then divorced a second time. We tried to make it work. She told me only the meanest, nastiest folks could survive what I went through in the war. You have to be damn sure of yourself to survive, she said. No, I never saw my boys much as they grew up. She knew I was struggling. She would still talk to my mama, but she'd hardly talk to me. I got to wondering if she was trying to protect my boys from their own father.

My mind became so distressed that I finally checked into a military psych ward in Palo Alto. They sent me up to two psychiatrists. I was nearly undone. Six months passed in that hospital with me rattling around in it. None of us was actually crazy, least we figured. Sometimes we joked around. It weren't all bad. But I felt alone. Real alone. Lots of things in life is like that.

Aw, maybe that's more than you want to know.

I get to telling these stories sometimes, and all you asked was about Perpetua. If she was the love of my life. Well, what am I gonna say? Did I think about her over the years—at least from time to time?

Shit. Never been a day gone by when I didn't. That night I dropped her off at the Catholic church, I wish I'd looked at her longer. Studied every inch of her face in the lamplight. Memorized exactly what she looked like so I never forgot. My first love was always with me, even when the memory of her face grew blurry. I tell you this much. That night at the church, my war was only beginning. Perpetua got me through every moment of hell that was to come.

CHAPTER 7

Horizon of Hurt

J oe wants to go home.

He writes his mother, hinting. He's lonesome and has an ear infection. He doesn't want to sound like a quitter to her, but maybe she'll pick up the cues and reveal his true age to the Army. A month will pass before his letter reaches home. Another month to have a message returned. Morning after morning, while waiting for a letter, Joe sneaks a look across the street from his quarters, hoping he'll glimpse Perpetua. He sees nuns in their black and white habits out on the lawn, but nobody else. All the adrenaline from the rescue has fled his system now, and the boy feels heartsick, depleted, attached to those he loves yet distanced from them all. Joe stops going out on weekend passes. He fears that Manny Tang and his thugs are looking for him, seeking revenge. When the soldiers are paid at the start of October 1941, Joe hands the loan shark the nine dollars he borrowed plus interest, repays Dale his two bucks, then slips another five into an envelope with the regimental insignia to drop across the street. He feels shaky. Cautious.

An older soldier in the company is Catholic, and Joe carefully inquires if he knows how the charity across the street operates. Joe learns that when a pregnant girl is close to delivery, she's moved to another sanctuary across town where a few of the nuns are midwives. After giving birth, the mother is trained in job skills and can seek employment. The nuns provide day care.

"It's a struggle, and money is scarce," the older soldier says. "A single mother has a hard life in Manila. But if things work out, she's able to make it. That's the goal."

When the first of November arrives, Joe drops another five dollars in another regimental envelope and takes it across the street. He wants Sister Carmella to know he's keeping his word. The boy is tempted to linger at the church gate, to knock and inquire about those inside, but he remembers his promise to stay anonymous. Already he has stopped looking across the street every morning for her. Despondency grasps at the boy. He misses his friend.

Feeling he's done all he can do for Perpetua, at least for now, he focuses his attention on trying to get sent home. Joe knows the futility of directly approaching his commanding officer with news of his real age. He's unable to prove it without a birth certificate. He writes his mother again, this time more specifically, adamantly, asking her to track down a copy:

> *Write to the commanding officer of the 31st Infantry, Manilla, and tell him I joined the army without your consent, and I am underage and to send me home at once. Mother, you may think I am a sissy pants and a coward and can't take it. But if I come home, I'll get an education and make something of myself.*
>
> *I have been telling you I was all right, but really this is the worst place in the world.... When I go back home, I'll not be a burden to you. Mister Jake or someone else may tell you to let me take it like a man, but they don't know what it's like.*

His mother has known for months where her boy is, but being in the Army is a job, and jobs are hard to come by. The boy is fed and clothed. Besides, Joe has reassured her he's okay. Shortly after Joe's adamant letter is sent, he receives a letter from his mother, but she evidently hasn't received his request yet. In a warm, chatty voice, she writes how she's thinking of him and hopes he eats a big Thanksgiving dinner. She promises she'll send him a little something for Christmas but doesn't know what to send, because "it takes so long to get there." She closes her letter, "Well, Joe, chin up and be a good boy. I love you lots, Mother."

Joe reads and rereads the letter and flops on his bunk. He is filled with remembrances—not just of his mother and siblings, but of his father's side of the family, too. He recalls the warm times he had as a kid before Mr. Jake entered the picture. He thinks of Alamo Downs and his grandmother's home cooking. His mind constantly drifts to Perpetua. He aches to see her. The girl he loves is right across the street, but she may as well be across the world.

Dale finds the boy huddled in a ball on his bunk. He can see the boy is spent and in need of encouragement. Dale sits on the opposite bunk and asks a few gentle questions. Joe tells him the story about what he did for Perpetua and why.

For a long time, Dale simply listens. Then he says, "What you did took guts and a good heart, Joe. You're a good soldier. You did your duty then and now. Besides what you did for the girl, I always see you doing your duty here correctly and on time. You're a damn good bugler, too. Everyone in the battalion talks about how well you play. Don't sell yourself short."

Joe sniffs and blurts, "I guess I've accomplished a lot for a fifteen-year-old kid from Memphis." He bolts upright, claps both hands over his mouth, realizing what he's revealed.

A slow smile breaks over Dale's face. "Relax, kid. I figured it out long ago. We didn't have you pegged quite as young as fifteen. But we sure as hell knew you weren't eighteen. Don't worry. We got your back."

Joe feels strangely loosened. He'd held the secret inside tightly for so long—now he feels released. He exhales. At last, someone in the Army besides him knows the truth.

———

November 1941 rushes by. Joe pulls guard duty twice, attends boxing matches on base with Ray and Dale, and is chosen to play "General's Call" on his bugle when MacArthur visits the compound. The battalion does two forced night marches in full gear. Fifteen miles each. Joe senses a new intensity and an upward arc to their training.

Near month's end, Joe is ordered to add an additional duty to his bugling responsibilities. He'll become the new battalion messenger and company runner, ferrying officers and messages between various bases in the city on a motorcycle with a sidecar. Joe has never ridden a motorcycle. He's both worried and excited as he trots down to the motor pool. An angular, pimply-faced sergeant glances at Joe's papers, then leads him inside to the building's back corner. Almost hidden from view is a dusty, low-slung machine with chipped green paint.

"There's the old gal," the sergeant says. "She'll shake your teeth out on these cobblestone streets, so I'd poke along whenever you're inside the wall. Help me push her outside. We'll hose her down and try to get her started."

Awestruck, Joe stares at the machine. They push her outside, dust her off, check the oil and gas, and put more air in the tires. The sergeant twists the spark and kicks the starter. The bike fires up with a hard rumble. He gives the kid a few pointers. Joe straddles the seat, examines the grips and switches, and taps it into gear. The boy lurches forward and shimmies down the narrow cobblestoned street. The bike has a front spring, but no rear shocks. She backfires every fifty feet, and blue smoke pours from the tailpipe but disappears after the bike warms. Joe rides up and down the street five times, testing the brakes, twisting the throttle, hearing the roar of the engine echo off the buildings. He returns to the motor pool and switches her off. A huge grin spreads across the boy's face. The thrill of riding a motorcycle feels electrifying, like a thunderbolt has cracked the sky.

Inside the building, the sergeant calls Joe over with a holler, tosses him a pen, and chin waves toward a form and a pass. "Sign here. She's officially checked out to you. This pass allows you to check your bike out if we're ever closed and a guard's on duty. Before you get any real orders, take her outside the wall a few times and make sure you can handle the traffic. Meanwhile, keep her parked in the back, out of the way." The sergeant lifts his head and smirks. "The city's yours now, kid. Stay out of trouble."

———

The morning of December 8 dawns rainless and warm in Manila. Joe stands beside Dale during roll call, and at first it seems like any other Monday. Since Manila is across the International Date Line, it's a day earlier back in the States.

December 7, 1941.

The formation is dismissed. First Platoon catches area policing. Joe and Dale and the rest of the men shuffle along with their eyes to the ground, picking up cigarette butts and empty gum wrappers, griping about all the careless slobs in the world.

They finish the chore and amble toward breakfast. Joe washes his hands, sits down, and loads his plate with bacon and sausage, scrambled eggs, hash browns, and toast with jam. The table scuttlebutt is of a wild party last night at the Manila Hotel's Fiesta

Pavilion. The hotel acts as MacArthur's residence while he's in Manila. Evidently, scads of officers, including American pilots and even Major General Lewis Brereton himself (commander of Army Air Forces in the Far East), attended an unbridled shindig thrown by the 27th Bomb Group. The party raged until 2 a.m. "I hear girls squealed until early morning," a private says.

Joe chuckles. After breakfast, he returns to his bunk upstairs in the barracks along with the others in his platoon. He's just about to head down to the motor pool to take his bike out for a practice run when the chow bell begins to clang in earnest. *Strange,* Joe thinks. *We already finished breakfast.*

Other bells in the cuartel begin to clang. A jarring cacophony of alarms, whistles, sirens, yells. A sergeant bounds up the stairs two at a time and shouts, "Everyone out into the street. Formation! This is no drill!"

The men jostle one another, clatter down the steps, and fall in by platoons. A sergeant shouts, "Attention!" A lieutenant strides to the front of the assembly and speaks in a surprisingly calm voice: "At ease. It's not official yet, but the wire services have announced that the Japanese have attacked Hawaii. We're awaiting word from Battalion Command as to what action we are to take. Personally, I find it hard to believe. We will stand by on alert until the company receives official orders. Each of you will return to your bunks, lock your personal belongings in your foot-lockers for safekeeping, and dress for field duty. Return to this area on the double, and we will issue pistols and gas masks by platoon. Dismissed."

The men scramble back inside the barracks and up the stairs. Joe and Dale help each other with their packs in the clamorous room, adjusting the straps and fitting them snugly. Joe squints sideways at Dale. "You think this is the real McCoy?"

"I hope not." Dale's voice is somber. "But I have a feeling we won't see this old barracks for a while."

Soon the platoon is outside again and assembled on the company street. From all over the city, sirens have begun to wail. For more than an hour, the platoons mill about on the street, awaiting further orders. The sun shines down hot. Each man is issued a gas mask, a .45 pistol, and two clips of ammunition. Machine guns and mortars are lined up and readied, but no ammunition is issued for the larger weapons. They wait, sweating. No one seems to know what to do.

At last, Joe is ordered to report to battalion headquarters. Eager to move, he sprints to the motor pool, where he tops up his motorcycle with gas. The pimply sergeant is keen for more news, but Joe has none. A radio blares inside the motor-pool office, and an announcer is only repeating everything they've heard so far in a rapid-fire voice. In addition to attacking Pearl Harbor, the Japanese have also attacked Singapore, Guam, Hong Kong, Wake Island, and the Philippines. No details about the attacks on the Philippines are revealed yet.

Joe kick-starts his motorcycle and heads out over the cobblestoned streets toward headquarters. The bike feels powerful beneath him, and the boy feels a strange sense of exhilaration and eagerness to help wherever he can. At headquarters, he parks his bike and sprints up the stone steps into the rambling wood building. He checks in and is ordered not to salute officers except once in the morning, then told to wait.

Battalion headquarters is crowded with brass. Officers and clerks hurry around with papers in their hands. Phones ring incessantly. From off in the distance, the boom of antiaircraft guns can be heard. Joe snatches bits of news in the fray. "Those damn Japs are scheduled to arrive any minute," barks an officer.

"Planes are coming at us from Formosa. A troop of boy scouts with kites could take these damned islands." A news report crackles over the radio and an announcer repeats the words that Philippine president Manuel Quezon issued earlier: "The zero hour has arrived. I expect every Filipino—man and woman—to do his duty. We have pledged our honor to stand to the last by the United States and we shall not fail her, happen what may."

Joe hears a thundering noise and runs outside. It is noon. Straight overhead is a formation of high-flying Japanese planes, hard to see against the bright midday sun. In V formation, they head toward the Cavite Navy Yard across the bay. Joe wonders if the American fleet stationed there will be ready to fight back.

Meanwhile, various troops are finally dispatched from the cuartel. Weapons Company is ordered to station machine-gun squads on most of the highest buildings in midtown Manila and scattered positions around the Luneta, the large public park outside the walls. Rifle Company is to establish checkpoints at the bridges crossing the Pasig River and at other key intersections around Manila. Machine-gun positions are to be placed atop the Post Office, the National Hotel, and the Manila Hotel. Joe is told to pick a bunk at headquarters and stick around. He's ordered to be on call around the clock until further notice. *It's a strange feeling,* he thinks. *So much happening, yet so little for me to do.*

Joe eats that night and grabs some sleep. Next morning on his motorcycle, Joe delivers a few messages. He zips a lieutenant out to a command post in midtown. He carries sandwiches to a gun position a few blocks away. With each ride, Joe's steel helmet beats a tattoo on top of his head. By day's end he's grown wise to the problem. Back at his bunk, he opens a first aid kit, removes a large gauze bandage, and tapes it inside the top of his helmet.

Over the next few days, Joe continues his messenger duties and gleans pieces of news. The Japanese have bombed the central and northern Filipino cities of Tarlac City and Tuguegarao and the base at Cabanatuan. Tragically, most of the American planes at Clark Field and Nichols Field never got off the ground the first day and were destroyed. Clark is about forty-five minutes north of Manila, and Nichols Field sits right on Manila's outskirts. The American forces at Cavite Naval Yard, which Joe spotted the planes flying toward, took a beating. Some 500 American men were killed or seriously wounded. The yard was destroyed. Any ships and submarines not sunk, except for a few PT boats, were ordered to head for Australia.

Japan has also bombed airfields in Zambales, Pampanga, and Fort McKinley, where Joe went through Basic Training. Outlying installations around Manila Bay have been hit, but so far the main areas of Manila haven't been touched. American antiaircraft fire seems light and sporadic—at least, that's what the guys are complaining about. Some 3,000 Japanese troops waded ashore on December 10, almost unimpeded, at the municipalities of Aparri and Gonzaga, on the northern tip of Luzon. Two days later, another 2,500 Japanese troops encircled Luzon and landed from the south at Legazpi City.

As enemy troops have advanced, American and Filipino ground troops have fought back, yet the immediate reaction at headquarters is one of surprising calm. Rumor has it that General MacArthur feels optimistic. He's waiting to concentrate Allied efforts against the main Japanese attack, which will come in perhaps two weeks' time. Many soldiers don't share the same sentiment. Ray runs into Joe and laments, "I don't think anybody knows what they're doing."

Joe tries to keep his head down. As a private, it's difficult for him to grasp the full picture of what's happening in the war, how much danger they're all in. Joe is able to juggle his time between headquarters and his barracks, and he knows meals are still being prepared in the company's kitchens in the cuartel, which he's happy to see, although the Filipino bunk boys and mess boys have been let go. A guard has been stationed at the door of each barracks, and Joe and the rest of the men are rotated by squads and allowed back in the barracks every other day to shave, shower, and change uniforms. Lots of soldiers in the quarter seem to be milling about, antsy, looking for something to do, wanting to get in on the action. In a few days, Joe finds time to head over to the supply depot, where he picks out a new, larger uniform. He's been shooting upward like the stalk of a sunflower in summer, and his old uniforms barely fit. He delivers more sandwiches. He gets a haircut.

The first week of the attacks passes without incident for D Company, 1st Battalion, 31st Infantry. For Joe, so far, it's an easy war.

———

Ten days after the invasion of the Philippines, following orders, Joe rumbles up to the Manila Hotel and parks his bike. He hefts a bag of sandwiches and a large container of coffee out of the sidecar and heads toward the hotel's front door. A priest, dressed all in black and wearing a straw hat, stands inside the front door as if waiting for someone. He's thickly built, expressionless, taller and more muscled than any priest Joe has ever seen. An uneasy feeling creeps over Joe. He boards the elevator. The priest follows him inside.

The hotel is one of the tallest buildings in Manila. Joe rides the elevator to the top floor, where he steps out, walks down a short hallway, and slows his gait. In front of him is a flight of stairs he must climb so he can deliver the food to gun positions on the roof, but the priest has disembarked on the top floor also. A sheen of sweat appears on the boy's forehead; Manny Tang's thugs have been known to adopt many disguises. Joe decides he'll be safer on the roof, so he speeds up, takes the stairs two at a time to the top floor, and delivers the food to the gun crew. They're relaxed and bored, and Joe talks to them for fifteen minutes, whiling away the day and forgetting about the priest until he walks down the stairs. The priest is standing in the middle of the hallway, staring in his direction. The man in black speaks first.

"Private Joe Johnson."

"Yeah?"

"I have a problem. A friend says you can help."

"Who's your friend?"

"Francisco Smith. The cabdriver."

"I don't know him."

"Here's what I need." The priest's voice is firm. "I do not know what your commander has told you, but our church has its own lines of communication. The Japanese are closing in on Manila from the north and south. No one is stopping them, and you young men will soon need to defend Manila with your lives. It will be a bloody fight, and Manila will become a far more dangerous place than today. Understand?"

"Who are you really?" Joe drops his right hand and unsnaps his holster, resting his fingers on his revolver. This goon is no priest.

"Do not be alarmed," the priest says. "I have no reason to harm you. I am Father Bruno, from Lady of Lourdes Church in Makati. We need your help to move the nuns and pregnant girls out of the Walled City. You know a girl there. Perpetua."

Joe doesn't blink, and he has a dry, unpleasant taste in his mouth. In the most controlled voice he can muster he says, "I don't know any girl named Perpetua."

"We have calesas," the priest says, ignoring Joe's denials.

"But we need somebody with a pass to get us through the check-points at night. You are a motorcycle messenger."

"Speak to our battalion commander," Joe says. "Go through the proper channels. I'm sure he'll give you an escort."

The priest steps forward. "Your colonel would say that if a truckload of nuns was seen leaving the city at night, it might incite panic among the civilian population. Already there are rumors the Americans will abandon Manila. Public morale must be kept up. He would tell us not to be worried and that we will be safe." He takes another step forward.

"That's bullshit." Joe keeps his hand close to his revolver, but doesn't draw his weapon. "If you really are a priest, which I doubt, our colonel wouldn't say that. I'm going to walk to that elevator and get inside. Don't follow me. Understood?"

The priest says nothing. Joe walks around him as widely as possible, never averting his eyes. He enters the elevator alone. The door closes behind him. He exhales. As the elevator descends, he shakes his head. The entire exchange was so strange.

Outside the hotel, Joe straddles his motorcycle. He's just about to kick the starter when he hears a familiar voice.

"So, can you help?"

Joe glances toward the voice. It's Frisco Smith.

"You told me to lay low, keep my distance from you," Joe says. "Here—get in your cab and follow me."

Wordless, Frisco hops in his vehicle and follows Joe to a nearby filling station. They stop. Joe steps off his bike but leaves the engine running. He's wary of everybody. Even Frisco.

"That guy really a priest?" Joe asks. "Or did they put the heat on you, too?"

"He's for real," Frisco says. "Father Bruno guided my mother through some hard times when she was young. They need your help, Joe. It's serious. Manila's going to take a pounding."

Frisco is street-smart and cagey, but he's shown himself to be truthful—at least as far as Joe has ever known. The boy makes a snap decision. "Tell me what I need to do."

———

That night a forced blackout shrouds the city in darkness. A rumor's going around that more than 43,000 battle-hardened Japanese troops will soon land near the northern provincial capital of Lingayen, about three hours from Manila, with the highly experienced Lieutenant General Masaharu Homma leading the charge. The atmosphere within the city is tense and foreboding. The streets are murky.

Joe meets Frisco in front of the church. Three calesas are already lined up, the ponies nervous in the evening air. Father Bruno is assisting girls into the carts. Joe glances this way and that. He's enlisted the help of Dale and a corporal who drives the commissary truck. They're loading bedding and belongings into the truck.

"You're looking for her?" Frisco asks Joe.

"Yeah."

"Sorry. I already asked Sister Carmella. Perpetua and another girl were moved to the sanctuary last week, the day after the attacks. Their babies are due sooner. Don't worry. They're fine."

Joe snorts with disappointment. The matter can't be helped. He returns to the task. The pregnant girls are loaded three to a cart. Four nuns squeeze into Frisco's cab. Sister Carmella is the last one out of the church. She turns and crosses herself, then closes the iron door. She'll ride in the truck with Dale and the corporal. Father Bruno climbs into the sidecar with Joe.

As quietly as possible, Joe kick-starts his bike, then leads the ragtag convoy out of a side sally port and toward the Pasig River bridge. Joe holds the motorcycle to a crawl, watching behind him to ensure the calesas are keeping pace. Business owners have already covered their shop windows with boards or thick adhesive tape. They've barricaded their doors with sandbags. In front of the bridge, Joe slows to a stop. He's been through this checkpoint before, but only in daylight. A guard approaches, holding his rifle in one arm. Joe's fingers twitch on the throttle.

"What the hell's all this?" the guard asks.

Joe sticks out his pass. "I'm supposed to guide these nuns and their wards to the Lady of Lourdes Church in Makati. We got off to a late start. This cab and these calesas were all they could round up. Father Bruno here is showing us the way to the church. Truck has all their bedding."

The guard points a flashlight onto the truck, then shines it at the pass. "This is only good for you. Not the rest of this bunch."

Joe raises himself from the motorcycle's seat. "Look, I ain't going to argue. All I know is the clerk at Battalion told me to get these nuns through this checkpoint. I know we're late, but it couldn't be helped. I was told you guys would be alerted for us to come through."

The other guard approaches. Joe blinks and does a double-take. It's none other than Coot, the soldier he got in a fight with back at Fort McDowell. Joe starts to sweat. Both men examine the pass with flashlights. Then, for reasons Joe will never understand, Coot squints at Joe and says, "I know this guy. He's the battalion messenger. He's okay." The guards take three steps in the other direction, confer among themselves, then return. The first says, "We just came on duty, and the other guys didn't say nothing about this. But we'll take your word for it. Get going."

Joe nods, motions to the others behind him, and hits the throttle. The convoy rolls through the checkpoint. Joe's still shaking his head about Coot. On the other side of the city, as they near the safer church, Joe leans over to Father Bruno and says, "Hey. Sorry I gave you so much trouble at the hotel. Not everybody in this city likes me these days."

The muscled priest nods. "You are doing us a great favor, my son. You cannot be too careful. All is forgiven."

Joe continues to lean. "Where we're going tonight—there's a girl there already. I wonder if I could see her. Just a few minutes."

The priest shakes his head. "I am sorry, my son. Some things are never allowed."

Joe senses the fragility of hope, but takes a slow breath and adds, "Then I'd appreciate it if you put in a good word for me with your boss upstairs."

"That I will do. What about?"

Joe selects his next words carefully. "If we're truly in for as much trouble as you say, we're gonna need all the help we can get."

———

Surprisingly to Joe, much is quiet in the quarter for the next few weeks, even though the Japanese have indeed landed at Lingayen and are pushing toward Manila. The 1st Battalion of the 31st, Joe's outfit, is ordered to guard the area around the cuartel against Japanese paratroopers who never materialize. The boy continues his messenger duties. He hears enough news to know that by late December 1941 in the Far East, the Japanese control wide sections of land, sea, and air. The tropical islands of Guam and Wake have fallen, as has Singapore. The Japanese have raced across the border into Thailand. Hong Kong is nearly toppled, its seizure imminent. Most of the fleet at Pearl Harbor lies in ruins.

In the Philippines, Cavite Navy Yard has been largely destroyed, and many of the American ships are smoldering wrecks. Most of the American planes at Nichols, Iba, Del Carmen, Cabanatuan, Batangas, and Clark airfields are destroyed.

Heavily reinforced Japanese forces have invaded the country in at least six locations—Batan Island, Aparri, Vigan, Legaspi, Davao City, and Jolo Island—conquering large sections of the country with their artillery and tanks. American and Filipino defenders have slowed the advance in places, but the enemy has proven relentless—too powerful to contain.

Joe has heard that no supplies or reinforcements can reach the Philippines. About this, he's particularly concerned. He learns that President Quezon packed a few belongings on December 24, fled the mainland on a moonlit night, and steamed to the small island of Corregidor, along with much of his staff. General MacArthur and his staff soon followed.

Orders come for the 31st Infantry's 1st Battalion to pull out of Manila, leaving a single rifle company behind. Joe has a hunch what the declaration means for the city. He thinks of Perpetua, and his stomach twists. Joe grabs only the bare necessities—extra socks, underwear, and his bugle mouthpiece. He cannot take the actual instrument. He must leave his motorcycle, too, another loss he winces at. On Christmas morning 1941, he and the rest of the men are barged west four miles across the bay to the island of Corregidor. Their departure feels unceremonious and anticlimactic, and many grumble that they've left Manila without firing a single shot.

On December 26, Joe hears that MacArthur has declared Manila an *open city*. All defensive efforts have been abandoned in an attempt to avoid the destruction of buildings and to preserve civilian lives. MacArthur expects the Japanese to respect the declaration. The day after MacArthur's announcement, the Japanese demand that all Filipino troops lay down their arms and cease all resistance throughout the country. When the Filipinos refuse to comply, five waves of Japanese bombers pound Manila for three hours. From across the bay, Joe can see smoke rising above the city. The enemy lays waste to entire blocks of schools, historic churches, government buildings, and modern shops. Joe will learn later that at least fifty civilians died that day. Hundreds more were wounded. Word around Corregidor, almost with universal sentiment, is that the Japanese don't play by the rules.

With sinking hopes, Joe begins to realize his personal plight. The few ocean-crossing ships that are still seaworthy aren't coming in or leaving Manila's port now—certainly not on a mission to take home an underage soldier. Even if his mother ever located a birth certificate and sent it to his commanding officer and he received it, what good would that do? Joe is in for the duration.

He will need to fight.

CHAPTER 8

Digging the Ashes

From outside the barracks on Corregidor, Joe looks down the rocky hillside and out across the dark bay. A somber atmosphere prevails among the troops. No one speaks in a loud voice. No one smokes. An order has been issued for weapons and ammo to be ready for use at a moment's notice, although Joe can't quite comprehend why. Corregidor's concrete bunkers are rumored to be bombproof. Japanese planes have so far avoided flying over the tadpole-shaped island, perhaps because the enemy believes the Americans' antiaircraft batteries are too strong.

A day passes in quietness. Then a second, and a third. Beach defenses are set up around the island. The soldiers clean their weapons and talk among themselves in hushed voices. Joe knows that US and Filipino soldiers from other battalions are fighting all over the mainland. Talk runs that the enemy has struck the 3rd Battalion at the village of Dinalupihan. Japanese planes dived out of the clouds and rained bombs on the men. Elsewhere on the mainland, troops are fighting valiantly—a tough fight made tougher for the Allies by the dense jungle underbrush and steep terrain.

The morning of Monday, December 29, 1941, dawns cloudless

and warm on Corregidor. After breakfast, a detail is ordered to head to the north dock to pick up foodstuffs and munitions. Joe is to help load supplies with the men and also is given a requisition form to hand to the supply officer at the other end. The soldiers climb aboard an electric flatcar and whir off toward the dock. The silent rail lines are said to be one of the best-kept secrets in the US Army. The lines link the island's various fortifications, as well as a power plant and an underground hospital. Joe and the other men sit on the flatcar's sides and let their legs dangle. The day feels routine. One man whistles.

Inside the supply depot at the north dock, Joe finds the officer and delivers the form, then joins the others in loading boxes of eggs, apples, and beef from cold storage. Some men use hand dollies to haul the boxes. Four men together tackle the heavy sides of beef. It's nearly noon. Joe hikes with laden arms from the depot to the flatcar. He feels a ground tremor and wonders if an earthquake is underway. Or perhaps thunder's approaching on an otherwise fair-skies day. He glimpses a man leap off the flatcar and scramble for cover. All this happens in a rush.

In the distance, enemy bombs explode. Heavy fire stutters and starts to spew upward from nearby antiaircraft guns. Joe's feet feel fixed, as if in cement. He eyeballs the sky and sees Japanese warplanes approaching in a V formation. Bombs begin their descent, heading in his direction. He finds his footing and sprints one step, two. A bomb plunges with an ominous *whoosh* and slams into the nearby ground with a roily burst. The boy flies uncontrolled through the air. The tumult in his ears suddenly mutes. His body hits the ground. Everything goes dark.

When Joe regains consciousness, he cannot suck in a full lungful of air. Bombs are still falling, exploding with thunderous blasts. Convulsive clouds of fragmentation and smoke lie heavy on the tangled horizon. The boy does not know how much time has passed since he was knocked out. He tastes dust, wipes his face with the back of his sleeve, tries to spit. He finds he's lying next to the opening of a small concrete culvert. He pushes himself upright and tries to climb to his knees. His brain doesn't want to work.

A motorman grabs him from behind and drags him inside the culvert. Two other men are already squeezed inside. The motorman lays the boy on his stomach and says, "We thought you'd bought it until you tried to stand." Joe can't work up enough saliva to answer. The stinging odor of exploded ordnance chokes the confined space. The four soldiers huddle inside the culvert, listening as flight after flight of bombers roar across the island fortress. Joe wonders if the bombing will last forever.

At last, a muffled calm sets in. The soldiers crawl outside the culvert. Joe bangs his palm against his temples, hoping his hearing will clear. He surveys the damage. The cold-storage plant has escaped destruction, but the train tracks are ripped apart and twisted. The heavy flatcar lies on its side. Other men appear from gullies and ravines. Everyone gathers near the flatcar. A corporal starts a head count and stops at nine. They'd arrived with eleven. The men fan out to look for the two missing soldiers. Both are found in the rubble, dead: George Gensel and Earl Petrimeaux. Earl was a tentmate of Joe's during boot camp.

Joe can't take it in. Their first dead. They gather the bodies and hike in somberness back to the barracks. He's still having a hard time breathing and hearing. The barracks are a mess. Chunks of concrete dot the ground, along with personal equipment and twisted weapons. Soldiers mill about, some in shock, others beginning the cleanup. Joe hears a familiar voice call out, "Thank God, you made it." Dale rushes to him, helps the boy sit, and gives him a drink of water from his canteen. "We were standing in line for chow when the first bombs hit," Dale adds. "It was pandemonium. So much for these barracks being bombproof. They've taken a truckload of wounded over to an aid station on the parade ground."

The boy still feels disoriented, and in his bewilderment he holds on to his emotions tightly. These are the first combat deaths they've witnessed, and Joe can't quite comprehend what's happened. When Dale hears about the death of their tentmate Earl, he breaks down and sobs. Joe is more stoic. He puts his hand on his friend's shoulder and lets him cry it out.

———

Two days after the attack, Joe's hearing has returned to normal. The 1st Battalion is loaded onto barges and motored from Corregidor across the bay to the Bataan peninsula. An outfit of Marines remains on the island. The 1st Battalion's orders are to join up with the rest of the regiment and form a main line of resistance to defend the thirty-mile-long peninsula until help arrives from the States. If it ever does. As long as Bataan and Corregidor stay standing, Joe learns, the Japanese will be unable to use Manila's harbor to land their larger craft—at least so it's thought.

Joe and his outfit unload at midmorning in the palm-treed port of Mariveles, at the southern tip of the peninsula. The sun shines brightly, and a riot of tropical swiftlets and jungle fowl trumpet the soldiers' arrival. The battalion boards a hodgepodge of vehicles—GI trucks, Navy trucks, and open-sided Filipino passenger buses—and the convoy climbs its way up a winding, unpaved road, heading north. The buses struggle under their heavy loads, inching through civilians in cars and on carts loaded with belongings, trying to get somewhere else. At the crest of the grade, the convoy enters a forest of tall trees and begins to make better time. A medical detachment is setting up a field hospital in a clearing. The convoy passes through small barrios and fishing villages. To his right, Joe spies the rocky inlet of Corregidor in the distance.

In late afternoon, at the town of Balanga, the battalion stops and is unloaded. The region looks flat and green and is built up around an outcropping of the bay. Joe hears chickens clucking. He smells woodsmoke from cookfires. Companies are formed, and the men are marched north up the road in columns of four. At dusk, they reach the small barrio of Abucay. Joe sees rice paddies and cornfields to his left, old wooden fishing boats to his right. Someone remarks that the name *Abucay* means *digging the ashes*. The men are issued C rations—canned corned beef and hardtack biscuits—and spend the night bivouacked near the road, slapping mosquitoes. Soldiers from other units are already stationed in Abucay and have set up defensive positions. They have been here for more than a week, their faces showing a mix of apprehension and exhaustion.

Early next morning, Joe's company is ordered to hike farther north. The men gather their weapons and ammo and march until early evening, when they're halted and positioned in sections off the road in the brush and cane fields. Darkness is falling. A sergeant barks: "From what our intelligence has reported, we should have nothing but Japs in front of us tomorrow morning. So stay alert." Dale and Joe start to dig in, but a sergeant strides over to them, pulls Joe aside, and hollers: "Get back with the captain. Go."

Joe says goodbye to Dale and trots toward the command post. He finds the captain and is immediately ordered to dig him a shallow foxhole in the hard, red-clay earth. Long past dark, Joe finishes the task, then helps erect a small triangle tent to be used for record keeping and dispatches. He considers digging a foxhole for himself, but is told he'll be on the run too much to warrant one. Joe lies in the back of the tent, using his gas mask as a pillow, and tries to sleep. But his mind races.

At the first gleam of dawn, the area in and around the tent bursts into a beehive of action. A corporal types a morning report under the canvas with a clatter. Signalmen scurry in and out, running lines from the command post to the various platoons and sections. The captain confers with junior officers outside the flap. Joe checks his gear and looks for breakfast, but no one's being fed. He's unsure of his new duties with the captain, so he lingers near the tent and tries to look useful.

A sergeant strides over and hands Joe a small brown envelope. "Get your butt up to Phillips's position. Give him this. Stay there till he gives you further instructions. Keep your head down. Watch for snipers. They like to hide in trees. Go."

Joe wonders how he can keep his head down while watching the trees. But he says nothing, checks directions with a corporal who has a hand-sketched map, and heads out. The boy hikes west past several squads of riflemen, then drops into a deep ravine with a brook trickling down its middle. He crosses the brook and heads north, counting his paces and positioning specific trees and topography in his mind as landmarks, just as he'd once read about in the training manual. When he reaches 100 paces, he climbs the bank for a look. He sees nothing but tall grass, wildflowers, and a shaggy brown carabao grazing contentedly, its great horned head deep in the weeds. Joe backtracks, heading east.

The directions given to him by the corporal had sounded so

easy back at the command post, but now Joe has his doubts. He stops and crouches low, searching for a landmark he remembers seeing on the map, but he feels exposed. Vulnerable. His skin begins to crawl. He swings his gaze toward a clump of trees. One looks like it's moving. He glances over his shoulder. The long grass sways in the sun.

"Looking for someone?"

Joe jumps. It's the familiar voice of a private from his company.

"Whoa!" Joe says. "You scared the last meal out of me. I'm looking for Sergeant Phillips."

The private motions for Joe to keep his head down and follow him. They flatten out, crawl under a low-hanging branch, and peer over the grass. First Platoon's guns are set up, ready for action. "Phillips is down the line east about fifty yards," the private says. "Watch for those damn riflemen of ours. They're antsy. You don't want them taking a shot at you."

Joe says thanks, hikes over, finds the sergeant, and hands him the envelope.

"So you're the captain's new runner, huh?" Phillips says while reading the message. "Did they tell you it's an easy job?" He removes a silver Zippo from his pocket, flicks open the lighter, ignites the message, and stares as it burns. "Watch out for both sides. Friendly fire will kill you sure as any bullet from a Jap."

The sergeant juts out his chin and changes his tone.

"You didn't happen to bring any chow with you, did you? I'm starved."

"Sorry," Joe says. "Larder's empty."

The sergeant lowers his eyebrows. "We're to vacate these positions once darkness falls so the Japs won't know we left.

They probably already have us zeroed in. You and Private Ybarra will lead us back to the company. We don't know where the hell we're going, so stick around. I've got to pass word up and down the line, and also to the rifle squads."

"No sweat," Joe says. "It's a couple hundred yards to the creek, then a few hundred yards south to the company. I'll wait for you guys near the top of the ravine."

Joe spots Private Rosbel Ybarra a few yards away. He's the bugler and runner from C Company, and they've talked a couple of times in the past. A wiry stick of a man, Ybarra walks over and smiles. "I guess it's all up to us tonight."

Joe nods.

Ybarra grimaces. "Say, have you heard when we're gonna get fed?"

———

Already the darkness feels violent. Joe paces under a tree branch near the top of the ravine, his stomach rumbling, his eyes on the alert. He doesn't have a flashlight or a torch. Lighting any sort of flame is suicide. He squints through the inkiness, hoping his sense of direction will provide accurate guidance for the men. Without warning from behind, Sergeant Phillips plucks Joe's shirtsleeve. Ybarra appears with him. The other runner holds a rifle under one arm.

"Both of you head to the bottom," the sergeant hisses. "Take Pilborn's squad and those riflemen with you. Wait for us there. I'll be along shortly with the rest of the platoon."

Joe nods. He and Ybarra continue their crouch and whisk through the tall grass over to where Pilborn's squad stands ready to go. Joe motions for them to follow. They plink their way down the gravelly path to the bottom. Joe whispers to Pilborn, "Head south. About 500 paces from here, you'll find the company. Save me some chow."

Pilborn nods and leads his squad into the night. Joe and Ybarra sit and wait for Phillips and the rest of the platoon.

"Where ya from?" Ybarra whispers with a soft twang.

"California." Joe tries to keep his voice down. "Before that, San Antonio."

"Texas? I'm from Texas. You like chicken-fried steak?"

"Love it."

"And beef brisket? My mom used to make it with garlic powder and black pepper. Man, what I'd give right now for some beef brisket. And ribs. Ever eat barbecued ribs?"

"Every chance I get." Joe's stomach rumbles again.

For the next twenty minutes, the boys discuss corn bread. Corn bread with butter. Corn bread with honey. Corn bread hot from the oven, eaten straight from the pan. A sliver of moonlight appears. Joe and Ybarra stop yakking and start listening for Sergeant Phillips and the other riflemen. Nothing.

"What's taking them so long?" Ybarra whispers.

"No guess," Joe says. "If they don't show up soon, something's wrong. Sergeant Phillips is no dummy."

Scattered rifle fire erupts in the distance. One location. Two. The firing dies down, then erupts again.

"That ain't all ours," Joe whispers.

The boys sit and wait, the sound of their breathing magnified. The firing breaks out again, this time louder, closer. A round zings through the branches above them. The crackle of automatic rifle fire joins in. Bullets slam into the wood.

"Let's get outta here!" Ybarra hisses. "Whole Jap army's on our ass."

Joe and Ybarra scoot down the final embankment that leads toward the bed of the ravine. After twenty yards of scrambling they rise and trot at a crouch, stopping every few yards to listen. They reach the brook. Gunfire is still heard.

"You counting paces?" Joe asks.

"No. Thought you were."

The boys crouch in the dark, wondering in whispers how far down the ravine they might have traveled. From above the boys comes the jabber of voices on the night wind. Ybarra elbows Joe. "Phillips has finally caught up with us. Now all we have to do is find our way out of here."

"Those aren't Americans," Joe hisses. "Listen."

The two strain their ears to pick up words. The voices become louder. More level. Joe hears water splashing. Footsteps on the bank. The words are neither English nor Tagalog.

"Run," whispers Ybarra.

He takes off, splashing through the water. Joe's one step behind. In fifty paces they stop and listen again. The wind has picked up. Leaves rustle in the trees. "Least I've got a rifle," Ybarra murmurs. "All you've got is that damn .45." They take off again, trotting at a quiet clip for perhaps ten minutes, pushing through undergrowth. A branch whips back and hits Joe in the face. They stop again, breathing heavily, and listen. The entire landscape has awakened. A monkey chatters through the darkness.

"Think we're any closer to the battalion?" Ybarra asks.

"No idea where we are," Joe says. "I think the best thing now for us to do is hole up till daylight. We're lost, and we're not gonna get unlost in the dark."

Ybarra agrees. The boys find a clump of trees and crawl underneath into the long grass. Joe worries about snakes but keeps his concerns to himself. He stays awake until dawn.

At first light, small-arms fire and mortars crackle up toward the east. Joe thinks he hears a horse's snort. More voices. The jingle of a stirrup. Another snort. He motions for Ybarra to stand and follow him. The boys glimpse riders emerging from the north section of the ravine.

"Americans!" Joe calls. "Don't shoot! We're 31st Infantry."

Joe hears safeties clicking off, the pull of reins and the utterings of *Whoa*. Three troops dismount and walk toward the boys. A string of horses stands behind the three. The first man has his pistol drawn. The other two advance with rifles aimed.

"You men lost?" a voice asks. A major.

"Yes, sir," Ybarra says. "We're sure glad to see you."

Joe speaks up, "Sir, we're both company runners. Last night, our men either lost us or we lost them. There was an intense firefight not far from here. And we heard a Japanese patrol. Close."

The major motions for his troops to keep in line. Small-arms fire is still audible. Without another word, he leads Joe, Ybarra, and his men along the ravine at a cautious pace for another ten minutes. The troops stop in a section of high grass. The major posts scouts to the north and east, then calls up his sergeant and tells him to locate a place where they can get the horses out of the ravine without breaking a leg. The rest of the troops take cover in the woods at the edge of the grass. A corporal wanders by and offers the boys some C rations. It's been two days now since they've eaten anything. To Joe, the C rations taste almost as good as Texas barbecue. Everybody waits. The day wears on. An order comes to bivouac overnight.

Next morning the major calls the boys over and says he and his troops are heading to higher ground. According to their calculations, the boys' outfit should be farther down the ravine—maybe half a mile, then about half a mile to the east. If they follow the ravine, then veer to the east, they should eventually run into their battalion. A Filipino scout rummages through a pack mule's load and hands Joe a musette bag and half a dozen cans of C rations. He picks out an old Springfield rifle and a bandolier of ammo, hands Joe the rifle, and slings the ammo over Joe's shoulder. "You look just like Pancho Villa," the scout says with a laugh.

Joe and Ybarra head south, their bellies full and their morale high. They stick to the east side of the ravine for cover, then veer farther east, just as the major had instructed. A bullet rips into the ground near Joe's foot. No warning. Another bullet whizzes into a tree at his side. The boys hit the dirt, rifles at the ready, trying to figure out where the shots are coming from. The air erupts over their backs. Bullets whiz past their skulls, then suddenly stop. American voices shout for them to come out. Joe and Ybarra call back, "Friendly! Friendly!" The boys rise and creep forward. They spy their own troops. "American!" Joe shouts. "Friendly! Friendly!"

"Get your damn butts over here!" a corporal shouts back. "We thought you were Japs."

The boys breathe easier. It's C Company, Ybarra's outfit. Joe asks directions to his company. He's told to head another couple hundred yards to the east; he'll find what he's looking for. Ybarra shakes hands with Joe and says goodbye. Joe claps him on the back and says with a jaunty grin, "We'll have to do this again sometime."

———

On Joe's home turf, D Company, a sergeant greets Joe with a scowl. "The hell have you been? You realize only half of Phillips's section made it back?"

Joe tries explaining, but the sergeant stands in Joe's face and shouts a string of insults, spit flying from his lips. *You're a horrible soldier. A waste of a uniform. You should be shot for desertion.* The sergeant rips the musette bag off Joe, insisting it's only for officers. He demands that Joe hand over the bandolier and rifle and says, "That stuff isn't yours, either. That's government property." He confiscates all of Joe's C rations.

Joe tries to tell the story again—how Sergeant Phillips never found him in the dark, how they hid from a Japanese patrol, how they were discovered by the cavalry—but the sergeant shouts him down again. "Don't tell me some cock-and-bull story! Hell, the cavalry's nowhere near this area, you little liar. You shirked your duty and hid. Cavalry's in the mountains."

The captain stands nearby, silent, his back to the tirade. Dale is twenty feet away, powerless to intervene. Joe feels confused and angry, on the verge of tears. He has no choice but to take the abuse.

Later that afternoon, the rest of Phillips's men straggle in. They describe their firefight with the Japanese and how the enemy broke through the line and sneaked behind them. They explain how the cavalry appeared and chased the enemy back, then pulled out and headed south. Every bit of Joe's story is confirmed.

The sergeant offers no apology.

He even keeps Joe's C rations.

Other soldiers murmur their support to Joe. The diatribe was uncalled-for. They wonder why the captain did nothing. Dale's fists are clenched. He wants to confront the captain for failing to act and demand an apology from the sergeant. Joe tells him thanks, but no; what's done is done.

In the evening, the same ornery sergeant calls Joe over and hands him a leather dispatch case. "Go to the command post. You're staying there from now on. Your job will be to carry reports between Battalion and us. You have a job to do, Private. And damn it, don't get lost again, or some trigger-happy sonuvabitch will shoot your ass off. Maybe *me*."

Joe glares at the sergeant, secures the leather case firmly under his arm, and strides away without saying goodbye to anyone. The Army can go to hell.

Ray is shooting the bull with some noncoms at the command post. Joe nods to his longtime friend without saying a word and sits on a log near the tent in a huff. Ray ambles over, sits next to the boy, slugs him in the shoulder. Gently.

"We heard about the shoot-out," Ray says. "You weren't at fault for those guys' getting lost. In fact, you and Ybarra were lucky to make it back in one piece. It's gonna be okay, bud. That sergeant's an asshole."

Joe shakes his head, stares at the ground.

"You don't want to be here, do you?" Ray asks.

Joe shakes his head again.

"Nobody does, kid. But you know, for a fifteen-year-old, you've already developed quite a reputation. Word got around about how you helped that priest get those pregnant girls to safety. The adjutant said you ought to get a medal. He thinks you got a big career ahead of you in logistics."

A smile tugs at the corner of Joe's mouth. "I didn't think anybody knew about that night with the priest except Dale and the corporal. And how'd you know I'm fifteen, anyway?"

Ray grins. "Dale's got a big mouth. Besides, I figured it out long ago." He pats Joe on the back and stands. "I gotta go. Stay safe. Dig yourself a foxhole close to the tent. Okay? Word is, we're gonna see lots of action real soon."

That night Joe dozes off in his new foxhole, his stomach growling. He's dug his hole near a clump of bamboo trees, where he feels a semblance of shelter. In a mix of dreams, his mind mingles the old and new worlds. Dale and Ray, his two best friends in the 31st, stand up for him as a sergeant shouts him down. Ybarra and the pregnant girls lift him gently, placing him in a civilian bus in Mariveles. The bus stops in San Antonio, where Joe climbs out. The boy sighs. Hugs his grandmother. Eats a plateful of honeyed corn bread at last.

CHAPTER 9

Ache from the Hacienda

The foxhole near the thicket of bamboo trees becomes Joe's new temporary nightly sanctuary. There, he can rest and dream. The bamboo acts as a wall, he thinks, providing a sense of protection. He hopes he's safer near the bamboo.

In the daytime, Joe mostly shuttles messages back and forth between the command post and D Company. He's ever on the outlook for food, but little can be found. Even C rations become scarce. The men have resorted to butchering carabao. Dysentery has set in, and many soldiers suffer from the runs. The medic says Joe has picked up a case of malaria somewhere; nothing can be done for it. Chills and a low-grade fever are troubling Joe. The medic says they will come and go. Dale has contracted malaria, too, and all medicines are strictly rationed. But Joe sneaks liquid quinine from the medicine locker at the battalion command post and gives it to Dale. Joe doesn't take any for himself. He figures he's younger; surely he can kick the disease.

One morning in the second week of January 1942, Joe runs the morning report over to D Company. On the way, he feels his bowels churn. There's no controlling this action, so he darts off the trail to discharge his diarrhea. Afterward, he wipes with fresh leaves and washes his hands with canteen water, wishing he had soap and a sink and a place to lie down. The boy is shivering and feverish, but his job still needs doing. Back on the trail, he makes it over to D Company, shoots the bull with Dale for a while near a gun position, asks about the older soldier's fever and how he slept, then trots back to the command post.

Joe is heading toward his favorite bamboo thicket to place his gas-mask carrier near his bedroll when he hears the unmistakable whistle of a mortar shell through the air.

"Incoming!" someone shouts.

Joe dives headfirst into his foxhole. He hears a solitary blast and feels strange, immense pain all over the back of his body — like he's been stung by a thousand bees. Dust envelops his eyes and face and is vacuumed up his nostrils. He blacks out and lies motionless for a few moments before regaining consciousness. No more mortar shells fly in, and the men slowly ease out of their holes. A corpsman rushes for Joe. The boy is hollering from the dirt. His mind starts to work, but he can't comprehend what's happened. All he can shout is, "Bees! Bees!"

"Stop moving! There aren't any bees." The corpsman's voice is firm as a brick. He jumps into the foxhole, crouches by the boy's side, and starts tending to his wounds.

"They're swarming all over me. Get them off! Ow, they're stinging! Help!"

"Son! Lie still. There are no bees."

Ray is about thirty yards away. He hears that trouble has found Joe and rushes over to help. "You're going to be okay, buddy," Ray says from the rim of the foxhole. "Lie still. Don't squirm. You're only making it worse." Ray eases into the hole near Joe's head and crouches, gently touching the side of the boy's face with the back of his hand to let him sense a reassuring presence. Joe lies on his stomach. His clothes are shredded. He's bleeding almost everywhere—top to bottom—from the back of his neck to the backs of his ankles.

"What's happening to me?" Joe spews the question.

The medic gives him a shot and goes to work on the boy's back.

"It's the bamboo," Ray murmurs. "Don't worry. It's going to hurt like hell. But you're one lucky son of a gun. You're gonna be okay."

Slowly Joe steals a glance over his shoulder. He moans. Gingerly he fingers the back of his neck. Lets out another moan. Every movement sends jolts of pain through his body. He understands now. The mortar has shredded clumps of his bamboo wall, sending shards of hard wood flying in all directions like shrapnel. Each shard is the size of a long, sharp horse needle. He's covered in the spikes. The corpsman begins the job of removing each long splinter, soaking each wound with a cotton ball loaded with fiery disinfectant. From the backs of Joe's legs. His buttocks. His back and shoulders. His neck and scalp. Joe tries not to scream.

It takes most of the day to remove all the shards—so lengthy an ordeal that the corpsman stops halfway through and lets Joe catch his breath. The boy's in so much pain. When it's all over, Ray hunts around and secures an intact uniform for him. Joe has no idea where Ray might have located an unused uniform but decides not to ask. The other guys can see the boy is walking now, so they razz him, calling him "Porcupine." It's good-natured, but no one doubts he could have died.

Next morning, Ray accompanies Joe on his hike up to D Company. Carefully, Joe delivers his dispatches. It's hard for the boy to move. Ray scrounges a rare cup of coffee, sits on a stump, and holds center court for the other soldiers, proudly describing Joe's incident to all who'll listen. Joe's almost at the place where he can laugh about it. One of the guys dubs Joe with a new nickname: "the Cockroach." Joe thinks it's an insult until he asks for an explanation. "It's a compliment," the guy says. "A cockroach lives through everything thrown at him. You can never kill a cockroach."

———

The Japanese are advancing. Despite the Allies' best efforts, the enemy can't be stopped. When Joe is out on his daily dispatch runs, he sometimes spots enemy troops moving through the fields and hills. The Americans are aided by Filipino troops, but Joe has heard mixed reports about their efficacy. Some fight valiantly and effectively, but others are ill-trained and underequipped; they withdraw and scatter. Joe has met Filipino troops on the trails in their ragged blue uniforms, carrying old Enfield rifles. Some have no rifles at all—only bolo knives. Some lack shoes. Yet they always smile at him and flash him the V sign for Victory. Once, a Filipino soldier shares part of his supper with Joe—a fire-roasted monkey.

Joe hears that almost 78,000 Allied troops are now fighting on Bataan—about 12,000 Americans, the rest Filipinos. Under the umbrella of MacArthur's leadership, wiry-framed Washington State native Major General Jonathan "Skinny" Wainwright leads the troops that fight toward the northwest. An affable Iowa native, Major General George Parker, leads the troops that fight toward the south. Major General Albert M. Jones of San Francisco, an expert tactician, leads the troops in the northeast. And the mustachioed Georgia-born Major General Edward King serves as MacArthur's artillery officer. Japan has initially landed about the same number of troops on Bataan as the Allies have, but the enemy is more experienced, more cohesive, and equipped with a larger and more advanced supply of weaponry.

Joe's battalion moves south about four miles as the front line is pushed back. Some soldiers grouse they'll need to dig new fox-holes, but Joe can tell that's the least of anybody's problems. If the war continues like it's going, soon there won't be anywhere for the defenders to go. Bataan is a peninsula. They keep getting pushed back. Soon the heels of their boots will be against the sea.

Joe's main job during and after the move is to guide various platoons and support personnel to their new positions. Everyone assumes the company runners know the trails best. Joe has no problem navigating in the daylight anymore, but it's a different story at night. Several nights pass with varying degrees of confusion, but Joe is able to sort out the problems and lead the troops where they need to go. During daytime, Joe keeps running all over the terrain, locating units and delivering messages, stopping every so often to crap in the jungle. Field phones rarely work, so Joe and the other runners are soon considered the only reliable way to send messages. Troops are repositioned again. Then again, and again. One officer gripes, "This is about the sixteenth move and the fifteenth foxhole I've had so far." When the battalion is finally settled, the men eat their first regular Army meal in what seems like ages. It's only tuna gravy over rice, but to Joe it tastes like a feast. He just hopes he can hold it in.

The food situation becomes more dire. One morning when supplies are distributed, only one can of rations is passed around to feed every four men. That evening, Joe's meal is a shared can of peeled tomatoes. The next morning a can of peaches. In the evening, a ration of mule meat is issued. The next night it's a ration of horse.

A few Filipino units are positioned closer to the line than Joe's outfit, which is ordered forward on January 16 to help plug some of the holes. For a few days the fighting is fierce and chaotic, and the 31st sees almost constant combat. The Japanese seize a position, then the Allies fight back and retake ground, then the enemy surges again and the Allies retreat. Joe is sent back and forth between the command post and the troops, running both ways now as fast as possible. He dodges artillery barrages and snipers. Once, shrapnel seems to rain down all around him. His main goal becomes staying alive.

At night, when Joe has a moment to himself, he wonders about Perpetua. He's heard that Manila is fully conquered, and that the enemy is harsh in their treatment and control of civilians. He wonders what life is like for the girl. She is so close to delivering her baby. He wonders if the priests were able to relocate the girls again, perhaps somewhere out in the country. Or perhaps the Allies were able to move the girls. He's heard that some 26,000 civilian refugees were shifted around the bay from Manila to the Bataan peninsula. For all he knows, the girl might be somewhere nearby, though Joe wonders if the countryside is any safer. He isn't sure what to hope for her—only that she's safe.

Pockets of the enemy are hidden throughout the area now, and most trails fall under enemy control. Joe continues to make his cross-country runs. He sees snipers who've tied themselves to the limbs of tall trees so they won't fall out, ready to pick off any Allied soldier they spot. Joe stays on constant alert. Every man in the outfit seems on edge, sick, hungry, and exhausted. The men were promised that if they keep fighting hard and hold off the enemy for just a little while longer, what's left of the US Navy is sure to fight its way across the Pacific, destroy the Japanese fleet in the Philippines, and land on Bataan with massive reinforcements. But hardly anyone believes that anymore.

On January 27, 1942, Joe eats his evening meal near the command-post tent. Half a can of tuna and a spoonful of cooked rice. He's happy for the tuna. Tuna is protein. Maybe it will stay down. The boy's been growing lately. He thinks he might be approaching six feet, though he doubts he's added commensurate weight. He was about 135 pounds when he joined the Army. He doesn't think he's much heavier now. His bowels gurgle. He runs a few steps into the jungle. The tuna and rice are lost. Joe cleans up as well as possible. Thick humidity has descended for the night, and Joe hikes back to his foxhole, nestles into the dirt, and looks up. He marvels at how bright the stars appear in such darkness. His back and legs are still sore, and he shivers. A malarial fever is rising. No one has remembered this day — and why would they? He considers many of the decisions he's made so far in his young life and chastises himself.

What a mess I've made, Joe thinks. *I had thought I was half-ass smart. But here I am on Bataan, alone in this hole, and no one except the Japanese is throwing me a party.*

He closes his eyes. Tries to sleep. It's his sixteenth birthday.

———

Between the bouts of fighting in Abucay, hustling food becomes a primary objective for many soldiers, and nearby lies a large sugarcane plantation known as Abucay Hacienda. The main buildings and sheds where the cane is processed have been destroyed by shellfire and bombings. The fields of sugarcane have been cut down to offer a clearer view for rifle and machine-gun fire. Barbed wire has been strung across the fields to make enemy advancement harder. But still intact are two large aboveground cisterns filled with sticky sugarcane syrup.

At night, opposing patrols sneak across the ground, load up their canteens, then slink back to their respective camps. It's become almost a gentleman's agreement. One night the Americans hike in and load up. The next night, the Japanese. As levels in the cisterns drop, the place becomes more dangerous. Joe experiences the strange results of the raids. Soldiers sit around small fires during lulls in the artillery barrages, boiling the syrup into juice or pulling it into taffy. The juice and taffy are neither filling nor particularly tasty, and too much of either will chap a man's lips and make them bleed, but at least it's something to help curb hunger pangs.

Late one evening, desperate for any sustenance, a lieutenant from Battalion Command decides to test the odds. He gathers as many canteens as he can carry and heads for the cisterns. Ray and two other soldiers go along to help. Joe hears about their mission only the next morning. None have returned. Had he known about it the night before, he would have tried to talk Ray out of going. By now, Joe is familiar with the dangers of the trails.

A patrol is organized to look for the missing four. Another lieutenant, a buck sergeant, and six riflemen are picked, and Joe is ordered to go along as guide. He has the most experience on the trails. Joe glances around at the men chosen for the mission and gives them a sharp look. "Stay on constant alert," Joe warns. "No talking—not even whispering. Don't have anything on you that rattles. If you see me point and hit the dirt, look where I'm pointing and hit the dirt too. Our main concern is snipers. Always check the trees, especially the tall ones."

The soldiers nod and follow Joe. He stays low, sticking mostly to drainage ditches and safer routes. His heart races. Heading out by himself is one thing, but having to guide others—particularly a lieutenant—means the stakes are raised. Joe's angry with Ray. Sure, everyone's hungry. But it seems like this was such a stupid decision. Joe vows to chew Ray out as soon as he sees him.

Far ahead they see the cisterns—huge steel vats broiling in the sun. A tall tree overlooks the cisterns. Joe motions for the patrol to halt. The men crouch. Joe scrutinizes the terrain ahead, the tree, the wind. Using hand gestures, he moves the patrol closer to their target. He can make out three figures. One sits on the ground, his back against the cistern. Two others are lying down, as if napping. Joe continues to eyeball the tree. Tiny razors bite into his calf, just above his boot. Without averting his eyes, Joe reaches down and swats away a fire ant. For about a week the bite will blister, itch, and burn, then fill with pus. Too many bites can kill a man. The riflemen are not watching the tree. They're checking themselves for ants. Still without averting his eyes, Joe reaches to the soldier next to him, grabs the M1 from his hands, and aims toward the tree.

"Hey, what do you think you're doing?" the soldier hisses.

Joe empties the clip. An enemy sniper topples from a branch, catches his ankle in the crook of a branch, and hangs upside down, swinging. The enemy's weapon clatters to the ground. Joe hands the M1 back to the soldier and waves his patrol on in. It's his first direct kill, but with every dark thing Joe has seen so far, he doesn't think twice about it, at least not with adrenaline rushing through his system. He's only glad he qualified as expert marksman back in boot camp.

The juice tanks are riddled with bullet holes. Juice still drips onto the ground. It has oozed from the tanks and saturated a large area around the cisterns. The men advance, stop short, and stare at the three bodies. One is the missing lieutenant. Blood oozes from his temple. They recognize the others as two of the missing men from the patrol. Their bodies are covered in fire ants, and all three have been stripped of their equipment. Joe walks a short distance around the side of one of the cisterns. There sits the fourth missing man, his back against the cistern, his head drooped against his chest. Fire ants cover the body, their fierce red shells glistening in the sun. It's Ray.

Joe stares at the lifeless face. The soldier's in his early twenties, with high cheekbones, arched eyebrows, and a dark-hued complexion. The boy wants to rush forward, to shake the young man awake. But a bullet zings in and pierces the dirt near where he stands.

"Let's get out of here!" the lieutenant hisses. "Nothing we can do!"

Joe's feet move before his mind does. Recovering the bodies anytime soon won't be possible, not with the fire ants and enemy small-arms fire.

Back at Battalion Command, news of the loss spreads. All the men are quiet. Joe has a hard time processing the events of the morning. He did fine with the guiding. He handled the sniper with coolness. But now he sits on the ground next to the command tent, his chin resting on his knees. He feels too trancelike for tears. No one bothers him and he likes that. Being left alone. He sits for a long time.

As he sits, Joe pictures Ray, once so full of verve. He was quick to shake Joe's hand back at Fort MacArthur—the first to befriend the boy. After Joe had stepped forward and volunteered to go to the Philippines, Ray had stepped forward, too. Only a week ago, he had sat on a log next to the boy and cheered him up. One by one, he had helped pick the splinters from the boy's back.

For the next few days, Joe is a ghost. His boyish grin has faded into the past. He performs his duties, but keeps to himself. He can barely absorb the truth. Ray Rico is dead.

From moment one, he's a force to be reckoned with. All ten pounds of Joseph Quitman Johnson arrive January 27, 1926.

When fourteen-year-old Joe joins the Army in Pasadena, California, he tells the recruiter he's eighteen, and that he has no birth certificate because it's back in Memphis, where he was born. In actuality, Joe was born in Ruston, Louisiana, in 1926. To this day, the Army lists his birth year as 1923.

Joe in 1929: a smiley, smart toddler

Joe's father, Joseph Johnson Sr., age nineteen, loves to box. He is working for the railroad when he meets Joe's mom, a teacher three years his senior. They're married June 12, 1925, when Joe Sr. takes a job at a soda counter. Two more children are born, and Joe Sr. leaves the family to look for a better job. He never returns.

Joe will do anything to put food on the table for his beloved little sister, Betty.

Joe as a boy, late 1930s. His mother is often gone, and Joe scavenges for coal, cooks supper, cleans the house, works odd jobs, and looks after his two younger siblings.

During the Depression, Joe's mother, Edna Johnson, works ten-hour days sewing flour sacks into dresses. Later, she lands a better-paying job at RKO Pictures, inspecting movie reels.

The out-of-work barkeep "Mr. Jake" (Jerkins) takes up with Joe's mother and struggles to find work, which sends Joe over the edge because it means another mouth to feed in the family. Later, Edna marries Mr. Jake, who turns out to be a decent guy.

ALAMO DOWNS
1940

The last days of boyhood: Joe, age fourteen, summer 1940, about six months before he enlists

A poignant post-script from a letter Joe sends to his mother, 1941. He's just heading overseas.

P.S. Tell Charles and Betty I love them a lot. I am getting kind of homesick but I'm sticking it out. Everyone gets kinda homesick. I guess. my address is, if you forgot

Private Joseph P. Johnson
31 first Infantry
manilla
Phillipine Islands

MANILA 1941 15 YRS OLd

After arriving in Manila in April 1941, Joe goes through boot camp at Fort McKinley. The new soldiers wore old World War I uniforms. Joe is fifteen here.

A boy among men, D Company, 1st Battalion, 31st Infantry Regiment, Fort McKinley, Manila. Joe, age fifteen, about five feet seven and 135 pounds, stands middle row, second from left, next to his friend Dale Snyder, who stands at the end of the row to Joe's right.

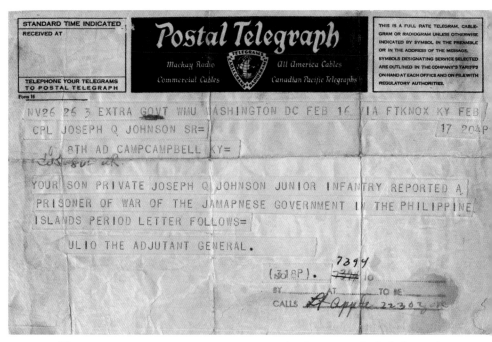

NV26 26 3 EXTRA GOVT WMU WASHINGTON DC FEB 16 VIA FTKNOX KY FEB 17 204P

CPL JOSEPH Q JOHNSON SR=

8TH AD CAMPCAMPBELL KY=

YOUR SON PRIVATE JOSEPH Q JOHNSON JUNIOR INFANTRY REPORTED A PRISONER OF WAR OF THE JAMAPNESE GOVERNMENT IN THE PHILIPPINE ISLANDS PERIOD LETTER FOLLOWS=

ULIO THE ADJUTANT GENERAL.

The message no parent ever wants to receive is sent to Joe's father, who enlisted after hearing that his son had.

Joe, a POW of Imperial Japan, is able to send word home that he's alive. The message is sent to columnist Eldon Roark care of the *Memphis Press-Scimitar* newspaper.

General Douglas MacArthur arrives at the wrecked dock on Corregidor, 1945, with Brigadier General Carlos Romulo, commanding general of Philippine Forces of Liberation. *(Photo courtesy the National Archives)*

As Allied soldiers advance through Manila City Hall in February 1945 on their way to liberate the Philippines, Joe has already been sent to Japan as a slave laborer. Note the pile of enemy bodies near a doorway. *(Photo courtesy John Tewell)*

Joe as a POW, age nineteen, summer 1945, near war's end. He stands six feet, four inches tall but weighs just 110 pounds.

Joe's hospital documents, October 1945

Fukuoka, Nippon
July 1945

408

1. Last Name, First Name, Middle In... Johnson   Joseph O. (RAMP)

2. Register No. 39 753   3. Army Serial No. 19 056 236   4. Grade Pvt

5. Organization and Arm or Service (if AAF personnel, see below)
Inf   Unasgd

6. Age 23   7. Race W   8. Length of Service 4-7/12   9. Date of Admission 20 Oct 45

10. Source of Admission Transferred from Letterman GH, San Francisco, (a)

*If AAF, indicate pilot, non-pilot flying pers., ground pers., or avn. cadet

II. Cause of Admission, Additional Diagnoses, Operations, Change of Status

(a) Calif., init adm 15 Sep 45, Nichols Fld, Disp, (Co D, 31st Inf) Manila, POA. (Patient was a prisoner of War from 6 May 42 to 15 Sep 45).

1. Wound, lacerating, posterior aspect right lower leg, severe, AI 6 Aug 45, Japan when a coal mine caved in while working as a prisoner of the Japanese. (Healed).
2. Dg 2 cured on admission.
3. Dg 3 cured on admission.
4. Malnutrition, severe, incurred while prisoner of the Japanese. (Cured).

Dgs on trfd card concurred in.

TDY at home 20 Oct 45.
From TDY at home 30 Oct 45.
Class III
Sp treatment: General Medicine.

12. Line or Duty
1-2-3-4-Yes

13. Disposition   Duty, General Service.

14. Date of Disposition   23 Jan 46

15. Days Lost → Total 100   Hospital 95-5 Tr   Quarters

16. Name and Location of Reporting Installation
Kennedy GH, Memphis, Tenn.

17. Signature
E. P. MOOMAU, Major, MAC

W. D., A. G. O. FORM NO. 8-24
1 July 1944

Joe with his iconic smile, shortly after being released from the hospital in Memphis. Although smiling, he still looks exhausted, (note the dark circles under his eyes), puffy from too-rapid weight increase, unhealthy, and older than his nineteen years here.

Joe with friends soon after he got home. For several months after the war, he said later, he did nothing but eat.

Joe, age nineteen,
healing in Memphis

After World War II, Joe reenlisted, first with the USAF
and later with the Marines. He
fought in Korea, where he was
wounded in the stomach.

Joe's second wife, Emma Lea, with whom he had two sons, Floyd Charles and Jerry *(Photo courtesy Audra Goff)*

Joe, the morning of his marriage to Marilyn, 1956

The lovely Marilyn Johnson, Joe's third wife

Joe and Marilyn with her daughter, Pamela, whom Joe raised as his own, 1964

Joe Johnson, finding peace at last

In his later years, Joe threw himself into volunteering, speaking, and advocating for POWs. *(Photo courtesy Richard and Michele Shirley)*

The guard detail at Joe's memorial service. Joe died June 24, 2017, at age ninety-one.

Joe's grave at Arlington National Cemetery

CHAPTER 10

Final Days of Bataan

Joe lugs a heavy machine-gun tripod along the jungle trail, keeping a sharp lookout for snipers while half closing his eyes against the ubiquitous dust. The soil rises in choking talcum waves. The soldiers of Weapons Company try not to be seen by the enemy, but they can't help booting up powder with every step. Some don their gas masks while carrying their sweaty, water-cooled guns. Others tie handkerchiefs over their noses and mouths as they haul ammo boxes along the trail. Joe is not sure where they are going. Their positions have been in constant flux, and often he doesn't know where he is, nor does he care all that much anymore. The boy knows that each day men are dying, and that he needs to put Ray's death out of his mind. He concentrates on the dust, the unspoken expectation to survive each day, and the order to put one foot in front of the next.

A dry irrigation ditch lies in front of them, and Joe and the men move at a crouch. The boy glances to his left and glimpses enemy bodies bloating in a tropical field. Without so much as a shudder, he turns his attention forward and keeps moving ahead. He guesses the dead men made a midnight charge some nights ago but were stopped by barbed wire and bullets. Yet he finds no reassurance in the ghastly sight; even though many enemy soldiers have been killed, more have kept coming. It's late February 1942, and the 31st has taken a beating. It's now a skeleton of its former self. Many men are dead, wounded, or sick with a lineup of diseases including malaria, dysentery, dengue fever, beriberi, and undiagnosed jungle sores. Joe's company of 183 men no longer seems like a company. It's more like a big platoon now, a fraction of its former size.

The men reach the rest of their outfit in a bivouac area north of a little barrio called Orion. The sky stays hot and cloudless even as twilight begins to fall. Soldiers are ordered to rest and regroup but to be ready to move at a moment's notice. By this time in the conflict, the 31st has clashed with the enemy in three hard fights—Abucay, the Pandan Line near the fishing barrio of Wawa, and an area farther south near the San Vicente River, as well as in other smaller skirmishes. Men hustle to dig foxholes, then tumble into an exhausted sleep. In the half-light of dawn, they're ordered to search for food. Joe and the men hike into the forest and hunt for wild pigs, stray chickens, bananas, edible roots, and snakes. Little food is found. Bataan has been stripped clean.

At midday, a Japanese bomber makes a run over the regiment's bivouac area, dropping a bomb indiscriminately. Several times that night, nearby enemy soldiers lob sporadic artillery rounds into the camp, just enough to keep the men from sleeping. This pattern of harassment continues for days. When not out scrambling for food, Joe and the men spend large parts of their days tucked into their foxholes. Joe is exhausted.

Captain Christopher Heffernan, commander of Joe's company, is severely ill with malaria. For a week, the captain never moves from his bedding near his foxhole. Joe knows a bit about the man. He's twenty-four, a graduate of West Point, has four sisters, and is a judge's son. Hovering constantly over the captain is a burly sergeant—the same one who chewed out Joe earlier. The sergeant brings the captain water from a canteen and keeps him as safe as possible. Few officers and noncommissioned officers are available for duty anymore, so a lowly corporal dishes out the company's assignments.

Joe scrounges up three cans of sweetened condensed milk and brings them to Captain Heffernan, who's lucid enough to receive the cans and thank Joe. But the captain hands the food over to the sergeant and says to give it to needier men than he. The sergeant carries the cans out of sight. At each mealtime over the next three nights, Joe observes the sergeant pouring a can of the milk over the captain's rice and feeding it to him anyway. The captain revives enough to get up and walk around a little for a few days but is soon overcome again. From then on, he stays lying near his foxhole.

In mid-March, all unit commanders are required to read a letter from General Douglas MacArthur. President Roosevelt has ordered the sixty-two-year-old commander of the Allied forces in the Philippines to head to Australia. The general's new assignment is to keep Australia safe, and from his new position, he's to organize an American offensive against Japan and hopefully return to the Philippines soon. The general, his wife, his four-year-old son, a doctor, and a few senior staffers have escaped on PT boats. They spent two days outwitting the Japanese navy on rough seas, then disembarked, drenched and exhausted, on the southern Philippine Island of Mindanao, some 500 miles from Corregidor. There they boarded a B-17 Flying Fortress at a pineapple plantation and flew to Australia.

A murmur of dismay rises among the troops. They feel

abandoned. In his note, MacArthur praises the troops for their bravery. He tells the soldiers how proud he is of them. General Wainwright has been left in command, and reinforcements are promised—again. But Joe knows the truth. The American planes on Bataan are wiped out. The bulk of America's ships are sunk or limping. Every soldier on Bataan is low on ammunition, famished, near the breaking point. The end is near.

That night Joe shivers in his foxhole and wonders about his fate. He's concerned about what his mother is hearing of the conflict, if she is worried sick about him. He wants to reassure her, even if he must fabricate news of his safety. But it doesn't matter. No mail is leaving—or reaching—the islands. The enemy lobs a random shell into the camp and it explodes. Joe huddles in the dirt. No one's screaming, so everyone must have lived—or, if not, their death was mercifully instant.

His mind turns to Perpetua. The boy discerns today's date, and a haggard smile spreads across his face. He knows nothing of her whereabouts or safety. Yet of these points he is certain: her conception date was mid-June 1941, and nine months have now passed.

Perpetua's baby has been born.

———

In the first week of April 1942, the enemy hits the main Allied line of resistance with new fury. Imperial Japan has brought in heavy artillery, more planes, and fresh troops. In daylight on April 3, under a dark and foreboding sky, arguably the most vicious artillery barrage of the entire campaign rips apart Allied troops near Mount Samat. Joe hears bits and pieces about the battle afterward. Shells shrieked down on American and Filipino troops. Men were hit and killed instantly. The not-so-lucky were blasted by nearby bombs and roasted alive. Fire spread rapidly in the dry jungle, and the dazed troops still alive retreated while lighting their cigarettes on the flaming bamboo.

April 4 begins with another fierce Japanese artillery and air bombardment. By day's end, the Japanese have gained so much ground they're reportedly more than a day ahead of schedule. That same evening, Joe and the 31st trek back through the jungle, heading north to the line again. In early morning of the next day, the Japanese pour in from the high jungle west of the line and flank the men, weapons blazing. The 31st holds off the enemy for a while, fighting fiercely, but fails in its attempt to push back the Japanese. Hour after hour, Joe fights with Weapons Company, working as Dale's assistant gunner. He handloads ammo belts and hustles water for the machine gun's water jacket. In late afternoon, Joe is sent back to the command post to work as a runner.

From the post, the boy heads up a trail with a message, stopping and hiding every few yards, listening, then moving on. Joe carries a rifle all the time now in addition to his .45. He delivers the message, then heads back to the command post. In front of him lies an open field, lightly grassed and pockmarked with abandoned foxholes. Joe passed through the same area not thirty minutes earlier. Now, a low-flying Japanese plane bursts out of the sun. The pilot spots the boy. The plane veers closer and zooms toward Joe, opening up its guns. Joe sprints toward the nearest foxhole and dives in headfirst, hitting with a *clump*. The plane screams overhead, guns strafing the ground around the boy.

Joe squirms. He's not on solid ground. His eyes are shut tight, yet in the confines of the foxhole he can comprehend he's not fully touching dirt. In a flash, he opens his eyes and stares straight into the face of a Japanese soldier. Alive. Panicked, the enemy moves to strike first, but Joe is already on top of him. The enemy punches, flails, tries to raise his rifle and shoot, but Joe slams his rifle across the enemy's sternum and upward to his chin, pinning him by the throat. The man's face contorts, his mouth opens in a scream. Joe grunts, pushes hard, then harder. The soldier strains to free himself. Joe bears down with all his might. Slowly the soldier loosens his grip, quits his struggle, gurgles. Joe keeps pressing until he is sure.

When the boy returns to the command post, he speaks to no one. He hikes over to his foxhole and lets his rifle clatter to the ground. He sits, leans across his knees, and buries his face in his hands. It's not his first kill. But it is his first in hand-to-hand combat. He has little time to process the horror. An hour later, he's ordered back to the line to work as assistant gunner again.

This time, the trail lies bare. The leaves rustle in the breeze, wilted and gunshot. For the last hundred yards, Joe is forced to a crawl. As soon as he reaches Dale's side, a Japanese machine gunner opens up, pinning the whole platoon. The gunner's location is spotted and men pour fire on the location, but the enemy keeps firing back. The sergeant hollers for a volunteer to sneak up close and lob a grenade. Joe inches his hand upward, but Dale grabs him and shoves it down. Another private volunteers, pulls two grenades out of his carrier, and crawls forward. Dale fires short bursts over the man's head as cover. The private throws his first grenade, but it falls short. He throws his second, but it's a dud and doesn't explode. The enemy gunner spots the private and rakes the area. The private is dead.

Dale grabs Joe's hand, places it on the grips of the machine gun, and shouts, "Cover me!" He wriggles forward before Joe can hold him back. Another private is also inching forward. He and Dale slide past the first private's body, rise, and both hurl their grenades at the same time. The enemy gunner is killed.

The next few days are full of fierce combat. Joe's outfit is rushed from position to position, fighting hard but always coming up short. Enemies pop up everywhere. They fire from head-on. They slip around the side, firing from the flanks. Sometimes Joe fights alongside Dale; other times he's ordered back to the command post to deliver messages. Joe finds he feels safer when he's with his machine-gun squad.

Back at the command post, Captain Heffernan's breathing has grown shallower. For several nights now he has hovered between life and death. The burly sergeant has tried to pick him up and take him to a field hospital, but the captain pulled his .45 on the sergeant and insisted on staying.

The captain falls weaker and weaker. By the morning of April 8, he's too frail to pull his .45, so Joe and a corporal are told to load the officer into the back of a Dodge WC Weapons Carrier and head for the field hospital. Dale is brought off the line to drive the truck while Joe is to care for the captain in the back under the canvas flaps. In the captain's absence, a lieutenant is put in charge. He wishes the medical evacuation team luck. Japanese have already overrun much terrain in the south. Roads are unsafe.

Dale inches the truck over rutted and bomb-cratered roads. Refugees trudge southward in long, desperate lines. It's slow going, but the truck finally reaches the aid station near the tiny town of Cabcaben. It's only a jungle facility, with no tents or buildings. Joe looks out over the wounded soldiers and estimates that more than a thousand men are lying in the open air. Dale and Joe have trouble finding a corpsman, much less a doctor, and when a corpsman finally examines the captain, he only shakes his head. The captain might have a chance of survival, he says, if they take him a few miles away to the better-equipped field hospital in Mariveles.

The men backtrack up the road, then circle around and head southwest, following the curve of the peninsula's bottom lip. An enemy plane zooms overhead, strafing the road. Dale and Joe have no choice but to leave the captain, pile out of the Weapons Carrier, and hit the dirt. The Dodge isn't hit, so they climb back inside and drive for another mile when another plane roars overhead, this one unloading a bomb. Again Dale and Joe leap out and dive for cover. Again they're safe. They climb back in and head up the road another mile. A third plane flies over. This time it banks and heads for the vehicle, guns spewing bullets. Again the men jump out and lunge toward any scrap of protection. The dirt kicks up around Joe. The plane passes and the vehicle is unharmed, but Joe can't move. When Dale tries to help him, the boy screams in pain. He fears his back is broken.

Gingerly, Dale lifts the boy, carries him to the truck, and lays him next to the captain. Lurching along the road as fast as he dares, Dale speeds to the field hospital, screeches to a halt, and shouts for help. Joe and the captain are carried into the emergency tent. Dale stays close. Joe is alert but moaning. A doctor examines the boy and says, "His back isn't broken. But he was hit by something. Maybe a rock. Maybe a piece of shrapnel that deflected off. He has a serious contusion on his lower left back muscle. We'll keep him here a day or so until he can walk again."

As the doctor begins to write up his report, he asks, "How old are you, son?"

"Fifteen!" Dale interjects, before Joe can utter a word. "Keep him here forever. He's too young to be up on the line."

With a puzzled look the doctor begins to write the number, but Joe gives a pained laugh and says, "Don't mind him, Doc. I'm eighteen."

The doctor writes the new age, then heads to a cabinet to find a heavy bandage.

Joe looks Dale in the eyes and quips, "Nice try, old buddy. But you got it wrong anyway. Late January, I turned sixteen."

———

Joe fights to take his next breath. His eyes open. The hospital air is choked with dust. Mattresses cartwheel through the air. The explosions are deafening. *Boom! Boom! Boom!* Corpsmen, doctors, and nurses are sprinting between patients. Joe slips to the floor, finds his boots and web belt. His back feels on fire. He counts the falling bombs. *Three, four, five.* Patients scream. *Six, seven.* Nurses shout for help. *Eight, nine, ten.* Tents are burning. Mangled bodies lie twisted on the ground. The explosions stop.

Joe can hardly move, but the wide, tight bandage wrapped around his torso helps him stand. He shuffles to the first wounded person he sees and helps calm the patient. He shuffles to a second. The man is gasping for air, with a hole in his throat. Joe tries to kneel to help, but the man dies before Joe can offer aid. The hospital looks like an alien planet. Walls are shredded. Cots and equipment have been tossed around as if in a hurricane. Joe knows his safest bet is to return to his company as fast as he can, but for the next aching hour he continues to move among the wounded, helping wherever he can. When things settle down slightly, he finds a corpsman and inquires about Captain Heffernan.

"Sorry," the corpsman says. "He died a few hours after he was admitted. You don't look so well yourself. Should you be walking?"

Joe mumbles an answer and turns away. In all, 73 people were killed in the hospital bombing; another 117 have been wounded. Dale left the hospital earlier to drive the Dodge back to the command post with supplies, and Joe's main hope now is to hitch a ride back. The boy sifts his way through the rubble, makes it outside, and locates the kitchen tent. No one is around, so he pockets two cans of condensed milk and a can of corned beef and heads for the road. Medical equipment shines from tree branches in the late-afternoon sun.

He flags down a jeep with two naval officers inside and climbs aboard. The road is so clogged with refugees and bombed-out equipment that a vehicle can hardly pass, but they manage to inch their way to Cabcaben, where Joe spots Dale's Weapons Carrier parked off the road, near the bay. Night is falling, and Joe smells salt in the air. He asks the officers to stop, wishes them luck, and hobbles over to the Dodge. Two Filipino scouts with tommy guns stand near the rear doors, guarding cases of C rations. They tell Joe to back off, but Dale quickly steps out from the shadows at the front of the vehicle and greets the boy.

Nearby under a tree near the dark ocean stands a major and a few other officers. Joe recognizes him as the same major he met a few months ago on horseback at the ravine. Dale helps Joe walk down a slope toward the tree and tries to help Joe sit, but the boy's back is aggrieved, and he can't do it. Standing, Joe tells Dale about the captain's death and the hospital bombing. Dale explains that he was heading to the command post, but couldn't get the larger vehicle through the throngs of refugees. A mob was just about to besiege the Dodge and seize its food when he spotted the major and asked for help. The major set the guard on the truck with orders to stay until the stream of refugees thins out.

"The officers say the Japs are only about six or seven kilometers up the road," Dale adds. "They're coming at us with everything they got. The major's trying to decide whether to try to make it over to Corregidor, or head west—up and over Mount Mariveles."

Before Joe can respond, the major strides over, smiles at the boy like he recognizes him, and addresses Dale: "We've decided to try to make it over the mountain and fight our way north. From all indications, each unit will need to fend for themselves. The two of you won't be able to reach your outfit from here, so you're welcome to join us or head off on your own. All organized resistance has collapsed. Either way, we'll take the food in your truck. I'll give you time to decide where to go." He turns and strides toward the other officers.

Joe tries to process this turn of events. Dale thinks for a moment, then says, "That major's going to have a hell of a time trying to get through those Japs and over Mount Mariveles. Then what? You won't make it through those mountains with your back all busted up. Hell, you can't even sit. Let's try for Corregidor. There's got to be a boat somewhere along this beach, and if we're lucky we can hitch a ride. Can't stay here—that's for damn sure. Won't survive if we do."

Joe grimaces and gives a slight nod. Dale strides over to the major to communicate their plans, then returns to Joe. The two set out along the beach in the moonlight, looking for a boat. Small-arms fire ripples over the rooftops in Cabcaben. Larger explosions ignite the night air farther in the distance. The enemy's heading toward them, gaining ground. No boats can be found, and Joe starts to think Dale made the wrong choice. His back is killing him, and it takes all his energy to keep walking. He's just about to ask them to halt a moment so he can rest when instead the boy cocks his ear and hisses, "Listen!"

It's the low throb of a boat engine, far in the distance. The engine misfires and dies. Then starts again.

"C'mon," Dale says. "Can you jog?"

Joe grits his teeth and breaks into a slow run. Pain shoots up his body with each step. His dysentery hits uncontrollably, but there's no time to lower his pants. He messes himself and keeps jogging.

"It's okay," Dale murmurs, then waves his arms and shouts toward the sound of the boat, "Hey! We're coming aboard!"

They can just make out a small Navy launch leaving the pier. Soldiers are already heaped on board. The launch sits dangerously low in the water. The small boat's engine misfires again, then restarts. The boat begins to move through the sea. No other boats are around.

"Wait!" Dale hollers toward the launch. "We'll swim to you."

Joe and Dale quickly undo their web belts, unlace their boots and kick them off, and plunge from the shore straight into the ocean. As they stroke toward the boat, a sailor shouts, "No room! We're already overloaded! We'll capsize if you guys try to board."

Dale struggles to grasp a rope that's dragging through the waves alongside the launch.

"Stay away!" another man yells. "You can't board."

Dale secures the rope, then helps Joe wrap it around his arm and hold on. The boat moves onward, slowly but steadily.

"We can't take you!" another man shouts. But others who sit on the side of the launch call out their encouragement. They pull the rope near to the launch and help Dale and Joe fashion slings, then let the rope out again. The boat picks up some speed, but not much.

As Dale and Joe are towed on their backs through the waters of Manila Bay toward Corregidor, they watch the shoreline slip away. The final battle for Bataan is being played out right before their eyes in the bright starlit night, and the enemy has all but won it. The terrain is illuminated like a Fourth of July fireworks display, and Joe hurts so much all he can think to do is lighten his mood by calling out to the guys in the boat: "Hey, fellas. If I didn't know any better, I'd say you were trolling for sharks and using us as bait."

The guys all laugh.

CHAPTER 11

So Utterly Alone

As the small launch chugs southeast through the dark waters toward the north pier on Corregidor, Joe can discern fragments of action around him. But his mind is focused on the throbs in his back, now seizing up from being dragged through cold water for so long. He glimpses a crowd on the pier in the moonlight. They reach out, grasp the launch when it bumps the pilings, and tie it fast. He hears someone shout, "We have two in the water! Take them first." He feels strong hands hook beneath his armpits, unwind him from the makeshift sling, and gingerly lift him up, passing him into more hands on the dock. A US Marine wraps a blanket around the boy and leads him to a nearby Army ambulance. Dale is already inside.

The launch has docked on the northern bank of the middle of Corregidor, the narrow ribbon of lowland known as Bottom Side. The ambulance driver rushes Dale and Joe half a mile up to the secret 1,000-bed hospital tucked inside the fortified tunnels of Malinta Hill. The duo is whisked inside, stripped of their ragged Army uniforms, and propped up under hot showers. After they thaw, they're handed hospital robes and steaming mugs of beef bouillon. A doctor examines them and pronounces them dehydrated and malnourished, but otherwise sound. Joe is given medication for his diarrhea. His back is heavily rewrapped. They're taken to the supply tunnel and issued new uniforms, boots, and weapons from the US Marines, now stationed on Corregidor with a few Army units. Joe gets a rifle and a .45.

It's nearing midnight, April 9, 1942. A Marine driver roars up to the supply depot in a jeep, greets them without smiling, and tells them to get in; he's been ordered to take them farther east on the rocky island to the Navy Radio Intercept Tunnel and fighting position known as Monkey Point.

On the ride over, as Joe absently surveys a serrated landscape of ravines and rocky cliffs, the driver explains to Joe and Dale what they already suspect. The Bataan peninsula has fallen completely to the Japanese, although it's taking a while for all fighting to cease. Against MacArthur's orders, Major General Edward King, the senior commander on Bataan, has officially surrendered—although it applies only to the troops on Bataan, not on the island of Corregidor. King is hoping to prevent further bloodshed. Joe isn't happy to hear of a surrender, but he knows the Japanese have scores of planes, whereas the defenders have none; the enemy has deep reserves of tanks and large guns, while the defenders have barely any left. Enemy forces on Bataan now number 200,000 well-fed and healthy troops, while the Allies have fewer than half that number. Plus, more than half the Allies are emaciated and sick—willing to fight, but no longer able.

The driver's been told it's the largest surrender ever of American forces against a foreign enemy. The only good news is that the Allies have held the enemy at bay for four long and savage months, buying precious time for the United States to ramp up the war effort stateside. Back in 1939, when hostilities were beginning in Europe, the United States had just 334,000 troops total. In 1941, immediately before Pearl Harbor and with the draft in effect, the American military had risen to 1.8 million troops. Now, by early 1942, that number has more than doubled to 3.9 million. Additionally, the United States has retooled factories and begun to build new ones to arm and equip the troops overseas. A massive effort is underway to meet President Roosevelt's new and urgent production goals, announced in January 1942: 60,000 new airplanes by the end of the year and 125,000 more in 1943, along with 120,000 new tanks. Meanwhile, US secretary of war Henry Stimson has declared to Americans back home that the surrender of Bataan is only a temporary loss, and the country will be avenged. The forces on Corregidor under General Wainwright are still itching to fight. Already MacArthur is rallying troops from Australia.

Joe and Dale spend a few hours in fitful sleep at Monkey Point. They wake, scrounge breakfast, and survey the area. The machine-gun positions are fully manned with Marines. Everyone is awaiting an attack. A Marine lieutenant tells them to join ranks and hold tight: the enemy is surely on its way.

A battery-powered radio broadcasts news from Manila. Some 65,000 Filipino and 10,000 American troops on the Bataan peninsula are being rounded up in the hot sun and marched toward POW camps in the north—a trek of up to sixty-five miles, depending on where the men are forced to join the march. Beatings, shootings, bayonetings, and beheadings are reported. Food, water, and medical care are virtually nonexistent. Thousands are perishing along the way. If Joe and Dale hadn't managed to grab the rope from the overloaded boat, they would have been part of one of the ghastliest American experiences of the Pacific war: the Bataan Death March.

Still dazed from the shock of battle and their escape, Joe and

Dale listen and wait. They're happy to see sandwiches brought out at lunch. Hot meals are served at suppertime, and Joe notices boxes of C rations stacked against one side of a gun emplacement. Compared to what they've just been through on Bataan, he considers the troops on Corregidor fortunate.

Later that night, Joe looks across the channel toward Bataan, sees fire in the sky, and hears the *boom* of explosions. Allied ammunition dumps are being destroyed. In the pale light of morning, scattered soldiers and civilian refugees begin to stumble ashore, exhausted. Some have swum through the shark-infested waters. Others have rowed across in pitifully small boats while enemy planes bombed and strafed them. Many haven't eaten for days. Joe helps wherever he can.

A few tense days pass in silence. Then the shelling begins. The Japanese have brought their artillery to the Cabcaben area of Bataan, knowing that the troops on Corregidor won't fire back because of wounded Allied POWs in a hospital in the Cabcaben area. The enemy unleashes its huge guns on Corregidor. At first, the shells target the coves and beach emplacements around Bottom Side. Then shells start exploding over higher ground. Japanese bombers fly a sortie across the island and drop bombs, but the initial damage is slight. Then another wave attacks, and another, and another—four in all. The damage becomes more pronounced. In retaliation, the Marines aim their guns at the planes and pour forth thunder. As Joe works in a machine-gun pit, his back begins to loosen.

The artillery and bombings continue for days. General Wainwright passes around news, assuring the troops that Corregidor can be held. Again and again, Japanese long-range guns fire their huge shells at them, while Japanese planes storm across the island and drop bombs, one after another. Joe and Dale crouch alongside Marines in gun nests and fire back. Most of the island vegetation soon disappears. Palm trees lie jagged and flattened. Rocky outcroppings turn to dust. Gone are the kingfishers, doves, pipits, and black-naped orioles. Toward the end of April, enemy fire strikes the powder magazine of a 12-inch mortar battery near the middle of Corregidor. A huge explosion reverberates across the island, shaking the ground under every man's feet. Steel fragments from the blast fall like hail on Joe's location. By May 1, casualties fill the beds in the hospital tunnel.

———

Late one afternoon in early May, Joe and Dale huddle behind sandbags near North Point. Joe nibbles on a candy bar from a D ration, cringing whenever he hears the whistle and burst of a close-landing shell. Dale smokes. A Marine sergeant moves around the emplacement, crouches next to the duo, and tries to grin.

"Did they rake you guys with this much artillery over on Bataan?" the sergeant asks.

"I didn't know the Japanese had this much artillery in their whole army," Joe says. "They must be using some of ours."

The sergeant spits in the dirt. "Scuttle is they're gonna try for a landing in the next few days. Probably at night, and probably here on the tail end. But we'll be ready for them. It's gonna get worse before it gets better. Just hang tough."

Joe checks the ammo supply. They're running low but are still okay for a while. Later that evening the fury of the enemy's artillery starts up again and surges to a new peak. Guns roar. The sky turns to brimstone. Hours pass in constant attack. Then, near midnight, the shelling slows, then pauses. Five minutes pass in silence. Ten. Joe climbs up on the edge of the emplacement and stares through the rare quiet across the bay toward

Bataan. Dale climbs up and sits next to him. The boy has tears in his eyes.

"What's wrong?" Dale asks.

"I dunno," Joe says. "I'm just sorry we ever came to Corregidor. You made this choice because of me—I know it. I was barely able to walk, much less hike over the mountains. I'm truly sorry for getting us into this mess."

Dale sucks in a long breath, then releases it. He slugs the boy on the arm, gently, and says, "Quit blaming yourself. I did the choosing, not you. Besides, what makes you think our fellas on Bataan have it any easier?"

Joe wipes his eyes on his sleeve, and his face becomes resolute. The boy gives Dale a glance, then speaks into the night sky, his words emerging without restraint. "Dale, I want you to know I love you like a brother. I always will."

His words are carried away on the wind. The lull in the shelling seems too prolonged. The enemy artillery is unusually quiet. Marines start moving about the emplacement. Dale stays silent, staring straight ahead. Joe glances at him again, and his friend's eyes are wet, though whether from poignancy or smoke Joe can't tell. Before anything further can be said, other men climb the emplacement. They sit next to Dale and Joe and stare into the darkness.

One gives a sudden start and shouts, "Japs are here! Barges out in front."

The gunners train their machine guns on the near shadowy shore and open up with fierce bursts. In a flash, Joe and Dale jump down, grab the ammo boxes for their squad, and hustle them up to the assistant gunner. Bullets whiz over their heads. Dawn is still a few hours off, and mortars begin to break overhead and explode. Joe can't tell exactly where the enemy fire is coming from. Japanese troops are running toward them from the beaches. They are bearing down on them from their flanks. The Japanese seem to fire from all directions at once. For some time, all is smoke and noise and bullets and mayhem.

In a rare lull, the boy works his way up the sandbags and sneaks a look over. Two assault barges are stuck against the barbed wire that's strung along the rocky beach. Both barges are loaded with dead bodies, piled on top of each other. A few bodies float in the surf. Yet more barges have already motored in behind them. Joe ducks his head again. It's barely daylight now, and bullets start flying with intensity again. Enemy howitzers start blasting again from the coast of Bataan. The enemy's huge guns fire at will, seemingly able to drop rounds into any deep ravine or gun emplacement they wish. In reprisal, Joe's outfit returns constant fire.

An hour passes in furious combat. The island is pounded by the bombardment. Another hour passes. Then another. Then another. It's the most horrific display of firepower the boy has ever witnessed. Fragments of hot metal fill the air. The enemy lands three tanks on the island, their long iron snouts blazing. Dust, dirt, and smoke choke the skies. All is chaos.

Then—suddenly—everything falls silent.

Joe blinks. Tries to find his bearings. Voices are heard approaching the emplacement. Booted footsteps. An American voice calls out: "Disarm yourselves! Corregidor has surrendered by order of General Wainwright. Fall in behind me and keep moving." Joe glimpses a Marine major surrounded by half a dozen enemy soldiers. A dozen disarmed Marines already follow them.

The sergeant of Joe's squad hesitates.

The major shouts toward him, "Damn it, Sergeant. Obey my order!"

The men in Joe's emplacement stare at their sergeant. He mutters, then drops his rifle on the hard-packed dirt. Joe looks at Dale. Dale looks at Joe. They let their rifles fall with a clatter. Joe unholsters his .45 and drops it, too. It is May 6, 1942 — five full months since the attack on Pearl Harbor. The troops on the island have been able to keep fighting for a month since the fall of Bataan. But now it's official. Corregidor, the last bulwark of organized Allied defense in the Philippines, has fallen.

The Allied troops group up behind the major and start hiking through the billowing smoke. The road up to the larger security tunnel at Malinta is littered with the bodies of US Marines, Filipino artillerymen, and unexploded Japanese shells. A Japanese commander halts the group outside the tunnel and orders the Americans to sit on some rubble near the entrance. The sun grows hot overhead, and Joe and Dale stay close as other Marines join the group of prisoners. The afternoon passes. Twilight overtakes them, and still they sit. Some are wounded. All are demoralized. They have no choice but to obey, their gloom as palpable as the surrender.

The first rays of dawn bring no relief. Joe finds a half-eaten candy bar in his shirt pocket and splits it with Dale. Their canteens are both half-full, and they whisper cautions to conserve their water. Rumors circulate. Some 10,000 men on Corregidor have become prisoners, along with 68 Army nurses. Of the troops still living, there are too many wounded to count. Some of the smoke has cleared overnight, and with the morning sun Joe and Dale are able to get a better look at the devastated landscape of what was once a lush tropical island. Dead bodies lie everywhere. The terrain has been pulverized. The boy stays silent, but Dale murmurs simply, "God help us."

Japanese soldiers approach and order Joe and Dale's group to start removing corpses. Four Marines are told to wield a large wooden wagon for collection. The prisoner detail moves slowly down the shell-pocked road, stacking enemy bodies on the wagon like cordwood. Two men try to load a dead Marine on board, but a Japanese guard pulls off the body, slams the butt of his rifle against one man's chest, then the other. Message received: the Americans are to load only Japanese.

Joe and Dale work as a team. Flies cover the corpses' faces. The bodies are already bloated. Joe tries to shoo the flies away, but it's no use. Flies swarm everywhere. The smell is almost unbearable. Joe ties a rag over his nose and mouth. His back aches. The day wears on, and the sun becomes broiling. Joe feels nauseous. The men fill the wagon, haul it to the tunnel entrance, and pile the corpses on a spot of rubble marked by the guards, about a hundred yards downhill. The men head back to the landscape to collect another load.

Later that night, the men on the grim detail are allowed to rest and fill their canteens. A guard opens a can of potatoes packed in water, tastes one and spits it out, then hands the can to a man from the detail. Sixteen Americans split the can—one small potato for each prisoner. They fall asleep on a patch of rocky ground close to the Japanese guard station. Early the next morning, the men are ordered to pour gasoline on the corpses and burn them. Afterward, the detail is ordered to pick up the American and Filipino bodies. Those bodies are likewise burned. The next night the Americans sleep on a concrete slab surrounded by barbed wire. In the morning, they are ordered to collect unexploded artillery shells. More cans of food are issued to the prisoners, and the amount is more plentiful than the first day. Joe looks both ways and manages to slip into his old gun emplacement. He grabs some D-ration candy bars and a couple of extra canteens.

When the cleanup is at last finished, a long column of

prisoners is marched down the winding road to Corregidor's south pier. It takes all day for the thousands of prisoners to make the hike. There is no shade. All that night and into the early hours of the next day, the prisoners are loaded onto barges. They are hauled east to Manila and unloaded as close to shore as possible. Joe and Dale slip over the side and splash ashore with their boatload.

At the city's edge, the prisoners are assembled in large groups, positioned into columns of four, and then marched down Dewey Boulevard in their wet boots. Civilians are forced to line the street, cheer, and wave small paper Japanese flags. The eyes of many spectators fill with tears. Japanese cavalry ride horses on each side of the columns, the riders brandishing drawn swords. Joe and Dale walk side by side, keeping their heads down. The boy understands what the procession is meant to convey. He can see the shame in the prisoners' faces, in each man's efforts to maintain a gritted countenance. The parade is a spectacle, an exhibition of defeat. Joe and his fellow soldiers are trophies of war.

Occasionally the boy looks up and stares through the crowd, wondering if he'll recognize any faces. Perhaps Frisco Smith. Father Bruno. Even Perpetua and her new baby. His feelings swirl. He longs to catch a glimpse of the girl—to reassure her, to offer some encouragement, to see what her child looks like. But he doesn't want Perpetua to see him like this. The column marches past the beautiful green Luneta park. Joe and Dale look across at the old Walled City. Joe longs for his barracks in the *Cuartel de España*. For the freedom of his motorcycle. The column is marched through the heart of Manila and into the stern concrete walls of the aged Bilibid Prison. Inside, groups are cordoned off and placed in larger cell blocks fanning out in a circle from the prison's center.

As each door slams shut, the sharp *clank* marks their new status: they are prisoners of war. Yet unlike ordinary criminals, they have no idea when they will be freed—if ever. Each man is given water and a bamboo cup of steamed rice topped with pork fat. Joe and Dale slide into a corner, sit, and lean back against the wall. The boy's hands tremble as he eats his meal, but he's glad at least that Dale is with him. When he finishes, Joe draws his knees up to his body's core. His eyes close from weariness and he can't help dozing off.

Dawn arrives early. The prisoners are pushed outside, lined up, marched a few blocks west to the railroad station, and ordered into waiting boxcars. Joe starts to move forward, but Dale elbows him and says to slow down and wait. The safest places to stand will be near the door. Prisoners are packed into the boxcars as tightly as possible. The men stand chest-to-back, sweating, stinking. The doors slide shut and are locked. The air inside the boxcar is stifling. The morning sun beats down on the metal roof.

"Just keep breathing," Dale murmurs to Joe.

Hours go by while the loading is completed. Finally the train begins to chug forward. Hours pass. There are no restrooms. A man in Joe's car faints but stays standing, buoyed upright by the press of shoulders. They are packed so tightly Joe finds it impossible to bring a canteen up from his side to take a drink. At last the train screeches to a stop. The door is opened. Joe inhales huge gulps of fresh air.

The prisoners are herded into columns again. They trudge four abreast along the dusty gravel road that leads out of the town of Cabanatuan, about 100 miles north of Manila. They hike for miles. A chain of lush green mountains lies in the distance, but Joe keeps his head down, focused on his gritty task. Finally, they arrive at an old Philippine army camp. It seems to sprawl for miles—rows of barracks after barracks. The roofs are thatched with cogon grass. A barbed-wire fence has been strung around the camp, and several thousand prisoners are already inside—the ones who surrendered on Bataan and managed to survive the Death March. Already, the survivors look skinnier than the troops from Corregidor, and stories are circulating about the horrors they endured. Every fifteen yards of the Bataan Death March, another man died. Mile after mile after mile.

In Cabanatuan POW Camp No. 3, guard towers dot the fence every fifty yards. Across a gravel road from the camp sits a Japanese administration building and several newer barracks for the guards. The prisoners are searched, organized into groups of fifty, assigned barracks, and ordered to fall out in formation in the hot sun. Joe and Dale stand for hours and wait.

Finally a Japanese officer appears from across the road. A placid-looking man in his late fifties with dark-rimmed glasses, he strides in front of the formation and stops. Two guards scurry to place a small crate in front of him. He stands on the crate and speaks to the crowd through an interpreter:

"This is Cabanatuan Prisoner of War Camp No. 3. I am Commander Mori of His Imperial Majesty's Army. You have surrendered like cowards. Therefore, you have given up your rights to be treated like soldiers.

"You will be required to work, and you will keep this camp clean. You will be assigned work according to your ability.

"If you attempt to escape, you will be executed."

He turns, steps off the crate, and heads back across the road. As the prisoners are allowed to mill around, Joe's able to sit and remove his boot. During the hike, a blister on the top of his right foot has grown to the size of a quarter. Now it has burst and is red and raw. The whole foot has swollen. Dale scrounges some rice powder from the kitchen, which he sprinkles on the blister in an attempt to dry up the sore. He finds bits of wood and helps the boy fashion a clog he can wear until the swelling goes down.

The next morning, the men are assigned work details. Joe and Dale try to stick together, but they're split up. Dale is assigned firewood detail. He and a group of about fifty prisoners leave the camp, hike out into the heavy brush, and spend the day sawing trees and chopping the branches and trunks into smaller pieces of firewood. They return at day's end exhausted, carrying bundles of wood on their shoulders.

Joe is ordered to the kitchen. He spends the day washing rice and cutting greens and fish—whatever might be available for the day's ration. His hunger is unrelenting. Occasionally he is able to slip an extra morsel for himself. Hearing of the jobs that other prisoners are forced to do, he considers himself lucky. Already he's seen a line of men carrying litters. Men lug corpses outside camp, dig mass graves, and bury the dead. The line never ends.

Days pass in the POW camp, and Dale grows irritable. He's concerned about Joe's foot, how it's healing, often asking how far the boy can walk on it without explaining why. Evenings, Dale and two other prisoners from the firewood detail have taken to standing outside the barracks, where they talk furtively. They never invite the boy to join, although Joe asks once. Dale declines, saying it's nothing important. But Joe feels peeved. Dale's his best friend—his only friend. Anything Dale can say to others, he can surely say to Joe.

Toward the end of May, the boy spends a day picking maggots out of dried fish. Other prisoners rinse off the fish, cut them up, and toss the carcasses into soup pots. Two small meals are served each day. By day's end, Dale has not returned to camp.

Joe notices guards at the camp's gate interrogating the men on the firewood detail, but Dale is not among them. When the interrogation is finished, Joe asks one of the firewood guys about Dale.

The prisoner breaks eye contact. "He took off."

"Took off?"

"Yeah. Him and two guys ran."

"Escaped?"

"I guess some of our guys never got captured when Bataan surrendered. They're still free in the countryside, fighting as guerrillas, harassing the Japs any way they can. Least that's what I heard. Hey—look sharp and shut up. Here they come." Joe is stunned by the news. Guards push their way into the barracks, rummage through Dale's bedroll, then question Joe on Dale's whereabouts. The boy answers honestly. He has no idea.

For the next few days, Joe goes through the motions of his work, feeling bewildered and hurt. He tries to give his friend the benefit of the doubt. Maybe Dale acted on the spur of the moment. Or perhaps the other two goaded Dale into running away. He understands now why Dale was curious about how far he could walk. Perhaps Dale hoped Joe could come with him, but had given up on the idea. He deliberately gave the boy no information in order to protect Joe. Yet Joe can't believe Dale would just abandon him, leaving without even saying goodbye. That's how it seems. The boy feels betrayed.

Late one evening a truck roars into the administration compound across the road. Three prisoners are unloaded, but Joe can't make out their faces in the distance and twilight. They are stripped of their shirts and tied to a fence. A guard beats the prisoners with a heavy stick. Joe hears their cries of pain. A crowd of prisoners gathers near Joe, muttering and cursing about the beatings. But nobody can do anything to help the men. The crowd watches a long time. When it grows too dark to see, the sounds of the beatings stop.

In the morning, all prisoners are ordered to gather in the large open area in front of the main gate and stand at attention. A dozen Japanese guards stand outside on the road facing the camp. An American officer stands near the guards. The three prisoners are still tied to the fence, slumped. Joe sees they're bloodied but still alive. The boy feels light-headed and sick to his stomach.

From across the way, the camp commander leaves his office and strides toward the bound men. He pulls out his sword and utters a loud shout. It all happens in a rush. A few rows behind Joe, a man begins to recite the Lord's Prayer.

With a mighty heave, the commander slices off the first prisoner's head. It falls to the dirt with a *thump*. The commander shouts again, beheading the second man, then the third. A guard scurries to the commander and hands him a cloth. The commander wipes his blade, returns his sword to his scabbard, pivots, and calmly walks back to the administration building.

The formation is dismissed, and the prisoners begin to head to their work details. But Joe stands frozen. Never has he felt so alone. The American officer walks across the road from the administration building to the camp, his head bowed. He's carrying something in one hand. Joe finds his footing and walks over to the officer. The boy has a despairing hunch, but he must be certain.

"Sir—do you know the names of the men?"

The officer jangles three sets of dog tags. He studies the tags, reads the names to Joe, each in turn. The first two pass in a whisper. The boy barely hears them being read. But with the third, a solitary picture passes through his mind from a lifetime ago, from way back at Fort McDowell. A lounging Michigan native rises on one elbow to shake hands and introduce himself. As Joe gets to know him in those early Army days, he makes a sure decision. His friend is a good egg.

Joe's pain is immediate. His grief inconsolable. Sobbing, the boy walks toward the kitchen at Cabanatuan, the final name ringing in his ears:

"Dale L. Snyder."

PART III

That major in our provost marshal's office, the officer who questioned me in front of Manny Tang — he was taken prisoner, same as us. He got real sick in Cabanatuan Camp No. 1, where I spent some time. I went to see him.

It was one of those days — no wind, hotter than hell. He was sicker than a dog. I took his hand. He was so frail I was afraid to squeeze it. He laid there a long time, not looking at me. Then he stared me straight in the eye, his voice real quiet, and said, "I'm happy you're still alive."

He had news. My mother had written the general and told him my real age. They were gonna send me home on a ship. This was right before Pearl Harbor, end of November 1941. I'd get a Fraudulent Enlistment Discharge when I reached the States. But my mother hadn't sent my birth certificate with her letter. They had to wait for it to get proof of my age. It never arrived.

When they'd first got the letter, they'd talked about putting me in the guardhouse until I could get sent home. But everybody liked my bugle playing so much they decided I could stay free. Keep doing my job. That was good of them, all right. After the attacks happened, well, weren't no way I could get sent home then, birth certificate or no. That's why they assigned me as a runner — so they could keep an eye out for me.

I stayed with the major as long as I could. He was a good one. He died in that camp.

About a month after Dale died, a guy sidled up to me one morning, asked me if I wanted to escape with him. He was itching to run, but didn't want to go alone. I said no. Didn't think long about his offer. It weren't no picnic trying to survive in the jungle. Weren't no coconuts left. No damn bananas hanging

*from any trees. No wild game anymore. Hell, we'd eaten every-
thing that moved before the surrender. Back in Abucay, we'd got
so hungry we tried to survive on sugarcane juice. That's how
starving we were. Escaping by sea weren't no plan. The whole
China Sea was controlled by the Japanese. They had a standing
offer of a hundred pounds of rice to any Filipino who turned in
an escaped American prisoner. That's what happened to Dale
and the two guys who took off with him. They'd been turned in
for a few bags of lousy rice, we heard. Later, the Japanese started
this other policy. If you escaped, they'd shoot five prisoners,
sometimes ten. Random guys. You don't want that on your
conscience.*

*So I didn't run from trouble. Weren't no place to go anyway.
But it was tough. Real tough. At least the fight on Bataan and
Corregidor had been bearable because I had Ray and Dale to
share those hells with me. But there in Cabanatuan Camp No. 3,
I had no one to share that with. That hell was mine, and mine
alone.*

*I wasn't mad at Dale. He had reasons for doing what he did.
Trying to escape like that. I just missed my friend. That's all. I
missed him bad. Dale was a hero. Ray was a hero. The major
was a hero. Every man buried under that soil is a hero. A man
gives his life so others can be free—he's a hero. We forget that
these days. We damn well do.*

CHAPTER 12

Prerogative of Madness

Eight months after Dale's death
January 25, 1943

For a moment in the predawn stillness, he thinks he hears his baby sister crying. Joe sits upright, rubs his eyes, peers through the gloom.

"Betty?" Joe's whisper is hoarse.

Maybe little Charlie has wet the bed again, Joe thinks. It's never easy for three siblings to share the same bed.

A figure stirs beside him but does not speak. Joe thinks again. He feels the hard, thin, woven bamboo mat beneath him that covers a patch of floor at the Pasay schoolhouse, a few miles south of Manila's core. His awareness becomes clearer. The whimper has not come from his sister. It's emerged from the lips of a fellow prisoner, nursing his blows from yesterday's beating.

Joe knows he ought to lie down. He should try for more rest before the wake-up order is given, but he wills himself to stay sitting. The daylight has almost come. Across from him in the schoolroom is a chalkboard covered with Japanese words scrawled phonetically with English letters. Joe squints and looks closer as the light grows. If any prisoner believes he has learned a phrase, he writes it on the board for the others to learn. *Hurry up. Come here. Lift this. Carry that.* The more of the Japanese language a prisoner knows, the fewer times he is hit. Already Joe has learned his numbers, close-order-drill commands, and basic work instructions. Some prisoners are too exhausted to expend any further energy on learning; every ounce of vigor has been spent trying to survive each day. Yet Joe has not resigned himself to complete despair. At least not yet. Each morning before the others awake, Joe studies the board.

Other prisoners are stirring now. Joe turns from the chalkboard and checks to see that his canteen, mess-kit bowl, and spoon have not been stolen during the night. Besides the clothes on his back, they are his only possessions. Thirty prisoners sleep in each classroom at the Pasay schoolhouse. The heavy wooden desks that were nailed to the floor have been pried up and stacked, leaving room for men to sleep ten to a row on the hard floor.

Joe pushes to his feet and heads down the hallway to the shower structure behind the kitchen. The rainy season has ended; the hot and oppressive temperatures have begun. As he eats his single bowl of morning rice, Joe reminds himself to keep a sharp lookout during the day ahead. A week ago, he and several hundred other prisoners were trucked to Pasay, and since Joe is still one of the new arrivals, he makes an easy target for the guards. On his first day at Pasay, a guard smacked Joe on the forehead with an open palm, plopped an old straw hat onto the boy's head, and motioned for him to stand still. On the straw hat was the number *176*. It had belonged to another prisoner who had since died. The guard painted another *1* in front of the original number. This is Joe's new name: *Prisoner 1176*. The higher number signifies his more recent arrival.

The sun has not fully risen yet, but the men are counted and marched from the schoolhouse to the Nichols Field worksite. The schoolhouse is only the sleeping quarters for this new detail; the slave labor happens three miles away, a forty-five-minute trek by foot. After he worked as a kitchen helper at Camp No. 3, and after he did some heavy salvage detail near the town of Cabanatuan, Joe worked as a barracks monitor at Camp No. 1, a larger, cleaner, better-organized camp than No. 3. The work was relatively easy, the food scant but enough to survive on. Just before he left, he was even ordered to send word home. The postcard had blanks to fill in and read *Imperial Japanese Army* at the top. Joe was ordered to address the card to the editor of the *Memphis Press-Scimitar* newspaper — perhaps, he wondered, for propaganda purposes? He was given the brief opportunity to describe his health, and he asked the editor to notify his folks that he's still alive. That was Camp No. 1. Here at Pasay, by contrast, Joe is already concerned about his prospects.

Dust rises with the morning sun as the airfield comes into view. A line of blackened houses and small thatched stores litter the horizon. Japanese bombers ruined the civilian residences and businesses in the air raids of December 1941. Now, at Nichols Field, the Japanese are forcing the POWs to extend an airstrip. It will become the longest runway in the Pacific. Joe's throat is dry. They are near the sea and he can smell salt air, but he can't see the ocean. He is handed a shovel and ordered to work. The day's sunlight has barely begun. Prisoners are already hacking into a ridge to his right, ripping away at the rocks and dirt with pickaxes. Moving a hillside by hand. More prisoners shovel the debris into railway carts, while others lug the loads to a destination he can't see. Sweat runs across bone and sinew. Every man is a scarecrow.

Joe is part of a four-man work crew along with Norman "Hicks" Hinckley, a lanky, twenty-five-year-old private first class. Hicks has painful open sores on his legs, yet for days now he's been affably whispering the rules and protocols of this new camp to the younger soldier. Chatting is forbidden, yet Hicks manages to reveal that his grandfather runs a boarding school in Maine for orphans. Hicks has been raised to show kindness to any youth who needs a helping hand. Japanese supervisors (some military, some contractors) roam the field giving orders, shouting, sometimes threatening the prisoners—who will work dawn to dusk, seven days a week.

"Pace yourself," Hicks says to Joe in a low voice, as they shovel dirt and rocks into their small wooden railway cart. "Not too fast. Not too slow. Keep your head down and your ass up. The one they call 'Cherry Blossom' is okay. He's second-in-command. 'Pistol Pete' can be brutal, and watch out for the one with the buck teeth—'El Lobo.' That's him holding the cane. No, don't look at him. And never cross paths with 'the White Angel.' You'll be dead if you do."

Joe keeps digging, absorbing Hicks's advice. He's heard of the White Angel already. It's the nickname given to the Nichols Field commander, a Japanese naval lieutenant. He is easy to spot because he always wears a starched white naval uniform. By his side, he always carries a sword. Joe doesn't like swords.

For the next half an hour all is quiet except for the grunts of men, the erratic percussion of dirt against steel. Joe has noticed that in this area of the worksite, ten crews are working to fill ten carts. Lines of rails, carts, and crews are scattered over the airfield, and each line has a quota of dirt and rocks to move each day. When all ten carts are loaded, each crew pushes its cart by hand to the end of the tracks. Joe and Hicks and two other workers dump the fill from their cart, then return to the hillside for another load.

A young prisoner off to the left has angered the guards. The work slows slightly as the others watch in short, furtive glances. Guards surround the prisoner. It's barely noon, and El Lobo beats the man across the back with his cane. Another guard strikes him hard across the mouth. It's not the first beating that Joe has witnessed at Nichols Field. Most beatings don't last long, but some are known to stretch through the afternoon if the guards feel so inclined. For this man, the guards stop the beating and make him dig a hole. Joe knows this can't be good. The prisoner is tired and cut up, yet all afternoon he is forced to dig— two hours, three hours, four, five, until it's late in the day. The sun sets about 6 p.m. in January in the Philippines. That's when the White Angel appears and strides over to the man in the hole. Just as the soft diffusion of twilight descends over the field.

The guards haul him out, tie the prisoner's hands behind his back, and force him to kneel in the dirt. The prisoner tilts his head downward slightly, but his eyes remain steely and focused ahead. The White Angel cannot tolerate this insolence. He shouts a long string of invectives, then steps forward, draws his sword with both hands, and raises it high over his head. Twinkles of twilight play along the glistening blade. It falls in an instant, the blow sounding like a meat cleaver slicing through a rump of beef. The headless body lurches forward. The legs give one final spasmodic kick. The body lies still in the grit and blood.

A murmur of dissent sweeps through the formation of prisoners but quickly is silenced by a guard's shout. Joe feels his stomach twist. He strains to keep from vomiting. The White Angel, his face flushed, wipes the blood from his sword. A guard nudges the headless body into the grave with his boot and motions for two prisoners with shovels to start covering the hole. The murmur from the prisoners grows again. The prisoners inch closer to the grave and form a semicircle out of respect for the man, still keeping a compliant distance from the commandant.

This time the White Angel himself calls for silence. In a low, barely audible voice he begins to speak. His English is perfect, and his timbre rises steadily to a high-pitched shriek. "This soldier died as a soldier should die! With bravery and courage. You will all die! I'm going to kill every one of you. When you die, you must die with honor. His death should teach you that escape is not possible. Any of you who break the rules shall meet the same fate."

Joe looks at Hicks, and Hicks glances up at Joe. The semicircle is breaking up. The two shake their heads and return to their work. The day is nearly over, and they cannot do anything but continue forward. After he is marched back to the Pasay schoolhouse with the other prisoners, Joe shivers the rest of the night. He's seen many horrific things in the war, but this is one of the worst.

Two days later, Joe turns seventeen.

For four long months, Joe and Hicks work at Nichols Field.

Far too much time, Joe thinks, and for a moment in the predawn stillness of another day, Joe feels Perpetua lying next to him. He reaches forward with two fingers, caresses the peachy glow along her neck. The warmth of the girl's body presses into him. Joe doesn't move. Doesn't rub his eyes. Doesn't peer through the gloom. He wants this dream to last forever.

It's May 1, 1943. His shoes have long since rotted away in the mud and the muck of Nichols Field. Now he wears wooden clogs that he fashioned himself. He shakes himself awake and checks his canteen, bowl, and spoon. Joe's been sharpening the spoon in spare moments when he can grind it against stone in the latrine. Sharpening, sharpening. Sharpening until it begets blood on his index finger when drawn across the tip. He's not sure what he's sharpening it for. But he likes the idea of carrying a weapon.

Joe has scaly sores on his legs and ankles now. He runs a constant fever—his body sometimes burning, sometimes freezing—and he often shakes throughout the night. He's lost some of the feeling in his hands and feet. The membranes of his mouth and nose are inflamed. His gums are bleeding and swollen. His stomach hurts all the time. He's grown to over six feet tall but weighs less than 110 pounds. One of the rooms at Pasay is a small infirmary, and a medic has diagnosed him with dry beriberi, pellagra, scurvy, and a persistent case of malaria. The hard labor and starvation diet intensify the mix of ailments that steadily beat him down.

This morning Joe rises once again. He reads one word, two, off the blackboard. Shrugs. If a man can walk, a man can work, so after the bowl of rice and morning head count, Joe trudges with the other prisoners to the field for the day. All the men walk slowly now, and the guards shout to move faster, prodding with rifle butts.

Joe and Hicks are still on the same work crew, but this morning Hicks has vanished. Hicks has been running a fever lately, plus he's suffered violent diarrhea every half hour for weeks. For a time, Hicks grew too sick to work. The guards put him on a softer detail, boiling water for their food. Hicks healed up just enough to return to pick and shovel. His once-affable spirit became numb and disengaged.

This morning, the guards have determined Hicks tried to run away.

Run, Joe thinks. *Now there's a word for a man who can barely walk.*

In an hour, Hicks is caught just outside the perimeter of the airfield. Joe witnesses the beating. Guards assault Hicks with rifle butts, spare pick handles—anything they can grab. The bucktoothed El Lobo is there, swinging his cane again and again.

Hicks survives the beating. He's tied to a post and left out in the sun. He loses all control of his bowels. The excrement runs down his legs and mingles with his blood. He is given no food or water all that day.

The next day, May 2, 1943, Hicks is still alive, his spirit unconquerable. He breathes without a sound. Hicks lives all that day, and all the next day, May 3. Sometime during the night before May 4, Norman "Hicks" Hinckley passes into eternity. For weeks afterward, Joe lies awake each night, picturing his friend's face.

In early summer 1943, the White Angel ups the pressure. He wants the Nichols Field runway completed. Quotas are raised. Beatings become more frequent. One prisoner is shot without provocation. Another is bayoneted. Joe notes the heightened irritability of the guards. They seem to look for any excuse to vent their anger. He vows, in remembrance of Hicks's advice, to keep his head down and his ass up. But late one afternoon Joe's luck runs out. His crew is sluggish. The men are exhausted. Joe tries to rally the men. He picks up the slack on behalf of the others. But El Lobo strides over to check things out.

"*Speedo*," El Lobo shouts to the men. It's the one English word all the guards seem to know. He clubs the closest with his cane. It's Joe. El Lobo shouts again. Clubs Joe again.

"Can't you see we're trying," Joe mutters, his eyes focused on his work.

El Lobo snorts. Clubs Joe again.

The burning fuse reaches the dynamite. Explodes. On reflex,

Joe snatches the cane out of the hands of El Lobo and breaks it across his knee. The moment the broken cane clatters on the gravel beneath his feet, Joe realizes he is dead.

El Lobo takes two steps back and yells for support. Two guards scurry over and grab Joe. The other prisoners in Joe's crew glance in his direction and shake their heads. The guards hustle Joe to a guardhouse at the main entrance of the work area. They order the boy to stand at attention while they take turns hitting him in the ribs with their rifle butts. Another guard runs over and joins the fray. They hit his face. Shoulders. Arms. The side of his head. Kick him in the crotch. They shout in Japanese, "Why did you break the cane? Tell us! Why?"

Joe refuses to answer. Silence is his final dignity.

An American officer, a fellow prisoner, sizes up the situation and runs over. He quickly bows to the guards and shouts at Joe to answer his captors. "Tell them something. Anything! You can't just stand with your mouth shut when they're asking you questions."

The guards interpret Joe's refusal to answer as defiance. Joe knows this but doesn't care. He's hungry. Sick. Worn-out. Furious. He tries to spit at the guards, but his mouth is so dry nothing emerges. Blood runs from one ear and marks a red trail down his face. His nose is bleeding all over his chin. One eye is swelling shut. He's light-headed and feels like vomiting. The boy has lost the desire to live.

He hears the American officer yelling at him once more. The guards have started up again on his face. Joe's world swirls and turns black. He collapses. A bucket of muddy water is thrown on him. He awakens to find two guards pulling him up and off the ground. They prop him against a shed and point to a shallow hole that two prisoners are already digging to receive him. The prisoners have been ordered to hustle; they're a foot deep already, and one pauses with his shovel just long enough to say, "Damn it, man. Just speak to them. They're going to bury you if you don't."

Joe hears the words but doesn't move his lips. A crowd gathers: several guards, a couple of American officers, and El Lobo. The guards are laughing at Joe, shaking their heads. For reasons he never understands, the two prisoners are told to knock it off with their shovels. Work on his grave halts, and Joe is shoved back in line as the prisoners march back to Pasay for the night. Maybe it's dinnertime for the guards, too. Nobody likes to kill on an empty stomach.

With the help of his fellow prisoners, Joe stumbles the three miles back to the schoolhouse. All he hopes for now is a chance to lie down. But the prisoners are lined up in the inner courtyard for evening roll call, and El Lobo stands with his arms folded. He calls Joe's number. Slowly and painfully, Joe steps forward. El Lobo and two guards drag him to the White Angel's office at the front of the schoolhouse.

The White Angel is finishing some paperwork behind his desk. When Joe enters, he doesn't even look up. The commandant's second-in-command also stands before the desk. He's a tall, thin officer known as Cherry Blossom due to an insignia on the collar of his dark green uniform. Cherry Blossom has called in the US Army medic who runs the dispensary. The medic looks at Joe but says nothing until the White Angel looks up, stares for a moment at Joe, and says, "Examine this man. He can't talk. See what's the matter."

The medic pulls out a tongue depressor, steps in front of Joe, and says, "Open your mouth." Joe complies. The medic looks long and hard down Joe's throat before stepping back and answering: "He has a badly infected and swollen throat. No wonder he can't speak."

The White Angel returns to his paperwork. Without looking

up again he says, "Okay. We need all prisoners working. Try to cure him. Dismissed."

The medic grabs Joe by the elbow and ushers him outside and to the infirmary. Once inside he says, "You lucky sonuvabitch. I don't know what you did to land yourself in there, but they bought my bull. You'd better sleep here tonight. I'll try to clean you up. They messed with you good." Joe slides to the floor while the medic grabs alcohol and bandages and hustles to swab Joe's throat with iodine.

Cherry Blossom stands in the doorway. His voice is sudden, quiet yet firm. "Stand up, Number 1176."

Joe struggles to rise.

Cherry Blossom hauls the boy to his feet. Like the White Angel, he, too, speaks perfect English. "I have a son in Japan who is about your age. We have a strong bond, father and son, and I wish to return home and see him again, just like I know your parents wish to see you again someday. Your survival has caused a loss of face for the guards. If you do not go to work tomorrow, you will be killed. But if you go to work, it will show them a strong character. They respect courage. Go to work tomorrow, and I will find you. I will arrange for you to have an easier job for the next few days. But you must show me that I have not misjudged your character. Am I understood?"

Joe nods. Cherry Blossom turns and leaves the infirmary.

The next morning Joe can barely walk to Nichols Field. Other prisoners in his column encourage him along. Once inside the work area, a guard singles out Joe from formation, leads him over to a cooking area, and points to two huge cast-iron pots filled with water. Another prisoner is already building a fire underneath the pots.

"You're supposed to help me today," the prisoner says to Joe. "Frankly, I'm surprised to see you alive. Everyone is. You stoke the fire and boil the water. Look useful. You'll live."

Every day for the next two weeks, Joe boils water and ladles it into five-gallon tin buckets to cool for drinking. Each day during the lunch break, Cherry Blossom sidles over to the fires and passes Joe some of his food. Rice. Eggplant. Slender white radishes called daikons. Joe can't help seeing the camp's second-in-command in a new light. Some Japanese guards are kind. After two weeks, Joe is healed enough to hoist two five-gallon buckets of water onto a pole and carry them to the guards on the worksite. He makes the rounds several times a day and soon is on a first-name basis with many of the guards. Some warm to him. One, named Tanaka, is even friendly.

"You know 'My Blue Heaven'?" Tanaka asks one afternoon.

"The song?"

"Hai. I like very much. Teach me words."

Joe chuckles. Soon Tanaka is crooning the song all over camp.

It's a brief reprieve; Joe is still in pain, though he's healing from the beating. Cherry Blossom notices the improvement and stops sharing his food. Joe is still feverish from malaria. His stomach aches continuously. The open wounds on his legs and ankles aren't getting better. His weight is dangerously low. He knows they're going to return him to pick-and-shovel work soon. Either the work will get him, or the diseases will. The walk to and from the field each day is becoming harder and harder. Escape is not an option—Hicks proved that. Joe knows he's going to die at Nichols Field. It won't be long now.

One night soon after this realization, Joe lies on his mat in the schoolhouse and fingers his spoon. It's sharpened to a razor's edge, and a dark temptation runs through his mind. There's only one way out of a place like Nichols Field. No one would miss him. Taking his life would be easy. He holds on to the spoon, waiting for the right moment.

Later that same night, the prisoners are awakened by a

commotion outside. They look out the window and see a short, portly guard chasing three other guards around the compound with a kitchen knife. The guards are bigger and taller than the first man and could surely subdue him, yet still they run away. The next day at the airfield, Joe asks Tanaka why.

"*Kichigai*," Tanaka says. *Crazy.*

Joe remembers back at Cabanatuan when a prisoner had gone insane. The Japanese hadn't killed him; they'd merely given him a wide berth. Mental illness in their culture is something to avoid, even to fear. Joe remembers that Bilibid Prison houses a larger hospital that can handle prisoners with mental illnesses. Joe had seen the patients there, many months earlier. A few American doctors worked at Bilibid, too. Good ones. They were still prisoners but allowed to practice. And the rations were more plentiful there.

The boy's mind shifts into overdrive. He lies awake for much of the night, sifting through the ramifications of his emerging plan, knowing he must be utterly convincing. Because his new plan is so desperate—so bold beyond common sense—that he needs to pull off the performance of a lifetime.

If not, he'll be the star attraction at the White Angel's next sword party.

———

For a moment in the predawn stillness, more than seven months after coming to Nichols Field, Joe imagines the gentleness of his mother's eyes, the sandpaper of his father's face against his cheek when the boy was still so small he could fit on his knee. He remembers his dog, Mippy, and how she liked to be scratched behind her ears. Joe recalls the warm, calming feel of the stables on a rainy morning back at Santa Anita Park. He thinks of Perpetua and sits upright. But he refuses to study the chalkboard anymore. Instead, he palms his sharpened spoon. His actions today will decide the remainder of his life.

He can hardly handle the trudge to the airfield. He stumbles to the fires for his last day on the easier detail, boils water and ladles it into buckets, loads the buckets on a pole, and heads to the worksite. Walking up to the first Japanese supervisor, Joe drops his water cans, removes his shirt, and whips the spoon out of his pocket with his right hand. He points to the man and shouts in a string of semi-fluent Japanese: "I'm going to cut your throat from ear to ear!"

The supervisor blinks once, twice. His jaw drops. Joe slices into his own arm with his spoon and begins to count in Japanese. "*Ichi. Ni. San. Shi. Go.*" With each number he whacks his arm again and shouts: "When I get to twenty-one, I'm gonna cut your throat." He continues to count and cut.

The supervisor stares transfixed, his eyes growing larger. In a flash he emerges from his trance, turns on his heel, and runs the other direction with a shout: "*Kichigai!*"

Joe has cut deeper than planned. Blood spurts with every heartbeat. Guards gather and stare at the boy. Joe takes the spoon in his left hand and slices three long lines up his right arm. He drops his weapon, runs each hand along the opposite arm, and rubs his face and upper body with his own blood. The guards have had enough, but they don't want to intervene in the mess. They motion for two prisoners to grab Joe. He puts up token resistance before the guards issue an order to hog-tie him.

Lying on the dirt of Nichols Field, naked and bloody from the waist up, Joe wonders if he's gone too far. Blood is everywhere. He's lost so much—and it only keeps flowing. He's dizzy and heaving, and the guards simply decide to keep their distance. They leave him tied for the rest of the day. At day's end they cut him free from the hog-tied knots, prod him to his feet with the ends of their bayonets, tie a long rope around his neck like a leash for a dog, and force him to march back to the schoolhouse. The blood has congealed on his face and body, although many wounds remain open.

Outside the entrance of the gates, near the main Japanese sentry post, lies an *eiso*—a boxlike cage made of rough-hewn lumber. About the size of a coffin. The guards strip Joe of his pants and underwear, force him into the *eiso,* and padlock it shut. The boy cannot stand, sit upright, or lie flat. He holds a naked fetal position throughout the sleepless night. No prisoner, to Joe's knowledge, has ever left the *eiso* alive.

No food is given to him the next morning. No water. The slashes on his arms are sore. The rough boards bite into his body, and his mouth feels like cotton. He regrets not loading up on water before he pulled his act. He feels a familiar urge; he's about to have an uncontrollable bowel movement. He tries to position himself into one corner of the cage, but he's so sore, and the cage so cramped, that the feces slide out and run everywhere. Flies buzz near and set up camp. The smell makes him gag. His excrement dries in a crust on his body in the sun.

That night he doesn't sleep. In the morning, prisoners whisper their encouragement to him as they march toward the field. Guards shout to stay quiet. Joe says nothing. He knows death will arrive soon.

Another day passes. Another night. No food is given. No water. His mind wanders to waterfalls. To lakes and streams. His mouth is sticky. He's barely able to massage it open.

On the morning of the next day, a Japanese guard pushes a rice ball through a small opening in the cage. Joe takes a bite and spits it out. Like the vinegary sponge lifted to Jesus on the cross, the offering is loaded with salt, inedible—a taunt and nothing more. That afternoon, two guards take turns poking him with a bamboo stick through the slats. Joe cackles like a maniac and throws his excrement at them, but he's not acting anymore. He wishes he had slashed his arms deeper. Anything would be better than this slow torture.

That night a sharp wind blows in from the north, slicing through the cage. Joe is so cold. He shivers and prays for death, shaking so hard he rattles the *eiso*. He remembers what Sister Carmella said to him after he brought Perpetua to the sanctuary: *If you ever need prayers said for you, remember me, and they will be said.* Joe closes his eyes. Words float through his mind. *Sister Carmella, pray for me.* Then a fragment of a Methodist prayer he learned as a boy: *Lord of life. In your mercy, hear us.*

It's the only prayer he can think of. The wind howls. In half an hour, the skies open. The darkness begins to rain. Water seeps in around the boards and soaks the boy. He runs his tongue over his lips.

Joe contorts his head, forces his mouth upright, allows the water to trickle into his mouth.

The rain falls the rest of that night. All the next day. All the next night. All the next day. He loses track of time. The water keeps him alive, cleanses his wounds, removes the crust of filth, but he has become so weak that every movement is an effort. He's chilled from the inside out. His skin is pallid and wrinkled. Voices and faces surround him, grinning, mocking. He can't understand the words. His mind wanders off for a walk. Or perhaps he sleeps. At last, the door is flung open. His eyes strain to adjust to the sunlight. The rain is over. Hands grab his ankles and drag his body across the boards. The pain is unbearable and he tries to cry out, but no words emerge. Other hands grab his wrists. His body lands on the splintery bed of a truck. His eyes stare ahead but cannot see or comprehend.

The ride is a slurry of bumps and bounces, swords of sunlight and smothering blackness.

He hears curses in English. Senses a sudden quietness. Lies still in a hushed room.

"Take it easy, son, you're going to make it."

The voice comes from someone above him. There's a jab in his arm. A needle. Something rushes inside him. He doesn't hear the voice again, and now he no longer feels any pain.

When he wakes, Joe's mind begins to clear. He opens his eyes, starts to understand his surroundings. Sees a doctor. Understands the voice.

"You're in Bilibid, son. I'm Doctor Emmerson. You just take it easy and rest."

Joe begins to laugh. He laughs and laughs, although the sound is only a whisper. He closes his eyes and sleeps in triumph.

His audacious acting has brought down the house.

CHAPTER 13

The Bilibid Prison Respite

September 1943

Joe doesn't know how many hours are passing by him. He sleeps and wakes and eats and sleeps again. His mind is groggy, his awareness of his surroundings dimmed. One morning early into his stay in the Bilibid Prison hospital, Dr. Emmerson and a corpsman help the boy stand. The seventeen-year-old is thin as a rifle barrel, and he can't balance on his feet except when supported. As the doctor and corpsman hold him upright, the boy moves to clasp the hand he feels underneath his right shoulder, and his eyes grow soft. Joe doesn't understand his sudden rush of emotions, but then it dawns on him. This is the first occurrence in a long while when he's been touched by someone who isn't hitting him.

They measure and weigh the boy. Joe stands six feet, two inches tall and weighs 109 pounds. They help him back into bed, tuck him in, and pull a sheet up around his sinewy chin. The windows of the hospital unit are open, and the breeze wafting inside feels humid and warm. Joe hears people talking above him. The doctor's voice is furious, shouting at someone. Joe tries to catch specific words, but he's so exhausted from the exertion of standing that his eyes collapse shut. He thinks it is nearing nighttime, but he is not sure. The shouting continues above him. He sleeps.

In the morning Joe opens his eyes. A corpsman holds a bowl of rice by the boy's chin and tries to spoon-feed him. Joe knows he needs to eat. He opens his mouth slightly, receives the spoon, chews and swallows the rice. Then another spoonful. And another. A canteen cup is brought to his lips, and something sweet and frothy flows in. He recognizes condensed milk. Joe gulps every delicious drop.

"Sorry, old pal," the corpsman says when the cup is drained. "We can't give you milk all the time. But you'll get another cupful the day after tomorrow. Promise."

Joe offers a slight wave of thanks and closes his eyes. His arms are thickly bandaged where he cut himself. His neck is wrapped where the guards tied a rope around him. The skin on his back, buttocks, and legs feels scraped and full of splinters from the rough boards of the *eiso*. His ribs and shoulders ache with bruises from being beaten with bamboo rods. The open sores on his legs have been dressed, and there's some sort of ointment on them. He's so weak he can barely lift his head. But he's aware enough to know that at least he's clean, not in a cage anymore, and his belly has something in it. He sleeps.

A week passes like this. Perhaps two. Dr. Emmerson stops by Joe's cot one morning.

"Good, you're awake," the doctor says. "How are you feeling today?"

"A bit better, I think." Joe's voice is hoarse; he croaks out the words.

The doctor checks Joe's chart, furrows his brow. "Son, I was so angry when you were brought in. Maybe you heard me. I was cursing those damn Japs. You were the most pitiful sight I've seen in a long while. We didn't give you much of a chance of making it."

Joe manages a wry smile. He whispers, "They don't call me the Cockroach for nothing."

In the afternoon, two corpsmen help Joe stand again. His blood pressure drops and there's a rushing feeling in his head that roars through his eardrums. They encourage him to try walking. Joe feels dizzy and pained. He shakes his head and asks them to help him lie down. They comply, but return the next day with the same request. With their help Joe manages to stand, then puts one foot in front of the next. Still supported, he walks three steps down the ward, turns, and walks back to bed. The next day Joe tries again and finds he can go five steps. The next day Joe can stand unsupported. He walks ten steps forward and ten steps back. But Joe isn't in any hurry. After where he's just come from, he likes lying down.

Joe manages to overhear bits and pieces of news from the corpsmen and other patients in the ward. Radios aren't allowed in the prison, but healthier prisoners are regularly sent outside the prison walls on work details around Manila. They seem better informed than those in the prison camps. Joe gets up to speed on the battle of Midway, June 1942, which happened more than a year ago now. Prisoners still whisper about it with smiles, calling it the major turning point in the battle of the Pacific. A corpsman informs him that the Marines have attacked the enemy on Guadalcanal in a series of hard, long skirmishes. Joe leans closer to hear the news.

"Our poor bastards fought like hell for six months," the

corpsman whispers. "But we got 'em in the end. We got 'em good."

The boy finds his Adam's apple bobbing, his eyes misty, as if he's trying to take it all in but can't. The upbeat disclosure has sent flutters into his chest, even perked up his senses with an air of readiness. Yet he has the strength only to lean back and rest his head on the old, stained pillow. It's been so long since he's felt this emotion, it takes him a while before he can name it. This feeling has been crushed so many times in his young life, it almost hurts to have it rise again.

Hope.

———

Four months pass while Joe slowly recuperates in the POW hospital unit. Each day he faces the simple challenges of moving, healing, eating, resting. At last he has convalesced enough to be sent to the work area of the prison. He knows he's one of the lucky ones. His slices and abrasions have mended. His skin ulcers have been treated with sulfur powder and are healed. His fevers and malaria are mostly gone, and his dysentery has abated. Mostly he feels optimistic, although he shies away from sharing his joy with anyone. He's found he likes keeping to himself nowadays, preferring to spend time alone and not speaking to anybody. He's wary of developing friendships again, particularly close ones.

The work-detail section of the prison is quartered in a large, one-story concrete monstrosity of a building near the back of the grounds. The workers' food is better than in the hospital ward — still small-portioned, yet more plentiful and diverse, with radishes and greens and bits of fish or nondescript meat every so often, besides the twice-daily rice. So far, the guards seem more relaxed than anywhere else Joe's been. To Joe's amazement, now and then a projector is set up and an American movie is shown, using a wall or an old bedsheet as a screen.

Joe is placed in a work detail with nine other prisoners. Early one late-December morning in 1943, his group and two guards are sent outside the walls into the city of Manila to load supplies for a Japanese detachment. It's Joe's first time outside Bilibid's walls since he arrived, and the day is cloudless and hot. Though dressed in rags and barefoot, the boy blinks in the sunlight and smiles at the day. As he walks on the city streets toward the bay, he breathes in the familiar scents of Manila: tropical flowers and woodsmoke, fried street foods, axle grease and diesel exhaust.

Joe scans the civilians walking down the streets, making eye contact with them when he dares, hoping to spot a familiar face. He longs to see Frisco Smith, Father Bruno, or Sister Carmella. Even the Big Rotunda. But all he sees are strangers. Half a mile from the prison, he spots a young Filipina girl crossing the street. The cut of her hair seems familiar from behind, as does something in the way she walks. He's twenty steps in back of her, but he can tell she's carrying a toddler in her arms. His heart beats faster. She stops on the far sidewalk to straighten the child's dress and smooth her hair. Joe's heart leaps. The distance between them lessens. The girl turns toward him, and he catches a fuller look into her face. He lowers his eyes. Then, as if on autopilot, he raises his eyes again and smiles at the mother and her child. The child stretches her chubby fingers toward him and offers a craggy grin in return. The mother is not Perpetua, and Joe's sliver of hope closes. But he urges himself to keep searching.

The next day, Joe's detail is ordered to load and deliver barrels of oil to a Japanese motor pool. Again, he is allowed outside. Today's work is heavier, and Joe is mindful of his bare feet, but he feels his muscles strengthening after being inside for so long. Another prisoner shows him how to lay a barrel on its side. He and Joe each take an end, cross their arms, and grab the edges of the barrel with their fingers. On the count of three, they snatch the barrel upward and in one quick motion roll it into the truck bed.

After the barrels have been delivered to their destination, Joe is ordered to take a broom and sweep out the truck bed while other prisoners tidy the nearby grounds. Two guards watch the prisoners. They laze in the sunshine near the truck's front bumper, then light cigarettes and look the other way. As he sweeps, Joe notices an older Filipino man and woman. They're on the sidewalk, walking toward the truck, leading a young girl by the hand, maybe five or six years old. He guesses they are her grandparents. Joe steps out of the truck bed and onto the dirt. As the distance between them lessens, the two grandparents stare at Joe, just a few feet away. Quicker than the sweep of a broom, the grandmother dips her hand into her dress pocket, pulls out a rice cake and a small bag of peanuts, and hands the food to Joe as she passes. No words are exchanged, and the three Filipinos keep walking, eyes now fixed straight ahead. Joe glances toward the guards. Absentmindedly, they continue to puff. He scurries behind the truck and devours the food.

Each day, Joe and his work detail are led out of the prison. Some days they clean buildings that have been commandeered by the Japanese. Other days they fix broken plumbing, or carry bags of powdered cement from trucks to worksites. Joe marvels at his job and the interaction it allows with Filipino civilians. Every other day or so he gets slipped a gift of a banana, a mango, a rice cake, or a package of Filipino cigarettes. He doesn't smoke, but he uses the cigarettes to barter with other prisoners inside Bilibid.

He asks another prisoner about the frequent gifts from civilians and if this sort of thing happens often.

"Beautiful people, the Filipinos," the fellow prisoner says. "They know what it's like to be hurting, but they still help others in need."

After a time, however, the guards begin to crack down on the gifts. The guards *inside* the prison, at any rate; the guards who take work details out and around the city are not the same as those who guard inside the walls. At the end of each working day, the prisoners are turned over to the Bilibid guards for a count and a search. The prisoners line up in front of the prison's main entrance. If a guard finds any contraband, he confiscates the item and slaps the prisoner around. Late one afternoon, Joe is given more peanuts than he can manage. He eats several large handfuls on the jobsite, takes a few swigs of water from his canteen, pours the remaining water out, then hides the rest of the peanuts in his empty canteen. His plan works, and that night and the next morning he enjoys a supplementary feast with his bowl of rice.

The plan proves to have limitations. A week later at day's end, the guards order every man on the detail to unscrew his canteen cap and turn the container upside down. Smuggled food cascades from several canteens, and Joe understands he's not the only prisoner who's used that technique. The offending prisoners are slapped or punched, and word is passed around to the other work details to fly under the radar for a while.

A few days later Joe is outside the walls when a civilian slips him an entire, unopened, two-pound bag of raw sugar. Joe rips open the top, hides the bag under a bush, and dips his hand again and again into the sugary goodness as the morning progresses. He refuses to let any calorie go to waste, so he ponders the conundrum. He can't take any sugar back to Bilibid, and he's not sure that he'll return to the same jobsite tomorrow. He can't see any safe way to share it with anyone, so he's out of options. He takes a deep breath and strengthens his gastronomic resolve. Before he heads in for the evening, Joe has eaten the entire bag.

Clothing is always in short supply, and most prisoners wear ragged shorts, shirts, and straw hats to keep the sun off. Several try to hide food under their straw hats, but the guards get wise to the scheme and at day's end order the prisoners to remove their hats and hold them upside down. The prisoners caught with food in their hats are punished. A few prisoners slip food into hats, then try to stuff their hats with rags so the food doesn't fall out when they're searched. That works for a few days until a Japanese sergeant takes a small bamboo stick and pokes all hats when held out for inspection. Contraband dumps all over the ground. Back in the workers' ward, the prisoners talk among themselves and vow to stay one step ahead of the guards. It becomes a game.

More months pass, and Joe considers how conditions at Bilibid have been good for him. He's put on some weight. He enjoys being outside. His muscles have hardened, and his body is filling out. He begins to pray sporadically, thanking God that he's still alive. January 1944 passes, and Joe finally turns eighteen — the age at which he could have legally enlisted. Still, he keeps to himself, preferring to spend his time alone. Occasionally a civilian passes him a book, which he smuggles inside and reads cover to cover, usually more than once. He becomes a thinker, even a schemer. He fears being transferred to another POW camp and often envisions ways to skirt the system if that happens again. He renews an unspoken pledge to survive the war, no matter what.

Even though life at Bilibid is plum compared to life at Nichols Field, Joe never forgets he's a prisoner. He dreams of sitting down at Frisco's restaurant, of gorging himself on fresh buttered bread, lobster tail, and martinis. He longs to go home to Memphis and see his mother and little Betty and Charlie. He yearns to freely roam the streets of Manila, searching in earnest for Perpetua and her child. A host of other prisoners begin to pass through Bilibid, and many are in bad shape. Joe reminds himself to stay sharp, to be ever vigilant. Anything can happen yet.

One morning Joe and another prisoner are sent to the hospital unit to help establish another ward. They get to work moving beds and cleaning. A doctor leads them to a small room near the back of the ward, instructs them to clean inside here also, and unlocks the door. Joe and the other soldier move beds and chairs out of the room, then spot a treasure of goods hidden in the back.

Clothes.

Bundles of clothes. Shirts and trousers and caps and shoes. Web belts and canteens and mess kits. Musty smelling, but far better than what they're wearing. Joe's biceps bulge through his old shirtsleeves. His waist hasn't grown much, so his ragged shorts still fit. But he hasn't worn a pair of boots or shoes since early in the Nichols detail. Joe and his companion pick out fresh shirts and trousers and sit down to try on boots. In no time, they've outfitted themselves anew.

"Hey, you look good," the other soldier says.

Joe laughs. "I haven't looked this good since boot camp."

When they finish their job, the same doctor finds them. "Ah," he says. "I'd forgotten about these until now."

"How can you forget a huge stash of clothes?" Joe raises an eyebrow.

The doctor offers a wry chuckle. "Well, I hope you can see the silver lining in this. Back in Cavite, if ever a soldier passed and his clothes were still usable, we bundled them up and stacked them in a corner of the hospital there. When the hospital was moved here, everything came with us. I hate to tell you this, fellas, but you're wearing *morgue* clothes."

Joe and the other soldier glance over their new outfits, then stare at the doctor. They all laugh.

In the summer of 1944, scores of prisoners begin to traverse Bilibid. They're brought in from any number of POW camps in the Philippines—Cabanatuan, Davao, O'Donnell, Los Banos, Santo Tomas, Puerto Princesa—and never stay long. One night, a few hundred prisoners from Nichols are dragged in. They're walking skeletons, glassy-eyed and haggard. Joe thinks he recognizes a guy and tries to ask him a few questions about conditions back at camp.

"It's rough. Real rough," is all the guy will say.

The prisoners from Nichols spend a night or two in the prison, then are marched to the docks and loaded aboard freighters. Joe asks around, trying to find out where the ships are headed, but he can never get a straight answer. He's still going out on his work details, but he's noticed the work has become erratic. Sometimes entire workdays are canceled. He senses things are changing at Bilibid—and not for the better.

On October 20, 1944, Joe is in downtown Manila on a work detail, cleaning a warehouse. He can hear snippets of news being broadcast from a nearby radio. A massive battle has raged, and General MacArthur and American troops have seized three strong beachheads in the Philippines. MacArthur waded ashore on Leyte, and American troops are now just over 500 miles away from Manila. The announcer finishes, and the general's familiar voice booms through the radio: "People of the Philippines: I have returned. By the grace of Almighty God, our forces stand again on Philippine soil—soil consecrated in the blood of our two peoples—"

A guard sprints to the radio and snaps it off. Joe's stunned. He wants so badly to cheer. But he lowers his gaze and focuses on his mop, thinking. He knows the significance of where the general has landed. Before the rest of the Philippines can be retaken, the Allies need to secure a landing point somewhere off the main island of Luzon to use as a base of operations. Leyte will become that base. He's sure of it.

The Allies are back.

———

On December 8, 1944, American planes drop bombs over parts of Manila. The bombing continues throughout the week—sometimes two or three raids a day. It's hard for Joe to tell what their targets are, but most of the explosions and smoke seem to come from the port area. He knows the Americans are increasing the pressure on the Japanese.

A large contingent of prisoners—perhaps 1,500, by Joe's estimate—arrive from Cabanatuan and are bedded down overnight in Bilibid, then marched down to the docks the next morning. There are so many prisoners, the marching continues all day into late evening.

The next morning, December 13, 1944, the Bilibid work details are ordered to line up at the prison's main gate and stay standing. Joe assembles in his regular group of ten and waits, the dawn air fresh against his cheeks. Trucks rumble up, and Japanese soldiers climb out. The order comes as a surprise to Joe: *Fall out in columns of four.* Joe and the workers are marched through the city toward the port area. Joe's heart lurches. He's leaving Bilibid for good.

A huge hulk of a Japanese freighter is moored at the docks. Joe can just make out its name: *Oryoku Maru.* Already it rests low in the water, heavily laden with the cavalcade of prisoners from the day before. He feels frantic. He knows he's being transferred—but where? He has a canteen full of water and a pocketful of peanuts, but that's it. He left his bedroll at the prison, a paperback he was saving to read, and a razor for the stubble that now grows nightly on his face. The items, he can live without. Yet his last fourteen months at Bilibid have proved such a respite for him that he worries about his next location.

The men in his work detail appear to be the last prisoners to board the freighter. A rumor makes the rounds that the Japanese are boarding the men on the Bilibid work details only as an afterthought. Joe can see that Japanese civilians—men, women, and children—have already boarded. They're kept separate from the Bilibid prisoners, who remain bunched on the dock. Civilians mill about on the deck, and Joe can see through the windows of the ship's staterooms that there are perhaps as many as 2,000 more inside. He had no idea so many Japanese civilians lived in the Manila area. Now, the civilians seem anxious to set sail. He realizes that trouble is coming for the Japanese troops in the Philippines from General MacArthur and his army. The civilians don't want to be caught in the cross fire.

Joe's detail is lined up, marched up the gangplank, and headed toward the most forward of three holds. In the brightness of the morning, Joe spots the large square hole in the ship's deck near the bow. A ladder descends into darkness. One by one, the prisoners ahead of him are prodded by guards with bayonets down the long ladder, deep underneath the ship's deck.

It's his turn. The wooden rungs feel rough in his hands, and the young man grips each one tightly, feeling his way downward into the gloom and musk. As Joe begins to descend, the larger perspective clicks into place. General MacArthur's return to the Philippines means the Allies are gearing up for a large-scale landing on Luzon. The Japanese have all but emptied Bilibid Prison in the last few days—not to save prisoners from the inevitable future bombings, but because Imperial Japan doesn't want to lose its slave-labor force. Joe hears shouts below him. Voices. Groans.

The boy does not yet realize he's descending into pure hell.

CHAPTER 14

Three Ships from Hell

As Joe climbs down the ladder into the dim light, he sees that the vast space underneath the deck of the *Oryoku Maru* has three levels, each already packed with prisoners. Joe stops at the floor of the first level and hangs on with one arm, his eyes adjusting to the darkness. Prisoners are crammed together as far as he can see, man against man, erratically jockeying for space. Later he will hear the exact count: 1,620 Allied prisoners are on board. He glances farther down and sees that several men have fallen from the ladder and lie on the bottom level in a heap, unmoving. The hold feels oven-hot, the air unstirring. Already it reeks of urine and feces. Many men—the ones who weren't from Bilibid—have been in the floating dungeon since early morning of the previous day. They yell and plead for air and water, cursing the Japanese and one another. Joe keeps one foot on the ladder and sets his other on the steel of the first level, making way for the prisoners above him to climb around and go lower into the dark. Some curse Joe, but he can see that any further movement downward is pointless. Fortunately, the boy is one of the last into the hold.

Hours pass while Joe holds fast, trying to conserve energy.

Late that evening, buckets of rice and water are lowered on ropes. Grasping hands and relentless fists surround Joe from behind. The prisoners nearest the ladder fight to grab food. Water and rice spill. Joe lets the buckets pass by. He still has his canteen and peanuts, but he doesn't want to draw attention to them in the mayhem. Night approaches, and the Japanese cover the hold with a heavy tarp, leaving a small hole for air. The bedlam intensifies, and the hold echoes with shouts, screams, and groans. One man insists he's losing his mind. Another calls out that he can't breathe: his tongue is swelling in his throat. After a while the men grow quiet, and a subdued apprehension reigns. An occasional shout or curse is heard, but the remainder of the night passes in an eerie semblance of silence. The young man does not sleep.

With dawn's first light, the ship's engines rumble to life and the *Oryoku Maru* begins to move. It is December 14, 1944. The tarp is rolled back, and Joe can see light. He catches a whiff of salt air. Joe helps pass dead bodies up and out of the hole. Men who died during the night. Rice and water are lowered again. Joe grabs a handful of rice.

A guard soon yells down the ladder for four prisoners to climb up. Men scramble for the fresh air, and Joe's the second man up. The bright sunlight almost blinds him. The deck is crowded with Japanese civilians, all walking about. They stare as the prisoners follow the guard to the stern of the ship. There, two contractors stand by a lumber stack. Joe grasps enough Japanese by now to understand that the prisoners are to build a makeshift toilet. Once completed, the prisoners below will be allowed on deck in shifts to use it. Joe and the others get to work as the ship rounds the tip of Bataan and heads north. Two hours later, a guard comes around with a pail of rice and eggplant sauce. The prisoners eat, then return to their labor.

Joe is intent on sawing a board when the ship's horns begin to blast. He gazes into the cloudless western sky and sees flaming flashes, then hears a roar. Allied planes hurtle over the ship, strafing and dropping bombs, unaware there are POWs aboard. Joe flattens his body against the deck and crawls toward cover. Bullets ricochet off the bulkheads. Something hard slams against his arm. Civilians run panicked in all directions, crying, screaming. The planes rise into the sun. Joe spies a Japanese guard lying in a pool of blood. Others are hit and bleeding. Part of the ship is burning. Joe feels for his elbow and sees a fragment of steel girding stuck fast into the skin. It's about an inch long, and without thinking he yanks it out. The blood oozes cleanly and Joe applies pressure from his hand to stanch the wound.

Crew members dash here and there, helping the wounded and trying to extinguish the fires. Guards shout orders. Machine guns are set up. A wounded guard sees that Joe has good cover and slides over to his position, along with the other prisoners who were working on the toilet. The five huddle together as the Allied planes bank, then roar again toward the ship. More bullets zip in. A great explosion rocks the hull. When the planes are at last out of range, the wounded guard orders Joe and the others down into the hold. Joe hesitates, but the guard points his rifle, insisting. The bodies of Japanese men, women, and children are strewn about the deck. Some are dead; others moan and cry out. Joe clambers down the ladder to his original spot. Prisoners are shouting, cursing, waving their fists. Others ply Joe for information.

No more planes attack, but that night Joe cannot sleep. At dawn, arguments break out among the prisoners again. More men have died overnight, and Joe pieces together that during the previous day's bedlam, a guard fired his rifle indiscriminately into the hold, killing several men. The stench in the hold is burgeoning, and once again the air is lifeless. A chant begins: "Water! Water! Water!" A guard's face appears at the top of the hold. He fires a short burst downward. Joe ducks. The men stop the chant. Only moans and whimpers remain.

In an hour, a different guard appears and motions for two helpers. Again, Joe clambers up the ladder. He and another prisoner are pointed toward a large canvas hose with no nozzle. They lug it across the deck, then lower the end and turn on the water. Joe yells downward: "Don't fight over it. Fill your canteens and the buckets. Pass it around."

The ship has a distinct list to starboard as it nears a rocky shore. Ahead, Joe sees a town with a small harbor. The ship's engines sputter and steam. He's rolling up the hose when the ship's horns blast again. Joe scrambles for cover beside a bulkhead. More Allied fighters roar over the ship. Their strafing pounds the deck, and the air fills with lead. Bullets bounce off bulkheads and into the open hold. A massive explosion rocks the ship's port side. Prisoners try to climb the ladder to get out. They're gunned down by guards. Smoke chokes the air. Shouts, screams, and cries fill Joe's ears. Dead bodies lie scattered on deck. Still huddling by a bulkhead, Joe whispers goodbye to his mother, brother, sister, and Perpetua. He says goodbye to his dad. He prays for forgiveness for the pain he's caused. Joe's sure his death is imminent. The ship is beginning to sink. Smoke billows from its stern.

A Japanese officer rushes to the hold and shouts in English: "Abandon ship! Come up in an orderly fashion or you will be shot. Sit on the deck until the next order is given." Prisoners surge from the hold, blinking at the sun. Some are wounded and collapse on the splintery deck. Prisoners from other holds also appear. They're ordered to line up and sit. Joe joins them. He can see civilians being lowered in slings to small waiting boats. The

Oryoku Maru's engines cough and die. The ship is powerless but still drifting, groaning from the inrushing water. Prisoners continue to pour from the holds.

Someone hisses that they're near Olongapo harbor, on the western coast of Luzon. Rope ladders are tied fast to railings and hung over the side nearest the shore. A Japanese officer shouts, "Abandon ship! Use the ropes and swim to shore. Do not attempt to escape or you will be shot. Hurry!" Some prisoners rush to the rope ladders. Others protest they can't swim. Others simply stay sitting, dazed. Joe eyes the shoreline, about three football fields away. No life jackets are available for the prisoners. He can see enemy soldiers patrolling the beach. The ship is rolling over. He unlaces his boots, unbuckles his web belt, and heads over the side and down a rope ladder.

Of the prisoners in the water, some are dog-paddling. Others hang on to broken boards while kicking their legs. Joe plunges into the water and searches for a scrap of lumber. None appears, so he swims slowly, trying to conserve energy. His canteen is deadweight, so he slides the strap from his shoulder and lets it slip away. Breathless, he rolls onto his back in the water and stares upward, watching prisoners climb down the rope ladders in the yellowish haze of smoke. He rolls onto his front again and renews his efforts to reach the shore. The water is clogged with struggling men. Joe strokes until his wounded arm gives way, then treads water, inhaling large gulps of air. For a moment he contemplates simply raising his hands and letting himself go under. The idea seems to have merit. Then he slowly shakes the thought from his mind and kicks forward, paddling with one hand. Each movement takes effort. His whole body aches. Each motion, each muscle twinge, is an act of desperation. He's barely above water. Gasping. One foot is kicking. Finally, his toe scrapes the bottom.

Joe stumbles forward. The ocean lowers to his shoulders.

Then splashes around his waist. At last he stands in the waves that lick the rocky shore. Some prisoners are stretched out on the gravelly beach, while others stumble around. The shore guards have rifles at the ready. A small motorboat heads from the harbor with a machine gun and snipers, looking for escapees. Joe reaches a sandy spot, sinks to his knees, flops onto his back. His chest and shoulders heave. He has no strength to care if he lives or dies. He closes his eyes. Dusk has begun to fall.

All that night Joe sleeps without moving. In the morning, he raises himself on an elbow and looks out over the bay. Bodies float and bob on the swells. The ship is nearly submerged, smoke drifting upward. His throat is parched. A guard spots Joe moving and shouts at him to join ranks farther up the beach. Joe struggles to stand and shuffles toward the group, studying the dead bodies on the shore, hoping to find a spare canteen.

The prisoners are loaded aboard trucks and hauled to a small town. They enter a deserted naval base and stop in front of six concrete tennis courts, newly ringed with a chain-link fence topped with barbed wire. One old water spigot on the side of the courts still works, and Joe and some of the other prisoners rush to make a line. The water trickles out slow and warm, and Joe, without a canteen, has no choice but to stick his head underneath and fill his stomach. More half-naked prisoners are unloaded. Soon they are jammed together, all sitting on the concrete, knees to backs. The sun rises and broils the men. American planes fly overhead, strafing and bombing enemy targets around the base. Prisoners stand and cheer as hope surges. The guards slam the gate shut, run a chain through, and lock it.

That night the prisoners shiver together on the court. Some throw up from having swallowed too much seawater during the swim. One man leaps to his feet and shakes the fence, screaming obscenities, until others pull him away and coax him to sit again.

In the morning, Joe notes that a number of prisoners aren't moving. Their bodies are gathered and stacked near the gate. American officers plead with the guards to unlock the chain so the bodies can be removed and loaded onto a truck. The guards agree. They also allow fifteen of the most gravely ill to be taken to Manila for hospitalization. Joe has his suspicions about the offer; later he will learn the men were driven to a cemetery and decapitated.

Back at the tennis courts, many prisoners are in sad shape. They're bleeding from bullet wounds and blows to the head. Many prisoners' feet are cut and bleeding. A corporal has a severely wounded and gangrenous arm. Two American doctors insist he will die unless it comes off. They have neither anesthesia nor scalpel, but they cauterize an old razor blade and amputate the limb. The corporal passes out but stays alive.

Late in the second day's heat, a few sacks of rice are brought in. American officers ration the food. Each man is allotted one spoonful. Some men reject their share, pushing the spoon away and spilling the food on the ground. Others gobble it up. Another night passes. It's the third day now, and when Joe awakes, the prisoner in front of him pitches forward, dead. The man sitting beside him is also slumped over, dead. Pragmatic, Joe removes the shirt from the dead prisoner next to him and wraps it around his head against the sun. From the body in front, the boy commandeers a canteen. Joe and another prisoner drag the two corpses to the gate, where Joe remains. If ever they're released, he wants to be the first one out.

Around noon, American pilots fly over again, strafing and bombing. This time the pilots wag their wings, indicating they've seen the prisoners below. Morale shifts slightly upward, and a few grins are seen. The day and night pass.

On the morning of the fifth day, the corporal with the

amputated arm dies. An hour later, the guards arrive with a convoy of trucks and load the prisoners into them. From the truck's bed, Joe looks back at the tennis courts and sees several dozen inert bodies on the concrete.

The trucks bounce along dusty roads until dusk, when they arrive in a small town. The prisoners are fed their first substantial meal in almost a week: rice and mung-bean soup. The food is unusually plentiful, and Joe gorges himself. The next morning, the sick and wounded are sorted from the able-bodied. Joe, considered able-bodied, is marched with others to a small train depot, where they are each given a rice ball wrapped in a banana leaf and loaded aboard boxcars. They're hauled to another small town and left at the station overnight. At dawn, they're marched three miles to a harbor. They are fed half a cup of rice each, then prodded up the gangplank of a Japanese freighter named the *Enoura Maru*. Someone remembers the date and begins to quietly hum a carol. Others join in and some quiet sniffling is heard.

It's Christmas morning 1944.

———

The hold that Joe enters this time is larger and not as crowded as before, but it reeks of horse manure and is buzzing with huge black flies. Joe searches for a safe haven, slaps at flies, and ends up near the ladder again. He figures it's the only chance to be called up on deck. His morale is sinking, and he wonders if his odyssey is coming to a tragic end. The temperature is dropping and he shivers, his bare feet cold against the wood and steel of the ship. All that day, the prisoners wait in the harbor. The next morning they're fed bran and dried fish while they wait again. The following day, December 27, the propellers of the *Enoura Maru* start to churn. The ship leaves the harbor and heads for the open sea.

What Joe does not know is that General MacArthur and more than 200,000 American forces have now reclaimed the Philippine islands of Leyte and Mindoro. Japan has fought back with ferocity, unleashing suicide planes on ships in the American fleet in a desperate attempt to maintain the upper hand, but the United States has prevailed. Troops are only days away from invading Luzon at the beaches of Lingayen Gulf. They are returning to the main island with battleships and heavy cruisers, airplanes and amphibious vehicles, tanks, rifles, a wealth of fuel, uncountable rounds of ammunition, and huge surpluses of food. Everything needed for the liberation of the Philippines. From the beaches, MacArthur and his troops will charge toward Manila. The capital is only 110 miles away.

Two guards peer down into the hold. One motions to Joe and shouts in Japanese, "You strong?"

Joe thumps his chest and answers in Japanese, "Strong!" He climbs the ladder. Five prisoners follow him. On deck they're led through a steel bulkhead door and down a flight of metal stairs to the boiler room, where a furnace rages. Two Japanese are shoveling coal through its open doors. The six prisoners are ordered to take over. They're to work in shifts of two men, each shift lasting thirty minutes, then they can rest for an hour before their next shift begins. Joe and another prisoner go right to work. A crewman soon appears and gives them canvas split-toed shoes, goggles, aprons, and red bandanas to cover their noses and mouths against the dust and ash.

Days pass. The *Enoura Maru* heads north through the South China Sea, the Philippines receding behind it. The ocean turns rough. The shoveling is difficult, yet Joe prefers work to being in the hold. Twice a day the shovelers are brought hot tea, rice, pickled radishes, and sour salted cherries. Once a day, their rice is mixed with steamed fish. Soon it becomes too cold to sleep on deck. A guard brings them thin straw mats and allows them to sleep inside the engine room. Joe doesn't know how the prisoners below are faring, but each day he sees bodies lifted from the hold with ropes and tossed overboard.

The ship docks, and Joe learns they're at the Port of Takao on the island of Formosa (now Taiwan). A few days pass, and the intensity of the shoveling dies down while they're in harbor. Joe's crew is allowed to stay on deck. The three pairs take turns keeping the furnace banked. The atmosphere among the guards seems to lift; one guard even brings them a box of leftover hard candies to wish them a fortunate new year. But Joe has an uneasy feeling. The harbor is in a blackout at night, and Joe fears the ship is a floating target.

On January 9, 1945, Joe awakes on deck just in time to see a blinding flash and hear a massive boom. Hatches and decking fly through the air. The ship shudders and dips. A section of one floor creaks and gives way, crashing thirty feet below. Joe hears pandemonium from the prisoners belowdecks. An air-raid horn sounds, and the harbor erupts with sirens and whistles. American aircraft zoom over the harbor, dropping bombs and torpedoes, and strafing ships. Joe and the shovelers are ordered to stoke the furnace as quickly as possible. Anchor chains are being pulled up. The ship is heading out to sea.

Then the attacks die down and a new order comes through; the shovel crew is ordered to halt and wait. All the rest of that day, the ship remains in the harbor. A second day passes, then a third. While they wait, Joe sees a crane hoisting a filled cargo net out of the front hold. Severed arms, legs, heads, and torsos protrude through the netting. Joe has seen so much death and carnage, he'd thought he was immune. But this sight rattles him. Someone murmurs that at least 300 men were killed by the torpedo blast that struck the hold. He turns away, feeling a new level of despair.

Joe and the survivors are unloaded onto the docks and packed aboard a third ship, the *Brazil Maru*. On January 14, 1945, the *Brazil Maru* heads for open water. Once again, Joe and several prisoners are ordered on deck to construct a toilet for prisoner use. A hard wind howls across the ship, bringing with it an icy mist. Joe finds a piece of old straw matting and wraps it around his legs while he works. Once finished, he and the work crew are ordered back into the hold. It's not as crowded anymore, and Joe and three others locate some loose boards that they set against the steel decking for insulation. That night, the four of them wedge themselves against one another for warmth.

In the morning, Joe and several others are brought up for more work. They hike back and forth, filling buckets in the galley and lowering them into the hold. On each trip, their buckets are coated with thin layers of ice by the time they reach the hold. The job takes several hours to complete, and when finished, Joe and the others are ordered back down the ladder again. Joe is chilled to the bone. Others have scattered the boards previously used for insulation, so the boy makes his way to the rear of the hold, seeking something new to keep himself above the freezing steel. He finds a broken crate with three sides still intact and crawls inside, growing sleepy. He knows he should stay near the ladder in case a call is made for more help, but his eyes are so heavy. His legs have lost feeling. All he wants to do is sleep.

When he awakens, Joe doesn't know how much time has passed. He feels a rumble underneath him from the ship's propellers. He sees some prisoners climbing the ladder and thinks he should rush to join them. But his eyes are bleary, his mind clouded. Again, he closes his eyes.

The days run together. Joe snags a handful of rice from a bucket. He drinks from his canteen until it is dry. But he finds it harder and harder to rise from his crate. At times he feels lucid and awake, and knows he should fight to live, but when he tries to stand his legs are like stone—cold, hard, almost immovable. He shivers constantly and wonders if his malaria has returned. At other times his mind wanders, almost drifting from reality. Mostly he sleeps. Once when he awakes, he sees dead prisoners being pulled up the ladder, but his moments of clarity are growing rarer. One morning he has a vague understanding of the date. It is January 27, 1945. He's almost sure of it, and Joe tries to smile, to chuckle, but he finds only a strange cackle emerging from his lips.

It's his nineteenth birthday.

He's certain it will be his last. He sleeps and awakens. Sleeps and awakens. On the third day after his birthday, the ship stops moving. He hears someone holler but can't make out the words. It seems as if men are ascending the ladder in a stream, straight up to heaven. Perhaps they're angels. Joe stares at the ascension, then returns in his mind to school. He's reciting history in front of his fifth-grade classroom, singing "La Marseillaise" as he used to. He's back in the Philippines, playing his bugle at Fort Santiago. He's riding his motorbike on the cobblestones of the old Walled City. One long, steady note blares in his ears. It sounds like a whistle, shrill and deafening. His crate is shaking. The hold is full of light. A hand pulls at his shirt.

"You still with us, soldier? Can you hear me? It's time to go. You don't want to be left down here. Let me help you up."

Joe opens his eyes. Tries to concentrate on the figure before him. A man helps haul Joe to his feet. The boy can barely make out the lieutenant's stripes on the man's sleeve. The two stand motionless for a long moment until Joe forces a leg to take a step. The lieutenant helps Joe shuffle toward the ladder. They step over and around dead bodies.

"Can you make it up?" the lieutenant asks.

Joe manages a nod. He grabs hold and tries to climb. His arms shake as he pulls himself from rung to rung.

The voyage from the Philippines has taken six weeks. The boy will learn later that of the 1,620 prisoners of war who left Manila on December 14, 1944, only 450 were still living by the time they reached their destination.

The lieutenant braces Joe as he gains another foothold upward, then another, and the last. It's cold on deck, and a light covering of snow blankets the ship. The *Brazil Maru* is tied up to a long pier. Groups of prisoners are being prodded off the ship and led nearby to a large warehouse. Joe is the last to leave the holds.

"Where are we?" the boy murmurs, his head beginning to clear.

"Moji, Japan," the officer says. "You were lucky, son. After everybody got up the ladder, the major got permission from the Japanese for us to make one last sweep of the holds. I had already finished my sweep when I noticed you in that crate. Nobody would have found you. You'd have frozen soon."

Joe offers the lieutenant a steadying stare. "Sir, I owe you one. Any idea why we're here or where we're going to next?"

"To the warehouse," the lieutenant says. "After that...damned if anyone knows."

CHAPTER 15

Under the Cold Ground

After a sleepless winter night in the warehouse at the pier in Moji, Joe sees light beginning to glow through the frosted windows near the ceiling. No food or water had been offered the day of debarkation, and when Joe opens his eyes, he's exhausted and parched, still struggling for lucidity. He huddles with the other prisoners on the chilly concrete floor for about an hour, then sees two large doors open. Joe counts thirty Japanese soldiers entering the warehouse, followed by a dozen Japanese civilians. A guard orders the prisoners to stand and snap to attention. Some prisoners try to rise but stumble and topple over. Many simply stay sitting. Others have died during the night and remain where they lie. Every man standing looks haggard and spent.

Joe rises. The civilians begin to study the prisoners, walking among them and looking them over as if they were beef at a cattle show. One scrutinizes Joe's build and height and says *"Koi"* (come here), pointing to a space near the door. Several other prisoners are directed to the same space, and when a group of eleven is formed, the same civilian and two guards lead the group through the door into another room in the warehouse.

Inside stands a cadre of Japanese women. They wear rubber

aprons over their simple dresses and have donned shower caps and rubber boots. The prisoners are ordered to strip. Joe sheds his filthy rags and sits naked on a long wooden bench, shivering, while a woman shaves his head. He's so skinny he can see his ribs outlined on his chest, and his veins stand out like knotted cords. Once all the prisoners are shaved, a guard tells them to stand, and a woman sprays them from head to toe with disinfectant. The guard orders the prisoners to bend at the waist so the woman can spray their genitals and buttocks. Joe can't help finding the scene comical, but he keeps his smile to himself. The prisoners are ordered to stand upright again, and another woman gives them a final hosing with cold saltwater.

Dripping and assaulted by indignity, the men are led into another room filled with stacks of clothing. It's surprisingly warm in this room, and the prisoners are told to find clothes and dress. Joe dons a heavy cotton shirt and a pair of long cotton trousers. A pair of black split-toed canvas shoes fit his large feet. A woman hands him a mustard-colored overcoat made of synthetic mohair fiber, which he puts on. For the first time in weeks he isn't chilly, although he desperately hopes for a meal. The men are led outside and loaded aboard a truck.

One of the prisoners grins at Joe and says, "Nice coat. You look like a golden retriever."

Joe finds it hurts to laugh.

———

The truck passes a slew of streets and buildings. The men are taken to a crowded pier and loaded onto a ferry that crosses a narrow strait. After disembarking, they're marched to a rail station and ordered inside a passenger car, where they're told to sit. The guards stay close. Two steamed buns and an orange are given to each prisoner. Joe stares at the orange, the rarity of fresh fruit not lost on him. He peels the orange and devours it. Then he eats the peel.

The train whooshes through villages and industrial areas without slowing. Near dark, the train chugs to a stop. Marched to waiting trucks, the prisoners are soon moving again. The road becomes steep and narrow. They pass through a small village with a coal mine on the outskirts, its cable-and-wheel system silhouetted against the night sky. The truck enters a gritty compound and stops. The prisoners are unloaded, marched to a mess hall, and fed cold rice and sour bean-paste soup. An American officer is already at the camp. He explains to the prisoners they're at Omine-machi, a coal-mining camp about thirty miles from Hiroshima on the main Japanese island of Honshu. The prisoners are assigned to barracks and ordered to sleep. Joe has no bedding, so he wraps his mustard overcoat around him to ward off the chill.

Again, Joe finds it hard to sleep. He's entered another season filled with unknowns, and as concerned as he is about himself, his thoughts soon turn to Perpetua and her plight. Joe can picture her hair, her face, the touch of his finger against her cheek. He wonders what chance she has alone, trying to raise her baby with her homeland now not only occupied but back in the thick of battle. He feels so far away from her, but vows anew that if he ever survives the war, he will return to the Philippines to find Perpetua and care for her and her child.

When morning comes, Joe and the other prisoners are assigned identification numbers to sew onto their shirts, then marched in the bitter cold to the opening of the mine. Joe is put on a conveyor crew. An earlier shift of miners has blown a rock face, leaving piles of broken coal. Joe's crew hikes into the mountain and assembles a large metal trough with a sturdy conveyor belt running through it. Men shovel coal into the trough. When the coal emerges from the mine, it is emptied into railcars. The day passes, as Joe's crew moves the conveyor to different locations within the mine. Of all the jobs at the mine, Joe considers his one of the easier tasks, although sometimes the setup and breakdown of the conveyors proves troublesome. He also soon realizes that any job at the mine comes with side effects. As weeks pass, Joe's skin darkens from the imbedded coal dust. When he coughs, his spittle is inky. When his nose runs—which it does continuously, thanks to the constant dust and biting winds—his snot is black. He wipes his nose on the sleeves of his big coat, and soon two long smears of sooty mucus are fixed on each sleeve.

Each day of February and March 1945 passes in the mines. On April 13, 1945, the Japanese commandant assembles the men before work for the day and announces that Franklin Delano Roosevelt has died. Vice President Harry Truman has become the new president. The commandant seems unusually reflective and offers more than bare-bones information. He tells them their president passed away suddenly the afternoon of April 12 from a cerebral hemorrhage. He was sixty-three and had been president for the last twelve years. Joe doesn't know what to think or feel. The commandant orders the ranking American officer to lead the prisoners in prayer, and then—to Joe's delight—gives all the prisoners the day off. The commandant's clemency is as rare as an orange.

Joe still keeps mostly to himself, yet he's ever on the hunt for news—either international or from around camp. At mealtimes he hears stories. A guard nicknamed Goldie carries a horsehide whip. He's been known to whip prisoners arbitrarily, so Joe learns to stay away from him. A different guard, known as Three Fingers, has a favorite habit of lobbing stones at POWs while they work. A prisoner named Bill Crowley is hit in the eye by a rock. Bill becomes a favorite target. Three Fingers smacks Bill in the head with a crowbar, then rubs coal dust into the open wound. Joe keeps the incidents to himself and steers clear of the more dangerous guards.

A likable Texan named Bob Mainer works on Joe's setup crew. He has a ruddy complexion, brown hair, and hazel eyes. One afternoon as they finish their task down in the mines, Bob looks both ways, then motions for Joe to follow him. He finds an unused tunnel away from the eyes of the guards, disconnects his lamp, and whispers for Joe to do the same.

"Ah, this is really living," Bob says, as he sits back against a rock face and stretches out his legs.

Joe follows the older soldier's lead. They sit in darkness and quietly shoot the bull for an hour, talking mostly of Texas, then head back to work, their absence undetected. A few days later they try it again. And again. The clandestine practice becomes Joe's lone respite.

Bob and Joe both like to eat. Civilian contractors often bring their lunches to the mines in bento boxes and wrap their boxes on a line with scarves before and after lunch. One day Bob lifts a bento, devours the food, then returns the box to the line, unnoticed. He gets away with it, so a week later he tries again. This also works. A week after that, Bob and Joe are sitting in the dark with their lamps off when Bob says, "Sit tight. I'll be right back." He returns with two bento boxes, hands one to Joe, and says, "Eat up." Inside is rice, a sour cherry, a pickled radish, and a small sardine. Joe devours the food. When the two finish, Bob takes the boxes and disappears. Later, Joe asks his new friend what he did with them.

Bob laughs. "I chucked them down a latrine."

When the shift is over, Bob and Joe march back into the camp with the other prisoners, but for some reason this evening everybody is ordered to stay in formation and stand, waiting. An hour passes in restlessness while the cold wind whips around the prisoners. Finally the commandant emerges with a civilian contractor, and announces through an interpreter: "A prisoner has stolen this man's bento box. It has been in his family for years and means much to him. You will all stand in formation until the guilty party steps forward."

Five minutes pass while Joe's mind races. He remembers what punishment was like at Nichols Field. He wonders what will happen to the rest of the prisoners if he doesn't say anything, but suspects the worst. The boy's throat bobs, and he tries to think. Finally, unable to resist the impulse, he squares his shoulders and steps forward. *Never give in to fear.* A moment later, Bob steps forward, too. The commandant orders Bob and Joe to the guardhouse and dismisses ranks.

Goldie and Three Fingers aren't around this evening to issue beatings, but another guard orders Joe and Bob into two *eisos*. Joe's muscles are twitchy and he fights panic, but the cages at Omine-machi prove more humane than the one Joe was in at Nichols. They're larger, plus they're located inside the guardhouse where it's warmer. Bob and Joe are left overnight. The next morning they're ordered to find the prized bento box. Bob leads the guards to the latrines, and both Bob and Joe are ordered to reach into the latrine, pick out the box together, and scrub it clean for the civilian. Joe still expects some roughing up, but much to his surprise, he and Bob are simply sent packing. They're escorted by two guards to the train station and ordered aboard a railcar. Joe is stripped of his shirt and his big mustard coat, which he hates to lose. They're both issued other shirts with Japanese lettering scrawled on the back. Joe recognizes what the word means but says nothing to Bob. As the train speeds south through mountainous terrain, the two prisoners receive unusually foul looks from the civilians aboard the train who read their shirts and frown, but Joe just chuckles. He wants to tell Bob what's written on the back, but decides it's worth more of a laugh if he doesn't.

Instead Joe asks, "Why did you follow me out to the front of the formation? I would have understood if you'd stayed put."

Bob furrows his brow. "I wasn't going to let you take the rap for me. I'm the jerk who thought it was cute to toss them in the can." He looks around at the civilians and adds, "Hey, can you figure why everybody's scowling at us so fierce?"

Joe just shrugs.

Their train reaches a station in the larger seaside city of Shimonoseki, and Joe and Bob are put aboard a ferry headed for Moji. Soon they're on another train on the southern island of Kyushu, heading south again. Everywhere they go, civilians glance at their shirts and glower. Joe falls asleep on the train. When it stops, he's awakened by a guard's kick to his leg. They're loaded aboard a truck and driven through the narrow streets of a small industrial town with billowing smokestacks, then several more miles up a narrow road, where they pass the ominous cable-pulley wheel of another coal mine. As they step off the truck, a guard hits Bob in the ribs with his rifle butt and shouts for them to hurry. Papers are exchanged between guards, and an American officer hurries over. He greets them with a flat smile and escorts them to their barracks. After explaining that these barracks are for prisoners who've violated one or more of the many Japanese rules, he warns the men to look sharp—if the guards don't kill them, the lice in the barracks will.

The officer departs, and since Joe and Bob have been given no further instructions, they gravitate outside and sit on some old wooden planks. Bob stretches back, but Joe keeps a keen lookout, studying their surroundings. He's wary of the camp, but he decides it's time to let Bob in on a piece of information. He rubs the back of his neck and says, "I probably should've told you earlier, but did I mention what word's scribbled on our backs?"

Bob shakes his head.

"*Thief.*"

"You sneaky bastard," Bob says. "You knew the whole time, didn't you?" He moves to punch Joe in the shoulder, then laughs.

All the rest of the day they sit. None of the guards pay them any attention. Toward dusk, when the work shift is finished, three Dutch prisoners and another American sit with them. They're not there long before a Japanese guard strides over with a thick bamboo pole, points to the four prisoners who've just sat, and barks out an order for the four to do push-ups. The prisoners comply, but the guard shouts at them more harshly and strikes them with his bamboo. Joe clenches his teeth and Bob looks surly, but since the guard hasn't ordered them to move, they dare not leave their positions. The pole is so long the guard can hit all four prisoners with the same swing. Lacerations form on their shoulders and backs. After several blows, the guard begins to tire. He stops, chuckles sadistically, and walks away. Joe and Bob help the four prisoners stand and try to help them with their wounds. Joe can't understand why the four were chosen for a beating when he and Bob weren't, but the message is received: This camp's rough.

———

For ten perplexing days, Joe and Bob stay at the camp without doing any work or receiving any orders. Then, inexplicably, they're placed on another train and sent to yet another camp. They're still wearing the shirts with the Japanese lettering on the back, and again they receive dirty looks. This time they both chuckle.

Their new habitation is Fukuoka POW Camp No. 17, located

near the medium-sized town of Omuta, some forty miles across the bay from the major city of Nagasaki. A wooden fence approximately twelve feet high, topped by three heavy-gauge barbed wires, encloses the compound. A fellow prisoner explains how the camp functions. Approximately 1,735 POWs of various nationalities are crammed into the camp—mostly British, Dutch, Czech, Norwegian, Korean, Australian, Indonesian, and American. Prisoners work twelve-hour shifts smelting zinc and mining coal. Conditions in the coal mine were so terrible before the war started that the mine was condemned. Even though conditions haven't improved since then, the mine has reopened using slave labor. Each prisoner is expected to fill three cars of coal a day by shovel. Food is scarce, but Allied loan sharks operate in the camp, and they'll trade you their bowl of rice today for two of yours later, on demand. Work is so tough that a number of prisoners have intentionally had an arm broken to be sidelined. You can pay one of the sharks to break it for you. You place your arm across a couple of two-by-fours and look the other way as they bash it with a full canteen. Joe shudders. The fellow prisoner has delivered all this information stoically. He offers no comfort.

Joe finds another prisoner and asks about exchanging shirts. The prisoner points toward the infirmary, where morgue clothes are sometimes available. Joe wants to get the word *Thief* off his back, thinking it might invite harsher treatment if he keeps it on. He and Bob head to the infirmary, where they find different shirts and dump their old ones. Inventory is limited, and Joe's shirt is too big for him. He sews his new number on the front: *408*. To his surprise, a guard snaps pictures of all the new prisoners near the administration building. Joe is weighed and measured. The young man catches his reflection in a window. His head is completely shaved. His face has become so pinched and gaunt that his ears stick out. His neck looks skeletal and pencil-thin in the circle of his collar. Joe buttons the garment to the top, but still he swims in the shirt. The guard speaks aloud to himself in Japanese as he writes Joe's height and weight on a chart. Joe understands what's said:

"Six feet, four inches tall."

"110 pounds."

——————

Bob is assigned to the timber crew. His job is to lug heavy wooden beams into the back of the mine, where the blasting and digging are most recent, then place the beams as supports for the ceiling. The ceiling settles fast after a blasting, and Bob tells Joe he has a hard time keeping up.

Joe is ordered to a drilling crew, where he quickly becomes the main drill operator, mostly because the two Indonesian prisoners with him refuse to carry the cumbersome machine as soon as the new guy shows up. Early each morning, Joe starts drilling holes in the coalface deep in the mine. He drills for the next ten hours, often as many as 100 holes. When all the holes for the day are drilled, he and his two helpers insert dynamite sticks in the holes, light their fuses, and run. It's arduous, dangerous work.

May and June 1945 pass like this. Joe continues working in the mine. It's warmer now, but flies emerge in huge swarms across the camp, prompting the prisoners to constantly swish the air and slap their skin. Bob develops a bad cough and struggles to live with it for some time, but it becomes so dire he's taken to the infirmary. Pneumonia is suspected. After work, Joe visits him. Bob is so weak he strains to lift his head off the pillow, but Joe talks to him about all the things his friend loves—Milky Way pie, jalapeño-and-pork tamales, and Texas. Bob manages a frail smile before closing his eyes, and Joe sits with him for a long while before adding, "We're gonna make it, you know. You and me both."

Bob gives a slight shake of his head and speaks with his eyes shut. "Doc says I got a bad lung infection. Weak heart. Says they can't do nothing for me. I'm outta time, pal."

Joe doesn't say anything further, but a deep sigh escapes his lips. He simply cannot lose another friend. Joe grasps Bob's hand, gives it a gentle squeeze, and promises to return soon.

That night, fleas emerge from Joe's thin straw mat and make high, whiny, buzzing sounds in his ears. It's a minor irritation compared with the change he notices in the guards. Over the next few days they become more petulant and more suspicious, yet Joe is unable to glean any news that might offer a clue. He hopes General MacArthur is making headway. Mostly, Joe simply tries to make it through each day. He sees Bob again, but his friend has taken another turn for the worse.

And Joe's not doing much better himself. The hard work in the mine, coupled with the meager rations and long hours, have taken their toll. Often when he drills, Joe must hold the heavy drill at chest height. Hour after hour his arms tremble in the dust, but he can't take a break. Not here.

What Joe doesn't know is that the Allies have spent a year since the Normandy invasion pushing into Germany from the west while the Russian army pushed from the east, leading to Germany's complete surrender. Victory in Europe was declared on May 8, 1945, and Japan now faces the full force of the Allies. MacArthur landed on Luzon on January 9 and reached the outskirts of Manila by February 3. American troops discovered a country in crisis. Resources, food, and supplies had been seized by the Japanese. Entire villages were ransacked. Philippine citizens were dying of starvation. A savage, monthlong battle took place within Manila, with Japanese troops losing yet indiscriminately slaughtering more than 100,000 Filipino men, women, and children before the city was fully liberated on March 3. Corregidor was retaken on April 13, and by the end of June only small pockets of Japanese soldiers remained in the country. MacArthur continued his Pacific island-hopping campaign, leading to the bloody battles of Iwo Jima and Okinawa, both victories for the Allies. Meanwhile scientists at Los Alamos are working furiously toward the completion of the world's first atomic bomb.

In July 1945, Joe and his fellow prisoners begin to see high-flying bombers make almost daily runs over Nagasaki, the city across the bay. Rumor has it that the Americans are hitting the port. Before long, a fleet of B-29 bombers rumbles over the camp, dropping their deadly loads on the nearby industrial town of Omuta. A thick, heavy smoke rises, making Joe suspect the town's oil plant has been hit. The guards become even more erratic. Joe is certain the Americans are bringing the war home to Japan. He just hopes he can hold on long enough. He sees Bob again, and Bob's still breathing. But barely.

Joe's near his own breaking point. It's late July. Soot-faced, exhausted, and coughing, at day's end he tamps the last sticks of dynamite into the holes, then motions for the helpers to wait a few moments before lighting the fuses. Joe shoulders the heavy drill and begins to trudge back up the shaft, wanting to get an early start on the task. The helpers will carry the drill bits and air hoses when they leave the shaft, but the drill itself is heavier, and the hike upward requires more work for him. Joe walks fifty paces, then stops to rest. He can hear his two helpers talking, preparing to light the fuses. He picks up the drill again and walks another fifty paces, then stops for another rest. He's just turned the corner into a main lateral when the ground jolts. He hears no sound, but a sudden, massive force lifts him off his feet and hurls him through the air. He lands hard on the rocky floor of the tunnel.

When he comes to, he tries to cough, but his lungs will barely force out air. He's covered with rocks. His legs are pinned. Thick black dust blankets the shaft. He feels that the drill is lying on his back, pressing its weight into his bony spine. His headlamp is still on, but the light is weak. He hears stray rocks falling behind him. He realizes the explosion caused the lateral to give way behind him and knows the tunnel is highly unstable now, susceptible to additional cave-ins at any moment.

He hears American voices calling to him. He discerns faces in the dim light. Other prisoners are crawling through the debris toward him. They grab Joe's wrists and try to pull the boy forward. Another prisoner removes rocks from Joe's legs. They're able to free Joe, and they carry him upward to the main shaft, where Joe is placed inside the cable car. He tries to sit up, but his right leg won't move correctly. He shines his light closer. The flesh is torn away in long, jagged chunks from the back of his calf, and the foot hangs loose. His Achilles tendon is exposed, blackened with coal dust.

"The other guys...?" Joe murmurs. "They okay?"

"The men you were with didn't make it," a prisoner says. "Good thing we found you. Your lamp was barely visible."

The loss of his crew descends on Joe like a new cave-in. His adrenaline is wearing off, and his leg has begun to scream. He's carted up the shaft and carried to the infirmary, where he's placed on a table. The American doctors imprisoned at Fukuoka have only a few implements and medicines. Joe feels like he's going to pass out. It's all he can do to hold himself together. One of the doctors examines his leg and scrubs it using a toothbrush without anesthesia. Two other prisoners must hold Joe down by his shoulders until the cleaning is completed. The doctor stitches up the lacerations as best he can, then wraps the ankle against a short, flat board. Joe is carried to a stray mat in a sick bay and ordered to dribble saltwater on his wounds each day. He's lost a lot of flesh, and no more can be done for him. He's placed next to Bob.

By August 1945, the boy's ankle isn't doing well. The split bone seems to be knitting, but the tendon isn't looking any better and the wounds have filled with pus. There are no nurses, and help in the infirmary is scarce, so Joe rinses out his own bandages and rewraps his ankle morning and night. The doctor examines his ankle and frowns. Flies swarm throughout the infirmary, and Joe tries to keep his wounds clean, but it's a losing battle. Rations are less in the infirmary, and the days pass slowly, painfully, hungrily. Sometimes Joe whispers stories of Texas to Bob, but he's not sure if his friend hears anymore. Bob still opens his eyes sometimes, but they are glassy and don't seem to focus.

One morning Joe awakes. He has slept hard, without dreaming, and later than usual. When he opens his eyes and looks toward Bob's mat, his friend is not there anymore. The mat is vacant. Joe doesn't need to ask the doctor what happened. Joe tries to pray. No words will come—neither from his heart nor his lips. He tries to think of something to comfort his grief. Of his mother and little brother and sister. Of his father and his dog, and all the good times they had at Alamo Downs. Of Perpetua and how his heart first felt when he realized her wellness meant so much to him. But he can't seem to fill his mind with anything good. He is finished. He can't stand any more sorrow. No more dying. No more hating. No more hurting. No more being alone.

Joe glances through the open window and sees a strange white smoke in the sky. He hears the roar of engines from a low-flying plane. The walls of the infirmary rattle, and Joe hears heavy thumps on the ground. The sounds of commotion fill the camp. Prisoners are yelling. Shouting. Cheering.

Singing.

Joe's eyes grow wide. A POW rushes into the infirmary. He's chewing gum and carrying three cans of fruit cocktail. His countenance bears the wild euphoria of a long-shackled man whose chains have just been broken. He calls to the patients with a full voice of promise:

"Guys, guess what?"

CHAPTER 16

Emancipation

Joe has little choice. Regardless of what's happening outside, he's too weary to leave the infirmary. The gum-chewing prisoner gives him a play-by-play. The Japanese have canceled all work details in the prison camp. The war is inches from being over. A huge white mushroom cloud hangs over Nagasaki, and prisoners speak of feeling the blast and seeing the cloud of smoke across the bay. Several radios are hidden in the camp, and it's reported that Nagasaki—as well as the city of Hiroshima—have been devastated by a new and dreadful weapon with capabilities that stagger the mind. Prisoners learn that Hiroshima was bombed on August 6, 1945, and Nagasaki on August 9. Both cities have been reduced to wastelands.

Joe can hardly absorb the news. Immediately the guards lessen their severity on the prisoners. The food supply increases. The next few days become devoid of activity, and with the heady anticipation of Allied victory in the air, neither prisoners nor guards know quite how to act. Joe's only job is clear. He must live. He lies on his flea-infested mat and wraps and rewraps his ankle, sprinkling saltwater on it day and night. He cannot put any weight on his leg, and simple actions such as crawling to the latrine and back have become onerous tasks.

Six days after the second city is bombed, more news arrives: Japan has agreed to a full surrender without conditions. The emperor orders all Imperial combatants to lay down their arms. The signing of surrender terms and a proclamation of V-J Day are still to come, but it's official:

The war is over.

A slow smile spreads over Joe's face. He soaks in the relief of the news. He knows his body is in bad shape, but his mind is still sharp, and his senses are alert to a wild and strange mix of melancholy and hope. The more he considers the news, the stronger the mix of feelings grows. The possibility of going home to see his family is so close now, yet the price he has paid over the last few years weighs on him. All his wartime friends are gone. He is nineteen years old, and he has been overseas since he was fifteen.

In time he will understand the full scope of Japan's advance, and what the signaling of war's end means for the world. At the peak of its conquests, Japan kept half a billion people enslaved under its iron rule and was threatening to subjugate another half billion. Precise death counts are difficult to pinpoint, even in time, yet all told from the Imperial invasion of China in 1937 until World War II ended, the Japanese political and military regime was responsible for killing anywhere from three million to ten million people—including Chinese, Filipino, Korean, Indochinese, American, and Western European prisoners of war.

Now, with all hostilities ceased, a contrite message is read to the prisoners at Fukuoka Camp No. 17 by the camp's Japanese commander.

"I am pleased to inform you that we received military orders for stop of warfare.

"Since you were entered in this camp, you have doubtless had to go through much trouble and agony due to the extension of your stay here as prisoners of war, but you have overcome.

"The news that the day for which you longed—the day which you could return to your dear homeland where your beloved wives and children, parents, brothers and sisters, are eagerly awaiting you—is probably your supreme joy.

"...I'd like to extend to you my most sincere congratulations, but at the same time I sympathize most deeply with those who have been unable due to illness or some other unfortunate reason to greet this joyous day.

"...I sincerely hope you will wait quietly for the day when you can return to your loved ones, behaving according to camp regulations, holding fast your pride and honor as people of a great nation, and taking care of your health."

Prisoners murmur among themselves in a range of skepticism, surprise, wariness, and guarded elation. Control of the camp is soon handed over to the Allied officers among the POWs. The Japanese guards and civilian supervisors flee the camp, fearing the prisoners will form a mob and kill them all. The newly freed POWs are ordered by the Allied officers to remain in the camp and await further instructions. Any prisoner caught trying to leave will be court-martialed. Some POWs jeer at the announcement; others laugh and make quiet plans to head for the gates.

But most of them, including Joe, stay put. He's dismayed to hear that it may be weeks—or even months—until help arrives and the POWs are able to leave. Joe knows that if he's going to

survive, he needs to get his ankle treated — fast. The reason for
the delay offers little consolation: some 34,000 Allied war prisoners are scattered in various POW camps throughout Japan. It's
simply going to take time to get them all home.

Meanwhile, more food arrives. The prisoners whitewash a
big X outside the camp near the coalfield to demarcate a drop
zone, and brightly colored parachutes fall from the sky with fifty-
gallon oil drums swinging underneath. The drums are filled with
soup, cocoa, C and K rations, fruit, candy, vitamin tablets, shoe-
laces, sewing kits, khaki uniforms, soap, toothpaste, razor blades,
medical kits, and canned beer. Joe eats and eats.

Mail also arrives, its delivery organized by the International
Red Cross Committee in Switzerland. A typed message on Red
Cross letterhead, dated August 17, 1945, finds its way to Joe at
Fukuoka. It's from his mother.

My Dear Son,

*Gee, I am so thrilled to have the opportunity of writ-
ing you a long letter again. And we are all so happy that
this awful war is over and all of you boys can be coming
home to us anxious parents. We are looking forward to
seeing you real soon, and we have a yard full of fryers
fattening for you.*

*...Son, if possible, as soon as you hit the States call
me, phone #48-2464. I want to hear your voice once
again.... Be sure and let me hear from you as soon as
possible.*

*Remember we love you lots and will be waiting for
your safe return.*

Keep your chin up.

Lots of love from all,
Mother

Joe reads and rereads the letter. He desperately hopes he can reach the States and make that telephone call, but his leg is in bad shape. Flies have laid eggs inside the wounds, and maggots are now working inside the bandage. The American doctor examines the leg again and informs Joe that the maggots may actually be helping. They're eating the dead tissue. Not much else can be done for the leg. Aside from vitamins and first aid kits, actual medicines are unavailable. Joe begins to have fainting spells.

An affable private from Baltimore named Raymond Ward Shipley finds Joe a pair of crude crutches. They're too short, forcing Joe to stoop whenever he shuffles about the ward, but he's pleased to be able to move a bit better on his own. The private tells Joe to call him Ray, but Joe asks if he can call him by his last name instead. In Joe's mind, there will only ever be one Ray.

The next day Shipley returns to the infirmary and whispers to Joe that a group's planning to cut out of camp and make a break for the railroad station. Joe's invited along. They plan to ride the train south to a city called Kagoshima, then hop a flight to Manila, then make it back to the States somehow. They're going home.

Joe's face lights up. "Man, I need to get out of here so bad. But I don't think I can make it more than 100 yards on these crutches."

Shipley grins. "Already thought about that. I snatched this big-wheeled turnip cart from the mess hall. You can ride while I push."

At daylight the next morning, September 12, 1945, with the breathless quiet of an approaching thunderstorm filling the air, a dozen soldiers kick through the boards in the back fence and head down the road to the train station. Shipley pushes Joe in the cart, chuckling under his breath and noiselessly calling,

"Tomatoes! Get your farm-fresh tomatoes! Bananas! Come get your fresh produce!"

A throng of civilians already crowds the train station. The wind picks up and rain starts to fall. Most people are loaded with luggage, cooking pots, even rickety chairs, and their faces are hardened and tense. Joe realizes the civilians are not just travel-ing — they're fleeing. The stationmaster announces that the only train of the day is late, and everybody must be patient.

Joe's concerned about the announcement, even suspicious. Due to all the violence he's seen over the past three and a half years, he doesn't trust his surrendered captors. A rumor has been circulating that the Japanese are ordered to kill any remaining POWs. He's anxious to clear out of Omuta, but if no train arrives, he knows they'll have little choice but to look both ways and sneak back to camp. They wait and wait. Morning passes, then afternoon. Finally, at dusk, a train is heard approaching the sta-tion. Loaded far beyond capacity, the train travels sluggishly, so slow it's barely moving, and it finally screeches to a tired stop at the station. Every car is already thick with passengers. People sit on windowsills, with half their bodies outside the cars. Passen-gers hold fast atop the train. They even huddle on the cowcatcher on the locomotive's front.

A couple of the soldiers in Joe's group storm the station-master's office, commandeer Japanese swords and clubs, and begin to scatter civilians out of the first passenger car. Two Americans climb into the locomotive and inform the engineer that the train needs to leave immediately — with the former POWs aboard. Other soldiers, with the help of the stationmaster, disconnect the locomotive and the first passenger car from the rest of the train's cars. They don't want any more delays. Joe feels bad for the civilians who will have to wait longer, but he's happy to leave as quickly as possible. Shipley helps him aboard the passenger car, and soon the lighter train is headed down the tracks at a much faster pace, puffing away the bad memories of Fukuoka POW Camp No. 17.

All the passenger car's windows have been blown out, letting smoke from the locomotive swirl through the open carriage whenever the wind hits. The ragged American soldiers sit and laugh and talk above the noisy locomotive's chugging. Near midnight the train slows, enters a large railyard, and stops. A huddle of important-looking Japanese railway officials stands alongside the train. The officials bow when Shipley and three Americans step down and talk, but the Japanese insist the train will not travel any farther that night. They offer food and sleeping quarters instead. Another train will be ready, they promise, early the next morning—a larger one that's able to climb the steep mountain grades to Kagoshima. But Shipley tells them to stuff it. He demands a new crew, a larger engine, and food—immediately. They're not waiting for tomorrow.

After some haggling, the officials agree to the demands and hurry to outfit a larger engine. Soon the prisoners are headed southward again. Joe tries to doze, but the day has been long, and surges of dizziness pass over him. His leg reeks, and he's alarmed and embarrassed by the smell. He sits with his arms crossed over his chest, consciously breathing through the discomfort and pain, hoping he can hold on long enough to get wherever they need to go. Shipley is smoking, cracking jokes, telling stories. Joe doesn't want to bother him or slow him down.

Daylight arrives, and Joe wakes from a doze to find the train racing along a wide, white beach. Scattered along the tracks every few miles are groups of Japanese soldiers, fully armed and outfitted, glaring as the train speeds by. The train begins to slow, then crawls to a stop. Joe props himself up and glances outside. They seem to be in the middle of nowhere. He can see no one. But then a solitary figure is spotted standing on the station platform. It's an American soldier wearing an M.P. armband. The M.P. glances through the broken windows at the ragtag American POWs inside the train and calls, "Whoa. Where the hell did you guys come from?"

Joe manages a chuckle.

The young man is lifted from the train. American GIs gather and help the former prisoners into trucks, then escort them to a big tent being used as a mess hall. No medical attention is available at this location yet, so Joe is plied with bacon and eggs, hot buttered pancakes and syrup, and as much freshly ground coffee as he wants—but no medicine. He hasn't much appetite. Soldiers ask him questions, offer cigarettes, and generally try to make the former prisoners feel welcome. It's not long before a major approaches Joe's group and tells them a plane is ready. A hurrah goes up from the other former prisoners, but Joe stays quiet. He's anxious to receive medical care, and no longer able to muster the strength even to cheer.

They fly all day and land in darkness on Okinawa. They're fed again. Joe can't believe the sight of all the food. He manages to eat a donut and drink a cup of coffee. In another hour, they're loaded onto a different plane and flying toward Manila. Joe asks the crew chief where they'll be landing.

"New runway," he says. "Nichols Field."

For the first time since leaving Fukuoka, Shipley takes a closer look at Joe and says, "Man, I've been so excited I forgot all about your ankle. When we get to the Philippines, they can dress your wound and pump you full of medicine. You'll be just like new." He looks at him more closely still and frowns. "You doin' okay? You look tired."

Joe asks his friend to lean closer. "You saved my life," Joe whispers. "I wasn't sure I was going to make it in the camp for much longer."

"Just keep breathing," Shipley tells him. "You and me, pal— we're finally going home."

CHAPTER 17

A Time to Heal

In a daze, Joe feels himself lifted from the plane just as the sun breaks over the eastern horizon. After so much darkness, the intensity of the morning light nearly blinds the young man. He's loaded into an ambulance. The door is slammed shut. He hears Shipley yell a final word of encouragement from beyond the glass. The ambulance speeds away toward the field hospital on the other side of the airport. Joe doesn't know it yet, but due to transportation schedules among troops going home, and an upcoming inability to locate each other back in America, he will never see Shipley again.

Joe feels nauseous and finds himself floating in and out of consciousness. He hears people talking above him. "What's left of this tendon is a mess. Nurse, get a pan and try to clean this up so we can see what we've got here."

"I'm fine, Doc," Joe tries to mumble. "All I need is a clean bandage and a drink of water. I'm thirsty as hell."

A kind female voice answers. "Just relax, soldier. How about a cold towel on your forehead? There, how's that feel? No, don't try to get up."

Joe feels needles going into his arms. Tubes run in and out of him. The voices fade and the sights blur. He takes a deep breath. Closes his eyes. Sees and hears nothing more.

———

When Joe awakes, he sees he's in a medical ward in the field hospital at Nichols Field. The airport is within city limits and about seven miles from the center of Manila. The breeze wafts freely through the walls of the field hospital, and everything smells sanitized and fresh. The roof is canvas, and the floor is made of wide planks jammed together. Beds line both sides of the tent, and a nurses' station is set up in the middle. As Joe takes in all this, he feels no pain except for a slight soreness in the left cheek of his buttocks. His mind feels medicated yet clear. He lies for an hour, maybe two, trying to collect his thoughts. A nurse approaches. She's smiling and carrying a small syringe, and he immediately sees her as a hearty sort.

"Hey, you finally decided to join us?" The nurse lifts the sheet, gives him another shot, rubs the spot with a cotton ball, and smiles again. "I'm Lieutenant Halstead. I'll be your day nurse most of the time. Welcome to our ward. We aim to please." She fills a water glass and hands it to Joe, who drains it and asks for another. She refills it and gives him a friendly wink. "You need anything else, just shout."

He tries to smile back. He wants to talk more, to ask her questions. But he finds himself too tired to speak words of substance. He closes his eyes.

Sleeps.

In the middle of the night he awakes with a jolt. Grasps the sides of his bed and feels cool sheets and a clean hospital blanket. No lice are gnawing at him. No flies are buzzing. Joe takes a breath and remembers where he is. He closes his eyes and tries to sleep, but his mind is an uncharted wilderness, and he fails to place his thoughts in any neat categories. Near dawn he dozes again, but not for long. He wakes early. His body feels restless, and he jumps at any unfamiliar sound, unsure of his surroundings. It's as if he's a caged animal, set free but unsure which way to turn. He tries to think some more, but his mind skitters from one thought to the next. Lieutenant Halstead approaches his bed again. She gives him another shot, refills his water glass, and promises that breakfast will be served soon.

"Nurse." He can barely rouse his voice.

"Yes?"

"Lemme ask you a question."

"Sure."

"I need to find somebody in Manila. A civilian. How soon till I get out of here?"

The nurse shakes her head. "You arrived with a bad infection. The doctors are doing all they can to get it under control, and they need to work more on your ankle, but until they get this infection cleared up, they don't want to mess with it. Honestly, it might take a while. Couple of months perhaps. You're going to be okay, but your recovery will take time." She pauses, then adds, "Filipina? A woman?"

"Yeah. She has a child, too. Three and a half years old now."

The nurse scratches her head. "You could try the Red Cross for information, but I wouldn't be surprised if it will be difficult for you to find her. Perhaps impossible. The civilians had it rough under the Japanese. Meanwhile I'll bring you some stationery. You can write home instead. How's that sound?"

Joe feels his anger rise and he finds a stronger voice. "What do you mean *rough*? Look, lady, I know you mean well, but I got too much on my mind to write a letter home just now." Joe turns his face away from her in fury but immediately feels sorry. He knows his brusque tone has caught her off guard, and that she's not the enemy. He returns his gaze toward her and apologizes. To his surprise, the nurse pulls up a chair and sits.

"You don't owe me any apologies," she says. "I didn't take it personally. You boys didn't get a lot of news in the camps, did you?"

Joe nods but doesn't make eye contact.

She purses her lips. "Last February, when MacArthur pushed the Japanese out of Manila, the enemy was really hard on the city as they left. Lots of stuff happened to the civilians—bad stuff, particularly to women. I'm sorry. You certain she was in Manila then?"

"No, not positive," Joe says. "But I think so."

"Well, can't be helped now. It'll take a while before you can..." The nurse doesn't finish her sentence. She softens her tone and adds, "Look, son, you're in safe hands now. Just relax. When I told you to write a letter instead, I just meant...well.... You're going to need your family. It'll be natural for you to feel angry for a while. We're all here to help get you well. You might have more on your mind than you realize. We can help you there, too. Just ask."

She looks finished in her words, but she doesn't move to rise. Joe stares at the canvas ceiling while moments pass. Finally he lets out a deep sigh. The nurse stays where she is, just sitting with him. A compassionate presence.

"You truly wanna know what's going on with me?" Joe says. She nods.

"I just lie here and think," Joe says. "I think about every friend I ever had in this world and how they're all gone. But I'm still here. I feel guilty for being alive. I know I should be happy, but I have no one to be happy *with*."

The nurse leans forward and takes Joe's hand in hers. "Johnson, you've been through a difficult time. The feelings you have are normal. They'll fade away eventually—not completely, but enough so you can get on with your life. Some days will be better than others." She pats his shoulder. "Now, I need you to get some rest. Try not to think too much, okay?"

Joe nods but bites his lip to stop from crying. He hasn't cried in three years. Not since Dale died in Cabanatuan. The nurse helps him sip some water. Joe lies back on his pillow and closes his eyes. Tries to rest. He's wrestling through what the nurse just told him. His mind still feels full.

A day later, Joe decides to take the nurse's advice. He picks up a pen and writes his first letter since being released. The words flow from him in bunches, and as he writes, he finds he has to wipe the wetness from his eyes with the back of his sleeve.

September 16, 1945

Dear Mother, and the whole family:

At last with tears in my eyes I am able to write you a letter.... Mother, I am in as good a shape as can be expected. On August 6 I was trapped in a cave in the coalmine I was forced to work in; 54 men were killed. I escaped with my right leg cut very bad at the back of the ankle. All the tendons were severed but due to the wonderful American surgeon we had they were mended. They are healing fine now, and I'll probably be able to walk in 3 or 4 months. Otherwise I am in good condition. I'm in the hospital here (in Manila) and it will probably hold me up coming home. They are giving us first priority on planes and ships. They sure treat us swell, like a bunch of babies.

...I'm not supposed to tell you how the Japs treated us, but I don't need to. Just believe everything you hear and then some. Boy, they can't be repaid enough. They're

not even in the human-being class.... Pardon my writing, but I'm so nervous and excited, I have forgot how to spell. I can't even talk English.

Tell Betty and Charles and Mr. Jake I can't wait to get back and see them. I guess we won't know each other. Write Aunt Ethel and all the kinfolks.

...Mom, I want to say so much, yet I can't get it on the paper. It's in my head, but it's packed so full of things.... We have about 26 men left in my company out of 183.

Hope you can make some sense out of the letter. It's all jumbled up and I forgot half of what I was going to say. But hang on Mom, till later.

Loads of love.

Joe

Your wandering boy is coming home.

Joe rereads what he's written and stares at one line: *Boy, they can't be repaid enough.* The line sounds more severe than he'd imagined when he wrote it. He studies it for a while, wondering if he should cross it out or maybe soften the presentation somehow. He decides to leave it as is.

Joe eats. He sleeps. Tries to sort out his thoughts some more. He continues to receive shots of penicillin. On September 21, 1945, he writes to his mother.

Dear Mom.

Received your first long letter in a long time. Was I happy to hear that you are okay. I was worried. Betty's picture was what I valued most. She sure looks good. Bet she's got lots of boyfriends. Write Chas and Dad and tell them to write me. I sure am anxious to get home.

...I got plenty of money coming, Mom. If you need any, let me know. Well, I got to go take a shot of penicillin. I have had 47 shots since I've been here. I feel like a pincushion. But I guess they know what they're doing.

Lots of love from your wandering son.

Joe

He rereads the letter. At least he hasn't lost his ability to poke fun at himself. *Pincushion.* That old humor. It's helped him get through a lot.

The next day, September 22, 1945, he writes his mother again. This time as he writes, he feels a strange sort of melancholy. He reminds himself he's finally free, finally safe, yet he can't deny the loneliness he feels. After he rereads his letter, he realizes it's a strange mix. Part of what he writes comes off as everyday chattiness. Another part conveys horror.

Dear Mom,

How are things coming along at home?

...They sure treat us swell here. Anything we want, we get. Three beers a day, free. Two cokes. Three bars of candy. Gum, peanuts, cigarettes. I don't smoke, but with all the cigarettes stacking up on me, I might as well start. Don't worry though, 'cause I won't.

Boy, Manila sure has changed since '42. I worked here on Nichols Field for the Japs, 18 months, the worst detail in the islands. They used to torture and kill someone at least every day or two.

Well, I won't burden you with a bunch of sob stuff of how bad we were treated, because I want to forget it myself.

...Mom, hang around that phone, because I hope to
be home soon. Fried chicken. Hot biscuits, and banana
pudding. That's what I want. Just as only you can fix it.
      Loads of love to all.

                                        Your loving son,
                                              Joe

A soldier who was with Joe at Omuta is released and finds his
way to the hospital in Manila. Before the soldier had left, he'd
commandeered a batch of photos taken by the Japanese. He finds
Joe in the hospital and gives him a picture the commandant
had taken of the boy. Joe stares at the photo and shakes his head.
He's seen his reflection in a hospital mirror. Already he looks different. His cheeks aren't as hollow. The lines in his throat aren't
as pronounced. A small brightness has begun to glimmer in
his eyes.

Over the next few days, Joe stares at his photo and wonders
about himself, grapples with his existence. He's lived his forma-
tive teenage years in such an unforeseen state. He wonders what
his classmates back home were doing during the war years. For
most of that time, they were too young to be drafted, too young
to enlist. Did they complete their schooling? Make plans for the
future? Go on dates?

A week later, Joe writes his mother again.

                                    September 28, 1945

Dear Mom,
      How are things at home? Am still in hospital here in
Manila. It don't look like I am going to get home by
Xmas. They say how many are leaving and all that, but
none of us are leaving yet. I went to the show last night

and seen Shirley Temple in Kiss and Tell. *We have a show three times a week.*

Mom, I hope this is the happiest Xmas of our lives. It's sure going to be great to see you and home. My hair hasn't been long since '42, and it's about 1 inch long now and sticking in all directions. The Japs made us keep it shorn all the time.

Keep your chin up.

Your loving son,
Joe

———

Not long after writing that letter, on a late-September morning in 1945, something happens to Joe that will change his sense of purpose. Something that causes him to change the questions he asks of Providence. Instead of wondering *Why do you allow so much evil in the world?* he will wonder *Why do you allow so much love?*

Joe has had several weeks of recuperation at Nichols Field by now, and on this morning of mystery and wonder, Lieutenant Halstead approaches Joe's bed and informs him about a new program they've just started. The American nurses are working in conjunction with local NGOs and the University of the Philippines. They're going to help young Filipina women become nurses so they can help rebuild their country. A new health aide has recently joined the program. She's eighteen and will be entering nursing school at the university soon. Her life is filled with the hope of second chances—just like Joe's.

"Be kind to the girl, and cut her some slack," Lieutenant Halstead says. "She's just beginning the program and a little shy. In fact, she just arrived at the hospital today. She's here to give you your bath. Ready?"

"A bath?" Joe sniffs his armpit. "I don't stink, do I?"

"Well, soldier," Lieutenant Halstead says with a chuckle. "You're certainly a lot more fragrant than when you first came to us, that's for sure."

Joe laughs.

The health aide comes around the corner, her eyes averted. She checks his bed tag and the name on her clipboard, focused on doing her job. Almost as an afterthought, she reads his bed tag again and gives a little start. "Private Johnson?" she says. She looks at the boy in the hospital bed. He is much taller, yet his nose is distinctly unchanged, the set of his cheekbones. His lips unmistakable. The clipboard slips from her hands and clatters on the floor. "It can't be. It simply *can't* be."

Joe's heart begins to pound. It's the same sweet voice. His eyes have been closed in preparation for the bath, but now they pop open. He pushes himself up on his elbows and stares hard at the girl. She has the same deep brown eyes, the same perfect strawberry mouth. Years have passed, but he would know her anywhere, anytime.

"Is there something I should know?" Lieutenant Halstead asks. Her voice sounds far away.

A magnificent lump has risen in Joe's throat. "An old and very dear friend," he whispers to the nurse. "We'll be okay." He opens his callused hand and extends his reach toward the girl. She's still staring at him, her mouth agape. She takes his hand in hers.

"It's you," the girl murmurs. "It is truly *you*."

A quiet and feral sound emerges from somewhere deep within Joe. They reach for each other and embrace. He draws her closer still, caressing the back of her hair, holding her tightly. Her embrace fills a cavernous hunger within him. Her warm and clean smell is intoxicating.

"My American soldier boy," she murmurs into his neck. "Oh,

how I prayed for you. My prayers have been answered. You have always been in my heart."

"I never forgot you," he whispers. "You were always with me."

They are both crying now, the saltwater of pure happiness. Clinging to each other in a tight embrace. The darkness they endured has been thick, but the light of hope has never been quenched. The scorching sun, the flag of war, dominated their circumstances for so long. But with this reunion they sense a greater spirit has been at work in their lives. The eternal sun, bright and blinding with pure radiance, has never ceased to shine.

Perpetua kisses Joe, again and again. On the mouth. Cheeks. Hair. Hands.

Joe dries his tears. Dries hers. Smiles at the one he loves.

Kisses her right back.

———

The miles between Manila and Joe will eventually widen, and time will change everything. It will become a time for peace, and a time for justice. A time for laughter, although also a time for mourning. Ultimately it will become a time to heal. Right before he leaves the field hospital, he is interrogated twice by American Army officers. He is asked to sign his name to his statements. His testimony will be used as affidavits in upcoming war trials.

Shortly after giving his testimony, Joe boards a C-54 hospital plane for an uneventful flight home. When it stops in Guam for refueling, Joe turns onto his side on the gurney and stares out the plane window with tears in his eyes. They land at Kwajalein Atoll, the Marshall Islands, to refuel again, and a flight nurse tugs gently on Joe's shoulder and asks if he would care for some coffee. His eyes are red and puffy, and she asks him if he's okay. He nods and declines the coffee, telling her he doesn't want to explain himself. Not now. Not anytime soon.

They continue toward Hawaii and land again. Joe lies on his back staring up into space, feeling relieved to be alive yet winded, guilty, and confused. He is carried off the plane on a stretcher and put on another plane, this one bound for San Francisco. He is given medicine to induce sleep, and he will barely remember touching down at Hamilton Field in Marin County, or being driven across the Golden Gate Bridge to Letterman Army Hospital in San Francisco, the main hospital for treating sick and wounded soldiers arriving from the Pacific Theater. Joe will sleep soundly his first night in his home country, and when he wakes, he will realize he is once again stateside.

A nurse comes into his room and asks, "Are you finally with us?"

She takes his temperature and pulse, all the time smiling and chatting. In the afternoon, Joe is given a complete physical and a new pair of crutches. It is October 9, 1945, and Joe sends his mother a Western Union telegram. It does not say much—only that he is officially back in the United States, and to wait for him by the phone. A short time later, Joe is wheeled to a dayroom at Letterman and handed one of the many phones so he can make the call. It feels surreal to hear his mother's voice, as though he never left Memphis years ago. They interrupt each other often and cry with each other, and Joe soon feels exhausted and emotionally drained.

After several more weeks of recovering at Letterman, Joe is carried on a gurney to a hospital train car. He is with five other patients, all former POWs from the Memphis area. A nurse and a cook are also on board. Soon after San Francisco is left behind, the cook asks, "What would you guys like to eat?" Almost in unison they yell, "Fried chicken!" The cook laughs and says, "You got it!"

They head south through California and east through

Arizona and New Mexico, and the train stops every so often. Patients who are more ambulatory step outside and walk alongside the car. Crowds gather, and people wave and cheer. When the train stops in Fort Worth, Texas, Joe takes his crutches and eases himself off the train. He sees that two patients have used wet towels to write in the dust on the side of the train: *POWs. Home at last.*

In time, the train reaches Union Station in Memphis. It is late autumn, and the trees have shed their leaves. Joe smiles with one realization. He still has a long way to go before he heals completely, but he's going to make it home for Christmas after all.

An Army captain boards the hospital car and formally welcomes the soldiers home. Joe wants to walk off the train. He doesn't want to be carried. The nurse hands the former POWs their records, and she and the cook wish them good luck.

Joe takes his crutches, stands, and steps forward to greet his family.

Joe, age ninety
Sun City West, Arizona, 2016

Mama and Mr. Jake met me when I got home to Memphis. Charles and little Betty were there. I can never describe that feeling. Hobbling off the train on my crutches and seeing them again. It was so good to see my family. So, so good. Mama and Mr. Jake had gotten married, you know. He turned out to be not half-bad. We got to be friends. Years went on, and Mr. Jake turned out to be the best thing that ever happened to my mother. They both lived long, full, and happy lives well into their eighties.

My father never wrote me after I joined the Army, although I heard he joined up himself, because he'd learned I'd been taken prisoner. That was something good. He was racing horses late 1945 when I returned to Memphis. I drove over to Hot Springs one weekend to visit him, and I guess he'd taken a turn for the worse. The old rascal. First words out of his mouth were to ask me for money.

Why didn't I stay in the Philippines, marry Perpetua? Good question. Sister Carmella and Lieutenant Halstead began to talk among themselves, see. The sister was responsible for Perpetua, and the lieutenant was responsible for me. They both had eyes, and they knew we was in love. Perpetua started coming around my room each day, lingering by my bed, which was a beautiful thing. The most blessed moments either of us ever had.

But they started up with us. Perpetua needed to finish her education, they said. I needed to go back to my family to let them know I was okay. We needed to get practical. It wouldn't be easy for me to take a war bride, and maybe someday—hopefully soon—I could return to the Philippines. Then Perpetua and me could plan our future.

Maybe we let ourselves get pushed around. I don't know. Perpetua agreed to their plan, although she was sad, and with some consternation, so did I. After that stretch of golden days, she weren't allowed to see me no more. I wrote her a note, and she was able to get a gift to me through Sister Carmella, right before I left the Philippines. When that big C-54 hospital plane was gaining altitude with me inside and still on a stretcher, I opened Perpetua's gift. It was a picture of a boy, and doggone if he wasn't the spitting image of me. My heart broke. I'm positive—her child was my son.

I returned home with many conflicted thoughts. Since I'd last left the United States, I'd spent nine months as a peacetime soldier in Manila, five months fighting the Japanese on Bataan and Corregidor, and more than three and a half years as a prisoner of war. Last stretch nearly did me in. Mostly now, like so many of the guys who'd fought, I wanted to forget.

Me and Perpetua wrote each other like gangbusters that first stretch. Love letters. Several months of writing back and forth. Then one sad week her letters stopped. Just like that. I didn't know what to make of it. I kept writing anyway. But she never wrote back. Never again. I kept writing and writing, but nothing.

I concluded she'd lost interest. Maybe the idea of marrying a former POW was too much for her. Or maybe she'd considered moving away from the Philippines to be with me, and she didn't like that. Or maybe she met someone else. It broke my heart, but I accepted it and kept my feelings to myself. Nobody in America during that time wanted to talk about nothing bad, or painful, or messy. We'd just won the war, hadn't we? It was a time for celebrating, for everybody getting on with their lives. Buying refrigerators. Houses. Having babies by the dozen. I decided to get practical. Married that other gal. Barely knew her, like I said.

That's when I had those rocky years when I was trying to get my head sorted out. Weren't all bad. I reached out to the families of Ray Rico and Dale Snyder, and that was good. We stayed in touch for years. But, you know, my troubles came to a head.

The doctors at that psych ward started talking to me. They said I had to leave the trouble behind.

I said, "How the hell you do that?"

They said, well, you don't pretend the bad stuff didn't happen. You don't push it all under the rug or say, "That's okay." But you got to set the hurt down. You got to forgive. When you're all mad and storming around, like I'd been doing, that only keeps hurting you.

I had written once to my mother saying my enemies couldn't be repaid enough. But I decided I wasn't going to spend the rest of my life filled with rage. No, sir. Wasn't going to dwell on it. The war was over, and I wasn't gonna make a stand against my enemies no more. Not in my head. Not in my heart. Not in my speech. It is so much easier to be forgiving than to harbor a gutful of hate.

Now, I had to make that choice more than once. I had to keep setting down that hurt and setting it down again. I had to forgive, and I had to forgive again. But I was okay after that. Those doctors worked my brain over and straightened my butt out. They were real great guys. We got along great. After that, I didn't hate anymore. I truly didn't. You can't live the rest of your life that way. You can't.

Did I tell you about me getting married to Marilyn? September 1956. Third time's a charm. Oh, we had our spats like everybody else, but this turned out to be a happy marriage. We never had any children together, but Marilyn had a daughter from a *previous marriage. Marilyn always said I raised that daughter like she was my own.*

In the 1970s, it was finally time. I made a pilgrimage back to the Philippines to search for Perpetua and our child. Marilyn gave her blessing. She knew I needed to make that trip. I looked around a long time and never did find my boy, but I found a grave. It was a hot day. Grass was withered. I stood a long time, sobbing. That's where Perpetua lay. I asked around in the neighborhood, and they figured both Perpetua and our boy were killed during the Marcos regime. Lots of folks went missing under him. I was real troubled with what I found. When I returned to the States, I kicked myself hard that I hadn't gone back to the Philippines earlier.

I kept kicking myself and kicking myself, beating myself up. Marilyn told me to knock it off. She was good like that. She said people live a lot of different ways, and it was real sad about Perpetua, but one consolation was I had helped her get on a better pathway, one that saved her from the streets. Marilyn said: Imagine if you'd never gone to the Philippines in the first place. What would have happened to Perpetua then? And what would have happened to you? You both helped each other. She helped you survive.

Maybe I had done a bit of good. Certainly Perpetua did. Perpetua had become a nurse. I'd found that out when I was there. She'd raised our son to adulthood. Found that out, too. She was a real good person. A priest in the Philippines told me that. I just hope Perpetua found love again. I do. She's the real saint of the story.

After my trip, even after hearing Marilyn's words, I wrestled with my head again. It wasn't easy to let go of the past, to forgive the world for all the wrongs it'd done to us. To forgive myself for the mistakes I'd made. Marilyn told me all folks have regrets, and often in the middle of our losses comes opportunity. You find new ways to grow. You heal. So I got back at it. I worked as a sheriff for a while. Then I worked as a marshal for some golf courses, helping out at tournaments and such. That's what I enjoyed most. Pay wasn't great, but being on a golf course hardly seemed like work. I didn't forget Perpetua. Never.

In our latter years, Marilyn and I moved to Arizona, where I retired and threw myself into volunteering. I started speaking all over the place, advocating for POWs, shining a spotlight on veterans, telling my story. Lots of good stuff came from that. Folks said they were encouraged to hear a guy can go forward, even when so much wrong is done to him. It helped them overcome their own hurts, they said. They gave me the Schow-Donnelly Award for heroism and service to our country. It was a real prestigious award, folks said. No, I ain't bragging.

Old age, you know. Creeps up swift and silent as an enemy with a rifle. I'm sorry to say Marilyn passed away last year. 2015. I was right next to her at her bedside. Her death left me shaken. I miss her so much. Yeah. Can't talk about that yet. No. All I can say for now.

This past year I was feeling so down with Marilyn gone. I rattled around in an empty house, me and the cat. When I turned ninety a bunch of friends came over and made a fuss. I had tears in my eyes. So many candles on a cake. Can you believe it? The guy who was supposed to have died all those times lives to this ripe old age?! On Corregidor, a bomb hit nearby, and I was covered up. I survived that. I was on Bataan, stupid enough to jump in a foxhole near bamboo. A mortar hit, busted all that bamboo down on me. Bamboo stuck in every part of my body. Nichols Field, of course, and slicing my arms and being thrown in the box. Survived that. Then the cave-in where my ankle was crushed. Oh, but it ain't easy being old. I've started having more aches and pains. A couple doctor's appointments haven't gone so okay. I haven't told nobody except you, now. You got to be brave to grow old.

Never been much for religion. Most of my life I searched and struggled. But I started listening to a preacher on TV. Smart fella, laid things out plain and simple. One day he was saying how God can spare you from troubles, but God doesn't always do that. Sometimes you go through the valley of the shadow, yet God walks with you. Only God keeps you going.

Well, I knew lots about that valley. So many times in the Philippines things happened, you know, where I just couldn't explain it. I don't know why one man dies and another man lives, and if you start trying to figure that out, you'll go nuts. But I knew I needed God more than ever. Right in my living room I bowed my head and made it official. Even for me. The grace of Christ is deep and wide.

After I prayed, I looked back over my last few years and noticed a change had been happening all along. Maybe God had been working in my life, even if I didn't know it was Him at work. Once I was bitter and untrusting. I was selfish and suspicious. I wasn't pleasant to be around. I was crafty. I knew just how far to push any situation and just when to stop so my ass was covered. Fortunately I had enough smarts to turn that around, to learn to love.

Several years ago I had started trying to become a caring, warmhearted, understanding, and tolerant human being. People seemed genuinely happy around me then. They didn't have to walk on eggshells around me anymore. They didn't seem to be afraid to accidently say the wrong thing and set me off.

I described it to my nephew over the phone. The old stuff had truly passed; the new stuff had truly come. I had learned to live by new values. Here they are in bullet form: trust in God, believe in God, listen to God, accept God, care for others, forgive others, change for the better.

One more thing you should know. It's up and down, but it happened, so I'll tell it. After the war, I was hospitalized at Kennedy General in Memphis for a couple months until I healed. At the hospital, I was using my mama's return address when I was writing to Perpetua, and that's where Perpetua was sending her letters to me. Then her letters suddenly stopped, like I said.

A couple years later I was visiting my mother, and one afternoon she teared up and said she had a secret to confess. Been nearly driving her mad. She went into the other room, came back with a stack of letters, held them out. She was crying then. Really sobbing. Said she figured she'd been doing the right thing at the time, helping me make the right decision. She thought I'd been too young to get involved with a Filipina girl halfway around the world.

All those letters spread out before me on the coffee table. All unopened. I leafed through them. Mostly I sat and stared. That's why Perpetua's letters had stopped. Mama hid them.

Well, it made me wince. If only things had been different. Such a statement for anyone. You can always look back and wonder what might have happened between you and someone you once loved. But you'll never know for sure. I was pretty messed up after I came home, and who's to say Perpetua would have put up with me? One thing you can know for sure is that you'll always hold a place in your heart for your first love. Perpetua and me—we weren't together for the rest of our lives, but we always had a great love. Of that, I'm sure.

There, that's the fuller answer to your question. Mine's an up-and-down story to be sure, but there's a happier ending than you might think. It's because today I ain't holding any of my hurt inside me. Not a lick. A life can get so messed by grievances, and all that messing can cause genuine damage. But the hurt don't need to destroy you. Life is too short to hold on to your hurt. Whether you're hurt from combat, or from being abused as a POW, or from a country that sent you back to war just so you could get shot in the stomach, or from your mama hiding letters, or from your daddy leaving you when you were young. You got to set that hurt down.

You'll only hurt yourself when you harbor hate and bitterness for deeds inflicted by others in the past. It is not easy, but time and patience will help you finally get over it. You learn more about life and surviving and human spirit from experiencing five years of pain, hardship, and tribulations than from fifty years of tranquility and contentment. It takes too much of your time and energy to seek revenge against those who inflicted pain and suffering and misdeeds on you. It doesn't mean you forget. You just file it in an unused chamber in your brain and go on with your life.

I'll stop jawing now, and maybe just take this straight up, because I'm doing a lot of soul-searching, even at this late hour. I've lived a charmed life. I have no complaints. I think about the guys I was so close to who are still over there, who didn't come home. They gave the supreme sacrifice. Me, I was lucky to live. You and me both, friend. We're both lucky to live. I have vivid memories of all my past years, and now I'm looking toward my burial ground with no fear. Find your peace like I found mine, because we don't get this world for long. No, we don't.

Heh.

That's for damn sure.

Acknowledgments

Profound thanks to Joseph Quitman Johnson (1926–2017) and estate executor Steve Graig.

To publisher and senior vice president Bruce Nichols and the entire team at Little, Brown and Company, Hachette Book Group, enormous thanks for your vision and careful stewardship of this project.

Rick Richter at Aevitas Creative Management and Madeleine Morel at 2M Communication Ltd., much gratitude for your continued championing of authorship and the written word.

First-draft readers Dorothy Brotherton and H. C. Jones — you are indispensable. Tosca Lee, Bob Craddock, and author and historian Donald Caldwell: thank you for your early notes on the manuscript. Mapmaker Pamela Fogle: it's always a pleasure to work with you. Research assistant and genealogist Karen Sue Clark; researcher Jay Gambol; Chief Master Sergeant Ricky Clark, USAF, Ret.: thank you for your helpful advice about this project.

All my love, always, to Mary Margaret, Addy, Zach, and Amie-Merrin.

A Note on Sources

All the information and stories in this book are presented as factually as possible. Joseph Quitman Johnson died in 2017 at age ninety-one. Before his death, he wrote two versions of a memoir, which were used along with other sources and interviews to help create this book.

One version of his memoir was independently published under the title *Baby of Bataan* in 2004, when Joe was seventy-eight. A friend of Joe's had published the manuscript on his behalf, and Joe had sold a few hundred copies out of his garage. After his death, his family believed that Joe's story was too remarkable to be allowed to fade away. Would I be interested in breathing new life into it? Literary precedent had been established. Two versions of Louis Zamperini's life story (*Devil at My Heels* and *Unbroken*) had been published, as well as two versions of Major Dick Winters's life story (*Biggest Brother* and *Beyond Band of Brothers*). Joe Johnson's story was something I wanted to tell — and tell with all my heart.

Incidentally, Joe hated the title *Baby of Bataan*. He wanted to call his memoir *Little Bird Walking,* but friends had talked him out of it because it didn't sound tough enough for military personnel. The phrase *Baby of Bataan* had come from the headline of a 1942 Memphis newspaper article. A wartime reporter had heard of an underage enlistee fighting in the Pacific, reached out to Joe's mother, and persuaded her to send in a baby picture of Joe. News of his imprisonment ran with the baby photo, and Joe was mortified to see a clipping of the article when he at last came home. The estate still has this clipping.

The other version of his memoir was so rare that not even his estate possessed it at first: an earlier, typewritten, first-draft version of Joe's life story. Only three copies were known to have been made, and Joe mentioned this document several times in other notes, first titling his story *My American Soldier Boy*. I was able to track down a copy from Judy Barber, who had been a close friend of Joe's along with her husband, Carl. The original writings proved wonderful and raw (Judy sent them to me in five large spiral-ring binders) and were peppered with news clippings and additional notes.

By studying the earlier version, I found variations between it and the version Joe eventually published. The first was longer and grittier, and I discovered new stories and gleaned new insight into Joe's direct thoughts, feelings, and actions. Interestingly, Joe typed *My American Soldier Boy* in the third-person voice—not first person, as a memoir normally would be written. It's almost as if he was reluctant to return to the difficulty. He wanted to observe himself as an outsider as he traversed the years of horror. He wrote to Judy and Carl: "The American POWs who survived returned home after the war with little fanfare. Most were reluctant to tell their stories. This is a part of our nation's history that has long gone untold and neglected. The stories now need to be told."

In both documents, I appreciated his unexpected lyricism. Joe had only a seventh-grade education, yet he wrote with fresh twists on words and phrasing. I quickly came to appreciate Joe Johnson as a true warrior-poet.

Joe also left behind a wealth of creative information in his

estate, including journal entries, musings, essays, bundles of wartime letters, photos, original poems, wartime documents, hard
copies of emails to friends and family members, and more than
ten hours of compelling video and audio interviews he'd given.
All were used to help create this book.

As I started the project, I augmented Joe's original narratives
with my interviews from his friends and family members. I also
studied Joe's taped interviews, read oral-history projects by other
former POWs, and pored over primary and secondary sources—
books, newspapers, articles, essays, military after-action reports,
and various research papers. Fortunately, this era has been
strongly documented by academics, journalists, and historians,
and I was able to cross-check Joe's story to ensure its accuracy
and make it understood in the wider context of the war.

Twelve living relatives and friends of Joe's were available for
me to interview. All had additional stories about Joe and insights
into Joe's experiences. Much gratitude goes to the family members and friends of Joe who were interviewed for this new book:
Steve Graig (who also provided five videotaped interviews done
with Joe in 2016), Benny Johnson, John "Buddy" Graig, Suzanne
Mickel, Jerry Watson, Bob and Carol Ottum, Tom Zmugg,
Richard and Michele Shirley, Greg Gantz, and Judy Barber.
Many thanks to Audra Goff for her information about Joe's
second marriage.

Special thanks to Barbara Hatch of the Veterans History Project at the Library of Congress for her 2007 interview
with Joe. To John General and his 2000 "Shore Talk" interview
with Joe. To C-Span, for its 2004 interview with Joe. To Memphis News 4, for its 2004 interview with Joe. To the Sun City
Grand Armed Forces Support Group, for its 2016 interview with
Joe. All of which were consulted for this book. To Anastasia
Harman for unpublished wartime journals. Thanks to Federico

Baldassare, Bruce Merrihew, Frank Aldridge, and Wes Injerd for correspondence with Joe. And to John Tewell for his historic Philippines photo curation.

In writing this book I consulted hundreds of resources, reference volumes, and books, which number too many to list here, although I would like to offer special thanks to the authors of the following books that proved most helpful to my research: Donald Knox (*Death March: The Survivors of Bataan*), William H. Bartsch (*December 8, 1941: MacArthur's Pearl Harbor*), John Toland (*But Not in Shame: The Six Months After Pearl Harbor*), Hampton Sides (*Ghost Soldiers*), John Whitman (*Bataan, Our Last Ditch*), Peter Eisner (*MacArthur's Spies*), Colonel Glenn D. Frazier (*Hell's Guest*), Bruce M. Petty (*Voices from the Pacific War*), Donald Caldwell (*Thunder on Bataan*), Anthony Weller (*First into Nagasaki*), Colonel E. B. Miller (*Bataan Uncensored*), Charles Underwood Jr. (*Deadline: Captain Charlie's Bataan Diary*), Clark Lee (*They Call It Pacific*), contributor Karl H. Lowe (*The 31st Infantry Regiment*), James M. Scott (*Rampage*), Bob Welch (*Resolve*), Elizabeth M. Norman (*We Band of Angels*), Michael Norman and Elizabeth M. Norman (*Tears in the Darkness*), Laura Hillenbrand (*Unbroken*), Manny Lawton (*Some Survived*), Bob Reynolds (*Of Rice and Men*), John W. Dower (*War Without Mercy*), Bill Sloan (*Undefeated*), G. C. Hamilton Middlesex and Alec Smith (*The Sinking of the* Lisbon Maru), John A. Adams Jr. (*The Fightin' Texas Aggie Defenders of Bataan & Corregidor*), Claire Phillips (*Agent High Pockets*), Mark Felton (*The Real Tenko*), and Adam Makos (*Voices of the Pacific*).

Additional thanks to the many research and archival sites used in preparing this manuscript, including the Roderick Hall Collection at the Filipinas Heritage Library, the University of the Philippines, the National Library of the Philippines, American

Defenders of Bataan and Corregidor Memorial Society, American Ex-Prisoners of War Organization, Bataan-Corregidor Memorial Foundation of New Mexico, the late Roger Mansell and the Center for Research: Allied POWs Under the Japanese (Mansell.com), the Children & Families of Far East Prisoners of War (COFEPOW), Corregidor—Then and Now (Corregidor.org), Far East Prisoners of War (the FEPOW Community), the United States Military Academy at West Point, the National WWII Museum, Manila American Cemetery and Memorial, the National Archives and Records Administration, US Army Center of Military History, the *Manila Times*, Newspapers.com, Ancestry.com, Arlington National Cemetery, Find a Grave, Google News Archive, the *Memphis Press-Scimitar*, POW Research Network Japan, Tim Gray and the WWII Foundation, Jim Erickson and POWs of the Japanese, and US-Japan Dialogue on POWs.

Notes

Part I

1. **Perpetua's rescue, Mama Rosa, and brothel.** Recounted in Joe's writings. Estate archives.

2. **Perpetua's her name.** Joe refers to the girl as Felicia in many of his notes and writings, as well as in later descriptions of her that he offers orally to family and friends. Yet in a private postwar note to a close friend (dated July 15, 2004), Joe reveals that while every description and incident he records about the girl is true, Felicia is actually a pseudonym he used for years to protect her true identity. Estate archives contain a handwritten wartime letter from Joe to his mother revealing that the girl's real name is Perpetua. Joe's letter to his mother doesn't describe the brothel, only that he has met a girl he particularly likes. He states her first name and offers a few defining features about her, notably that she is "lovely." No last name is ever recorded. Estate archives.

3. **Secret knock.** From Joe's notes. Estate archives.

Chapter 1: Little Bird Walking

4. **Description of Christine Elementary School.** *Memphis Daily Appeal,* "Our Finest Public Building," January 8, 1872. http://historic-memphis.com/memphis-historic/marketschool/market-description.pdf

5. **from one foot to another.** Joe journaled about this experience in his mid-eighties, the event still clearly etched in his mind.

6. **Works Progress Administration.** The WPA was renamed the Work Projects Administration in 1939. Eric Arnesen, *Encyclopedia of U.S. Labor and Working-Class History,* Routledge, 2007: 1540.

7. **He devours books.** Joe described in a 2006 email to his friend Frank Aldridge how much he always loved books, in particular from ages nine to thirteen. In an undated essay, Joe described teaching himself throughout adulthood using the public-library system. Estate archives.

8. **races mix without qualms.** Joe remarked this in a taped interview with his nephew Steve Graig in 2016.

9. **Edna likes Mr. Jake's look.** Details of the new arrangement were gleaned from Joe's writings and additionally offered by family members in present-day interviews, including the rock-throwing story. Joe used the line "She liked his look, so they started going together" in an interview with Steve Graig.

10. **the Humes school.** Elvis Presley graduated from this school in 1953. Peter Guralnick, *Last Train to Memphis: The Rise of Elvis Presley,* Little, Brown, 1994: 36. In 2004, the school was listed on the National Register of Historic Places. https://npgallery.nps.gov/NRHP/GetAsset/NRHP/98000368_text

11. **a carefree wanderer.** These descriptions of Joe Johnson Sr. are drawn from interviews with Steve Graig, Benny Johnson, John "Buddy" Graig, Suzanne Mickel, and other family members. The "fifth of whiskey" line came from Joe himself. Steve Graig interview, 2016.

Chapter 2: Last Days of Boyhood

12. **only a broken arm.** "Hurt Trying to Board Train," *Chattanooga News,* July 17, 1939: 1.

13. **crushed too badly to identify.** "Trains Cause Death of Two," *Chattanooga News,* July 17, 1939: 2.

14. **Encounter with tall man on train.** Recorded in several 2016 interviews with executor Steve Graig, estate archives. The man also gave Joe this practical advice: "When you ride the trains, wear coveralls over your regular clothes. That way when you're done riding, you take your coveralls off and your clothes underneath are clean."

15. **All the aunts are crying.** Joe recounts in his notes: "They cried on any occasion, even the men. When anything made them extremely happy, sad, or angry, they would cry. They were an emotional clan." Estate archives.

16. **Description of Alamo Downs.** Joe described the bats and guano-covered seats in his notes. The track closed for racing in May 1937, when pari-mutuel betting was outlawed in Texas. Afterward, Alamo Downs was mostly "a training track [and] a cow pasture." Paula Allen, "In '30s, Alamo Downs Had a Short Run," *San Antonio Express-News,* July 3, 2011. https://www.mysanantonio.com/news/article/Alamo-Downs-had-a-short-run-in-the-30s-1447995.php

17. **tamales for supper.** After precisely recording the foods they ate in the tack room at Alamo Downs, Joe added, "It was plain fare, but I loved the newness of it." Estate archives.

18. **working as a section hand for the railroad.** Whenever describing his father's first job, Joe used the slang term *gandy dancer,* a worker responsible for laying and maintaining railroad tracks.

19. **Father's occupation, parents' wedding date, Edna's birthdate.** *Fifteenth Census of the United States, 1930,* Department of Commerce—Bureau of the Census. Joe's father listed his occupation as "Salesman at a Soda Counter."

20. **an entry in his baby book.** Estate archives. Incidentally, another entry in the baby book notes Joe's birth weight of "10 pounds."

21. **"don't say nothing at all."** The evasive line comes verbatim from Joe. Steve Graig interview, 2016.

22. **then slides behind the wheel.** In his writings, Joe described his father's drunken behavior, and how it became a pattern in San Antonio. Estate archives.

23. **for actors and producers in the movie business.** Estate archives.

24. **two exercise boys.** Journalist Ernest Havemann describes the job this way: "The exercise boy is racing's unsung hero, practically worth his weight (around 120 pounds) in gold. He is out at the stable at dawn, when these frightening creatures are at their friskiest. He puts the exercise saddle on the horse, rides him at a walk to the track, steadies him with the feel of his confident hands on the reins and withers, calms him, reassures him, hangs on when he bucks or shies, teaches him manners, corrects his bad habits, gets him used to standing up straight in the starting gate, gallops him a slow mile or gives him a fast workout that is a marvel of split-second timing. Then he takes the horse back to the stable." Ernest Havemann, "The Boys with the Horse-Sized Job," *Sports Illustrated,* May 23, 1960. https://vault.si.com /vault/1960/05/23/the-boys-with-the-horsesized-job

25. **flush wages for a Depression-era kid.** The median monthly wage for an adult male in 1940 was $79.67. *The 1940 Census: 72-Year-Old Secrets Revealed.* https://www.npr.org/2012/04/02/149575704/the-1940-census-72-year-old -secrets-revealed

26. **to Seabiscuit and flies on past.** Joe recounts this story in his writings, noting it wasn't a real race. Estate archives.

27. **five feet seven and 135 pounds.** These details were related by Joe in an interview with Barbara Hatch on April 18, 2007. Veterans History Project, Library of Congress.

28. **"If they take you, you got my blessing."** Joe recounted this interchange with his father in an October 25, 2000, interview. Joe also noted that the Pasadena recruiter was skeptical, and that he told the recruiter he'd been born in Memphis to throw him off the trail of tracking down his birth certificate. In fact, Joe was born in Louisiana.

29. **seventeen with a note from your parents, eighteen without.** In his 2008 master's-degree thesis entitled *Children at War: Underage Americans Illegally Fighting the Second World War,* Joshua Ryan Pollarine writes: "Joining the military underage was a daunting task. Although there was the obvious need for manpower, the military would not accept just anyone who walked in and

asked where to sign. Enlistment required proof of age, a physical examina-tion, and written consent of parents or guardians for those under eighteen. In a few instances, a recruiter would pretend to ignore youthful appearances and believe the kid standing in front of him was eighteen. Most times, how-ever, they were sent home with parental consent forms and told to get signa-tures stating they had permission to enlist. Some tried with forged documents, and a few were actually successful, depending on how good of a job they did. Most were not. Sometimes they succeeded in joining underage through an elaborate scheme. For others the task necessitated relentless per-suasion in front of their parents. Even so, many underage volunteers first attempted to join without even notifying their legal guardians." Graduate Student Theses, Dissertations, & Professional Papers, 191 (2008), Univer-sity of Montana Graduate School: 8, 28. https://scholarworks.umt.edu/cgi/viewcontent.cgi?article=1210&context=etd

30. **His birthplace is...Ruston, Louisiana.** Although Joe told the recruiter he was born in Memphis, he was actually born in Lincoln Parish 1, Ruston, Lousiana, according to his birth certificate. Author interview with Steve Graig.

31. **the titanic struggle of World War II.** See, for instance, the editorial page of the *Knoxville Journal,* which stated on June 21, 1940: "A vote for [FDR] will thus become a vote for active involvement in the European struggle." "Ex-Republicans Stimson and Knox Desert to Accept Cabinet Posts in New Deal War Party": 4.

32. **the nation's first peacetime conscription bill.** The new law obligated some 16.5 million American men to register for military service. Associated Press, "Roosevelt Signs Draft Bill Today," *Meriden Daily Journal:* 1.

Chapter 3: Where Sea and Sky Meet

33. **how much his butt aches.** Joe's writings. Estate archives.

34. **three nations have been running loose.** "Comment on Foreign Affairs: The *Enquirer* Reviews the Week's News," *Cincinnati Enquirer,* September 5, 1937: 1.

35. **one of the...best-equipped armies in Europe.** "Poland's Motorized Artil-lery—Ready for War," *Santa Rosa Republican,* March 29, 1939: 1.

36. **Italy had...conquered Ethiopia.** "They Cry 'Peace' but Push Toward War," *Muncie Evening Press,* December 27, 1937: 1.

37. **Imperial Japan had attacked China.** "Fascists Warn the World of Three-Power Might," *Daily Democrat* [Tallahassee, Florida], November 7, 1937: 1.

38. **300,000 civilians...slaughtered.** Christopher Bodeen, "Beijing Marks Anni-versary of WWII Atrocity," *The Record* [Hackensack, New Jersey], Decem-ber 17, 2017: A-20.

39. **until they're sworn in.** Musing on his underage enlistment, Joe wrote, "The urgency and necessity of the times likely influenced the Army in accepting me." Estate archives. During World War II, approximately 16 million Americans become part of the military; some 200,000 of them were underage, and nearly 50,000 of those were detected and sent home. "Don't Count Him Out Yet," as told to Tony Welch, American Veterans Center. https://www.americanveteranscenter.org/2012/02/veterans-of-underage-military-service/

40. **stifling the sobs.** Joe's notes. Estate archives.

41. **to figure out what to do with them.** President Roosevelt had been authorized to enlarge the American military to 375,000 troops in June 1940. But few Americans willingly joined, so a peacetime draft was instituted on September 16, 1940. A large number of soldiers had begun to flood the Army's intake and processing system. Geoffrey Perrett, *Days of Sadness, Years of Triumph: The American People 1939–1945*, Coward, McCann & Geoghegan, 1973: 31.

42. **driving his car far too fast.** Joe relates specific discussions and his early friendship with Ray in two of his writings. Most of those stories are recounted almost word for word in both places, and some stories lean toward the salacious and extreme. But Joe mentioned Ray's exploits with Kitty only in his earliest draft, removing all mentions of her in a later draft, as if he'd had second thoughts. Kitty may have been a pseudonym. Estate archives.

43. **in early February 1941.** Joe enlisted in early January of 1941, when he was still just fourteen years old, mentioning that it was three weeks until his fifteenth birthday, which would arrive on January 26, 1941. He was sworn in just after his birthday: February 11, 1941. Joe's military records, estate archives.

44. **assigned to the 31st Infantry Regiment.** Activated in the Philippines on August 13, 1916, the 31st had the distinction of being the only Army unit never to have served on US soil, earning it the unofficial nickname "America's Foreign Legion." On August 7, 1918, the regiment was sent to Siberia for two years to protect the Siberian Railroad from the Bolsheviks (prompting the regimental insignia to briefly become a polar bear). The regiment returned to the Philippines on April 17, 1920. The regiment's Latin motto, *Pro Patria,* means "For Country." *The 31st Infantry Regiment,* prologue by Karl Lowe, McFarland & Company, 2018: 9–14, 46.

45. **Joe loses count.** In one version of the story, Joe drinks only two beers and gains "a fuzzy head." When Joe told the story to friends, however, it was far more. Estate archives.

46. **return to base to sleep.** Joe noted this in his writings. Estate archives.

47. **boot camp overseas.** Patrick Feng, *History of the 31st Infantry Regiment,* National Museum, United States Army. https://armyhistory.org/31st-infantry-regiment/

48. **"It's dog eat dog when it comes to chow."** Specific, from Joe's notes. Estate archives.

49. **But mostly they just sit around.** "For several months following conscription [in September 1940]...the army could not adequately house, train, or arm the influx of soldiers." Daniel Blumlo, *How the Common Grunt and Prostitute Changed Military Policy* [master's-degree thesis], Florida State University, 2004: 25.

50. **being true friends.** Joe recounts this story two different ways in different writings. Dale and Ray are kind in both versions, but in the first telling they give him a much harder time before acquiescing to his desire to return to the room. Estate archives.

51. **some servicemen who are heading overseas.** Joe refers to the first girl as Sally in one section of his notes and Dottie in another, although Marie and Ginger are named thus consistently. Joe never mentions an exchange of money, nor does he clarify if they were prostitutes or so-called "pickup girls" or "victory girls"—potentially promiscuous young women attracted to servicemen out of a sense of adventure or duty. In a 1943 story for the *Washington Post,* Agnes Meyer described the wartime phenomenon: "girls with a perverted sense of patriotism who would not think of having sex relations with a civilian, but feel they are doing something for their country when they enter into such relationships with members of the armed service." Agnes E. Meyer, "Puget Sound Area, Washington: Seattle Fights Venereal Disease," *Washington Post,* April 1, 1943 (quoted in Meyer, *Journey Through Chaos,* Harcourt, Brace, and Company, 1944: 114).

52. **to take care of some personal business.** Later, Dale admits to Joe and Ray that he left the hotel room to call his sister, revealing the young man was far more chaste than he had initially let on. Estate archives.

53. **between him and Dottie.** Joe recounts the hotel-room experience several ways in various drafts of his writings without ever specifying if the relationship was consummated. His vague answers in light of Ray's detailed questioning suggest that the boy kept it to conversation and drinks. Estate archives.

54. **"He's humping you every night."** Joe indicated in his writings that the slurs from Coot were pejorative and specifically insinuated that Ray and Joe were a sexually active couple. Estate archives.

55. **even to different battalions.** A word on unit designations: In World War II a squad was up to 24 men, a platoon up to 50, a company up to 250. Four or more companies constituted a battalion (up to 1,000 troops), while a regiment consisted of two or more battalions (1,000 to 2,000 troops). Three or more regiments made up a division (about 10,000 to 15,000 troops). Mack Dean, "WW2 Army Units and Sizes," October 8, 2020: http://www.world war2facts.org/ww2-army-units-and-sizes.html

56. **"I'll be careful."** The totality of Joe's first postcard to his mother, post-marked March 17, 1941, is this: "Dear Mom, am leaving for Philippines, Island, either 17th or 18th. How are you all? Write soon. My address is: 31st Infantry, Manilla, P.I. Love, your son, Joe." Later he wrote her a five-page letter (postmarked March 26, 1941, and mailed from Fort McDowell) mentioning that he had also written his father and Aunt Ethel. This letter contains the phrase "Don't worry, mother, I'll be careful" along with this admission: "Tell Charles and Betty I love them a lot. I am getting kind of homesick but I'm sticking it out. Everyone gets kinda homesick, I guess." Estate archives.

57. **named Dewey Holtclaw.** In 2004 Joe wrote, "Dewey Holtclaw always sticks in my mind. In such a short time he made such an impression on my young life. I have fond memories of him." Estate archives.

Chapter 4: Lost Babes in the Woods

58. **the vast chain of docks.** See the 1941 photo of the Manila docks in "The Philippines Come into the War Picture," *Fort Worth Star-Telegram*, August 17, 1941: 2.

59. **more than eight million people.** *Report of the Philippine Commission to the President,* vol. 1, 56th Cong., 1st sess., S. Doc. 138 (1900): 15; *The World Almanac and Book of Facts,* 2015: 824.

60. **closer cooperation was eventually achieved.** The Philippines became a colony of Spain in 1521. Several bids for independence were attempted over the ensuing years. After Cuba sought independence from Spain just before the turn of the twentieth century, the United States aided Cuba and won the Spanish-American War. Afterward, Spain ceded the Philippines, Guam, and Puerto Rico to the United States for the sum of twenty million dollars. American opinion was divided on the transaction. *History of the Philippines,* California State University, Bakersfield: https://www.csub.edu/paci ficrim/countryprospectus/history.htm; *The Philippines, 1898–1946,* History, Art & Archives, US House of Representatives: https://history.house.gov /Exhibitions-and-Publications/APA/Historical-Essays/Exclusion-and -Empire/The-Philippines/

61. **toward independence within the next decade.** The 1934 law that set the Philippines on the road to independence was the Tydings-McDuffie Act, or the Philippine Independence Act. Over the next few years, a constitution was written and citizenship was reclassified. The Philippines would not achieve full independence, however, until July 4, 1946. Then, based on the provisions of the Tydings-McDuffie Act, the Philippines was transformed from a commonwealth into an independent republic. Sonia M. Zaide, *The Philippines: A Unique Nation,* All-Nations Publishing Co., 1994: 314–315.

62. **Exports slowed, oil embargo, Tripartite Pact.** *Japan, China, the United States and the Road to Pearl Harbor, 1937–41,* Office of the Historian, US Department of State: https://history.state.gov/milestones/1937-1945/pearl-harbor

63. **peacetime defense, not troop buildup.** Joe arrived in Manila on April 22, 1941. Not until three months later—on July 25, 1941—did US Secretary of War Henry L. Stimson explain to FDR that "all practical steps should be taken to increase the defensive strength of the Philippine Islands." *Hearings Before the Joint Committee on the Investigation of the Pearl Harbor Attack, Congress of the United States,* US Government Printing Office, 1946: 4366.

64. **fewer than 20,000 US troops remain.** Trevor K. Plante, "Researching Service in the U.S. Army During the Philippine Insurrection," *Prologue,* Summer 2000: https://www.archives.gov/publications/prologue/2000/summer/philippine-insurrection.html; Jennifer L. Bailey, "Philippine Islands: The U.S. Army Campaigns of World War II," US Army Center of Military History: 6: https://history.army.mil/brochures/pi/pi.htm. Bailey notes that by December 1941, the number of US troops had risen to 31,095—a 40 percent increase in four months, though "it remained perilously inadequate for the task at hand."

65. **1st squad.** Seven men are in the squad: Joe, Dale Snyder, Earl Petrimeaux, Wayne Seiling, Winford Couch, Paul Jackson, and Thomas Taylor. Joe's notes; Lowe, 436–446.

66. **and a .45 caliber automatic pistol.** Joe lists the following gear: Class A uniform, fatigues, dress shoes, field shoes, canvas leggings, cap and campaign hat, pith helmet, steel helmet, belt, skivvies, socks, towels, insignias, web belt, two blankets, backpack, entrenching tool, .45 caliber pistol, leather holster, two ammunition clips, a can of brass polish, a tin of shoe wax, and toilet articles. Estate archives.

67. **beans from a can.** Joe detailed the meal—dry bologna-and-cheese sandwiches, cold pork and beans—in his notes. Estate archives.

68. **Telegram home.** Amateur radiogram, May 1, 1941, to Mrs. Edna Jerkins from Joe Johnson. Estate archives.

69. **a test requiring good eyesight.** Joe notes the sexualized nature of the jeers in his writing. Estate archives.

70. **sits a convent.** Joe calls this convent the Sisters of Charity in his writings, but he is probably mistaken in his memory of its name. The convent was most probably the Beaterio de la Compania, a community of lay sisters that later became the Religious of the Virgin Mary. Regardless of the name, the sisters were devoted to prayer and charitable work. The motherhouse was destroyed in 1945. *History of the Congregation of the Religious of the Virgin Mary,* Religious of the Virgin Mary: www.rvmonline.net

71. **Two tall, squiggly trees.** Joe carried home from the war a picture of the front of his barracks and noted *Two "gecko" trees* in front of the structure. Estate archives.

72. **peas, beans, and relish trays.** Joe lists the menu of his first meal. Estate archives.

73. **fifteen cents a slug.** "With an exchange rate of two Filipino pesos to one Yankee dollar, [in the Philippines] even a lowly Army private could claim a share of the good life on his $21-a-month salary. A half-liter peck of gin cost about 15 cents." Bill Sloan, *Undefeated,* Simon & Schuster, 2012: 3.

74. **slipped him a mickey.** A mickey—a drink laced with chloral hydrate (or some other drug) that acts as a strong sedative—is often the tool of pickpockets and rapists. Joe notes that the driver said he could smell it, but mickeys are typically odorless. https://www.independent.co.uk/life-style/drink-spike-how-to-stop-protect-clubbing-bars-drinkaware-spiking-a8546726.html

75. **"May the good Lord watch over our two dumb asses."** Joe's toast is verbatim from his notes. Estate archives.

76. **Conversation in front of brothel.** Joe records this dialogue more than one way in his writings, implying that both Dale and Joe offered their hesitancies at first, yet Dale ultimately did the leading. In one draft Joe describes leading the way up the stairs with Dale right behind him, suggesting that Joe was more eager than Dale. Yet in another draft he says Dale was indeed behind him, but the older soldier had his hand on Joe's back and was pushing the younger boy up the stairs. Estate archives.

77. **to put them back on.** Once he was inside the room, Joe stated, he regretted his decision ever to walk up the brothel's steps. Estate archives.

Chapter 5: The Girl Named Perpetua

78. **and 7,000 artillery pieces.** "Nazis Declare War on Russia; Attack by Land, Sea and Air; Rumania, Finland Join Drive," *Philadelphia Inquirer,* June 22, 1941, Newspapers.com; "Germany Launches Operation Barbarossa—the Invasion of Russia," History.com: https://www.history.com/this-day-in-history/germany-launches-operation-barbarossathe-invasion-of-russia

79. **from each soldier's pay.** Joe's notes. Estate archives.

80. **ordered to double-time.** This was the fastest rate of marching for troops in the US Army, requiring that 180 paces be taken in a minute. Dictionary.com.

81. **for contracting a sexually transmitted disease.** Joe noted that this breach brought an automatic thirty days in lockup, plus the loss of one stripe. Estate archives.

82. **a bugler is reassigned to headquarters staff.** "Bugle Calls," FAS Military Analysis Network: https://fas.org/man/dod-101/sys/land/bugle.htm

83. **Prewar prostitution in Manila.** "Most of the prostitutes in Manila came from the local population. They belonged to the working class, although some were foreigners. Their ages ranged from thirteen to thirty. Many of them started young. Almost all were illiterates, owing to their poverty.... They were isolated young women...driven by empty stomach[s]." Luis C. Dery, "Prostitution in Colonial Manila," *Philippine Studies* vol. 39, no. 4 (1991): 475–489. http://www.philippinestudies.net/files/journals/1/articles /2248/public/2248-2246-1-PB.pdf

84. **diminutive in stature.** Joe writes that he didn't really notice Perpetua's height during their first encounter. Later, he noticed she was "quite short." Estate archives.

85. **"Tang's. Placido Street."** The quote is verbatim from Joe's notes, but it's doubtful the Placido Street he mentions is the modern street of the same name in Quezon City. Quezon City was chartered only in 1939, although the barrio of Novaliches, where this street lies, is an old settlement. Still, it's nine miles from Intramuros, and Filipino researcher Jay Gambol says it's doubtful that a little calesa pony and its driver would take a fare there (essentially the next city over) and back, given that even to this day it takes ages to get to Novaliches from downtown Makati. In his *MacArthur's Spies* (Viking, 2017: 74), author Peter Eisner notes, "Unemployment was high.... Women working in the clubs did not brag about the nature of their jobs; the bars were a perfect setting for prostitution, which offered much more income than bar tabs and tips." Gambol notes that the bars and nightclubs where girls might end up taking business were either in the wartime equivalent of the modern Ermita district (just south of Intramuros) or in Escolta (just across the river). The Chinese ghetto of Binondo and nearby Sampaloc, both likewise across the river, were known to contain houses of prostitution. If Manny Tang was Chinese-Filipino, Mama Rosa's might have been based in those districts.

86. *She's just a little girl in a cruel and noncaring world.* This line comes verbatim from Joe's notes. Estate archives.

87. **Morning sickness, corresponding with Joe's third visit to Perpetua.** Morning sickness typically starts after the sixth week of pregnancy. Megan Dix, RN, BSN, "When Does Morning Sickness Start?," *Healthline,* October 22, 2019.

88. **"an emergency in the far east."** United Press, "American and Philippine Armed Forces Consolidated After Economic Order Freezing Japanese Credits Is Announced by President," *Visalia Times Delta,* July 27, 1941: 1, News papers.com.

89. **in the American League, 0–0.** Ibid.

90. **"I've heard it's sure not an egg in your beer."** "An egg in your beer" was World War II slang for too much of a good thing. Rebecca Onion, "Some

Choice Bits of Slang from American Soldiers Serving in WWII," *Slate,* November 11, 2013: https://slate.com/human-interest/2013/11/military-slang -terms-used-by-soldiers-in-wwii.html

Chapter 6: She'll Make You a Star

91. **he's aged ten years since arriving in the Philippines.** In a fall 1941 letter to his mother explaining his health, Joe writes, "You age 10 years in this climate, and you feel it the minute you hit here." Estate archives.

92. **replete with old mouthpieces.** "They were all pretty crummy," Joe writes. Estate archives.

93. **Filipino love song.** The now-traditional "Kundiman" was composed by Francisco Santiago (1889–1947), with lyrics by Deogracias A. Rosario (1894– 1936). Quiliano Niñeza Anderson, *Kundiman Love Songs from the Philippines: Their Development from Folksong to Art Song and an Examination of Representative Repertoire* [doctor of musical arts thesis], University of Iowa, 2015: 24. https://iro.uiowa.edu/discovery/fulldisplay/alma998377714 8002771/01IOWA_INST:ResearchRepository

94. **"You bring out all the good in me."** This dialogue from Joe's fourth meeting with Perpetua is based on his notes. Again, their relationship was not consummated this time. Estate archives.

95. **Joe doesn't want his friends to be involved.** In Joe's notes, he mentions casually floating the idea of helping the girl with a couple of guys on base. It's unclear whether he spoke to both Dale and Ray, or just Dale. He did this long before he worked out a plan. He was told not to stick his nose where it doesn't belong. Estate archives.

96. **Nun's secret knock.** Verbatim from Joe's notes. Estate archives.

97. **"You may call me Sister Carmella."** Joe refers to her as Sister Carmella in all his drafts, but in a 1994 email he noted this name is a pseudonym. Estate archives.

98. **a white sharkskin suit.** Researcher Jay Gambol has verified the authenticity of this detail.

99. **Major's actions and Manny Tang's apology.** Verbatim from Joe's notes. Estate archives.

Part II

100. **That was a riot.** Joe's first marriage was to a young woman named Betty Jean Anderson, though no records of the marriage can be found. The author's research assistant, Karen Sue Clark, combed through state marriage records for Tennessee and all surrounding states and came up empty. Variants of names were also tried. Because they were married in Betty Jean's

mother's backyard, perhaps the ceremony was not performed by an officiant who required Joe and Betty Jean to register their license with the county or state. Or perhaps the officiant didn't have them sign a license at all. Unfortunately, divorce records were sparsely compiled for that region during that era. In taped interviews, Joe describes the experience cavalierly: "I was home about 30 minutes and fell in love [with her]. She fell in love with me. She was in 11th grade at Humes High School. We got married at her mama's house, backyard." Joe's interviews with Steve Graig, 2016.

101. **how banged up I was back then.** Joe was hospitalized both in the Philippines at war's end and stateside when he came home. He was released from the hospital in January 1946. John General interview with Joe Johnson, October 25, 2000. Estate archives.

102. **"Malnutrition—severe."** Joe's hospital records, October 20, 1945. Estate archives.

103. **precursor of the USAF.** Joe was honorably discharged from the US Army on January 25, 1946. He entered the United States Army Air Forces the next day and served until January 25, 1949. He enlisted with the Air Force (as it had been renamed in 1947) again on April 23, 1949, and served until November 4, 1949. His serial numbers were the same for the Army and Air Force, but changed when he joined the Marine Corps in 1950. Dates of military service are from estate archives.

104. **I joined the Marine Corps reserve.** Joe joined the Marines on November 9, 1950, and served until June 7, 1951. He enlisted in the Corps again on January 10, 1952, and served until February 10, 1953. Military records, estate archives.

105. **being too close to Nagasaki.** Veterans Administration letter to Joe Johnson from Tony Guagliardo, Director, Health Eligibility Center, VA Health Care, January 3, 2012. Estate archives.

106. **I was real messed up.** Joe's second wife, whom he met in San Antonio, was Emma Lea Richardson. Their son Floyd Charles was named after her older brother and Joe's little brother. Interviews with family members, estate archives.

107. **a military psych ward in Palo Alto.** Joe tells this story several different ways. His family members agree he attended the clinic, but many of the details remain a mystery. Joe vacillates between serious descriptions of his time in the ward ("I went crazy. My mind was warped") and lighthearted ones ("None of us was crazy. Actually, I started bucking the system"). Family members don't doubt his severe PTSD. They interpret Joe's offhanded telling of the psych-ward stories as his minimizing the experience in a spirit of retrospective bravado. In one interview he notes, "Being back in the military [the Marines], I got to where I was up to here [motions to

his chin]. I could get people pissed off at me, and I was a smart-ass. You can't live your life like that....I was living in the Bay Area, Palo Alto, and they have a hospital there. They sent me up to two psychiatrists." One quote perhaps best summarizes his experiences: "I survived all that shit." Steve Graig interviews; Tom Zmugg interview; family interviews. Estate archives.

Chapter 7: Horizon of Hurt

108. **reveal his true age to the Army.** Joe's letter to his mother, October 8, 1941. Estate archives.

109. **Prewar letter begging to come home.** The wording of this undated letter is verbatim from the estate archives.

110. **Edna Jerkins's letter to her son.** November 1941. Verbatim from estate archives.

111. **The bike.** Joe describes the motorcycle a few times in his notes without ever mentioning the brand. It may have been a Harley-Davidson WLA, eventually nicknamed "the Liberator," the main motorcycle used by US armed forces after 1939. Other bikes saw limited circulation in Allied war efforts, including several versions of the Indian brand, which was more often used with a sidecar. Robert Kim, "D-Day History Classic: The Harley-Davidson WLA in the Second World War," CurbsideClassic.com, June 6, 2019. https://www.curbsideclassic.com/blog/history/d-day-history-classic-the-harley-davidson-wla-in-the-second-world-war/

112. **including American pilots.** *Invasion of the Philippine Islands.* C. Peter Chen, "Invasion of the Philippine Islands," World War II Database, https://ww2db.com/battle_spec.php?battle_id=46

113. **"girls squealed until early morning."** Lowe, *31st Infantry Regiment,* 87.

114. **"This is no drill!"** News of Pearl Harbor first arrived in Manila at 2:30 a.m., when PFC Norman Tant from the 409th Signal Company pulled a coded message off the teletype machine from the Hawaiian Department and began unscrambling it. The message read simply, "Attention all commanders. Japan has begun hostilities. Conduct yourselves accordingly." By 4:15 a.m. the message began to circulate among the upper brass. William H. Bartsch, *December 8, 1941: MacArthur's Pearl Harbor,* Texas A&M University Press, 2003: 275.

115. **Lieutenant's calm words after Pearl Harbor attack.** Verbatim from Joe's notes. Estate archives.

116. **Japanese attacks on December 7 and 8, 1941.** Louis Morton, *The Fall of the Philippines,* Center of Military History, United States Army, Washington, DC, 1953: 77. https://history.army.mil/books/wwii/5-2/5-2_5.htm

117. **"boy scouts with kites could take these damned islands."** Bartsch, 60.

118. **Words of President Quezon.** *World War II in the Philippines,* Official Gazette, the Presidential Communications Development and Strategic Planning Office. https://www.officialgazette.gov.ph/araw-ng-kagitingan-2013/world -war-ii-in-the-philippines/

119. **will be ready to fight back.** In his notes, Joe reported seeing the V formation of Japanese planes. These were twenty-seven Mitsubishi G4M Navy attack bombers, nicknamed the Betty by the Allies and the Hamaki ("cigar") by the Japanese. "The Mitsubishi G4M3 Model 34 BETTY," National Air and Space Museum, Smithsonian Institution. https://www.si.edu/object/mit subishi-g4m3-model-34-betty%3Anasm_A19600336000; John Toland, *But Not in Shame: The Six Months After Pearl Harbor,* Random House, 1961: 66.

120. **and the base at Cabanatuan.** The bombing of these three sites occurred before 10 a.m. Kit C. Carter and Robert Mueller, *Combat Chronology: 1941–1945,* Center for Air Force History, 1991: 4. https://media.defense .gov/2010/May/25/2001330283/-1/-1/0/AFD-100525-035.pdf

121. **never got off the ground . . . and were destroyed.** John T. Correll, "Disaster in the Philippines," *Air Force Magazine,* November 1, 2019. https://www.air forcemag.com/article/disaster-in-the-philippines/

122. **The yard was destroyed.** Jason McDonald, "Cavite Navy Yard Burns After Japanese Air Raid," World War II Multimedia Database, 2010. https:// worldwar2database.com/gallery/wwii1434; John A. Adams Jr., *The Fightin' Texas Aggie Defenders of Bataan & Corregidor,* Texas A&M University Press, 2016: 27.

123. **Japan has also bombed airfields. . . .** Ibid.

124. **surprising calm . . . to concentrate Allied efforts against the main Japanese attack.** Louis Morton, "The Fall of the Philippines," from *U.S. Army in World War II: The War in the Pacific,* Center of Military History, United States Army, 1952: 103–121. http://www.ibiblio.org/hyperwar/USA/USA-P -PI/index.html#6

125. **"I don't think anybody knows what they're doing."** Ray's comment is verbatim from Joe's notes. Estate archives.

126. **a new, larger uniform . . . He gets a haircut.** Joe records these quotidian activities in his notes. Estate archives.

127. **Father Bruno.** Joe explains in a 2004 email that this is a pseudonym. Estate archives.

128. **rumors the Americans will abandon Manila.** Early rumors around the city abounded—among them that the Americans would abandon the islands entirely, that the Japanese were landing paratroopers on the islands (the parachutists sighted were in fact American fliers escaping their burning planes), and that saboteurs were ready to strike Manila's water systems.

Toland, 69–70; Morton, 115 (the latter writes, "No one knew what to believe").

129. **troops will soon land near…Lingayen.** The main attacks on the Philippines would begin on December 22, 1941. Adams, 26–27.

130. **The streets are murky.** Morton, 115–116. ("The criminal element in the city took full advantage of the darkness and confusion.")

131. **barricaded their doors.** Ibid., 116.

132. **"I know this guy….He's okay."** Joe writes, "I couldn't believe it when Coot let me through the Pasig River Bridge checkpoint with my ragtag convoy of pregnant girls. For whatever reason, he let us through." Estate archives.

133. **Japanese paratroopers who never materialize.** Lowe, *31st Infantry Regiment*, 93.

134. **conquering large sections of the country.** "Attacks on the Philippines, Guam, and Wake," Naval History and Heritage Command, July 8, 2019. https://www.history.navy.mil/browse-by-topic/wars-conflicts-and-operations/world-war-ii/1941/philippines.html; Morton, 77–96.

135. **President Quezon flees to Corregidor.** Morton, 164.

136. **MacArthur has declared Manila an *open city*.** John W. Whitman, "Manila: How Open Was This Open City?," History Net. https://www.historynet.com/manila-how-open-was-this-open-city-january-98-world-war-ii-feature.htm

137. **The enemy lays waste to entire blocks.** Associated Press, "Manila Promised Safety After Raids Ruin Center," *Charlotte Sunday Observer*, December 28, 1941: 1, Newspapers.com.

138. **ships…aren't coming in or leaving Manila's port now.** Joe notes in a 2007 interview with Barbara Hatch that only four military vessels left Manila each year bound for the States—one every three months. Joseph Quitman Johnson Collection (AFC/2001/001/60167), Veterans History Project, American Folklife Center, Library of Congress.

Chapter 8: Digging the Ashes

139. **and rained bombs on the men.** Lowe, 91.

140. **The silent rail lines.** Ralph Forty, "The Corregidor Tramway," Historic Corregidor. https://corregidor.org/chs_campbell/rails.htm

141. **if the bombing will last forever.** The December 29, 1941, bombing of Corregidor went on for three riotous hours. John McCullough, "Manila Bay's Forts Bombed for 3 Hours; Army on New Line," *Philadelphia Inquirer*, December 30, 1941: 1, 2.

142. **Both are found in the rubble, dead.** Joe lists the names as Private Earl Petrimoux (different spelling) and Sergeant George Gensell, whereas historian Karl Lowe spells Earl's last name Petrimeaux and lists George Gensel (one

l) as a private (Lowe, 96). Lowe reports that Earl suffered two broken legs initially, then died the next day; Joe reports that Earl was found dead, while noting that he didn't look too closely and was still suffering the aftereffects of the bombing. In an unpublished diary (https://philippinediaryproject.com/1942/01/04/dec-24-1941-jan-4-1942/), Lieutenant Colonel Edward H. Bowes lists the names and ranks slightly differently: Corporal Earl Petrimously and Private George Gensel. The 31st Infantry Regiment Association lists Corporal Earl Petrimeaux with a date of death as December 31, 1941 (two days after the initial attack) and Private George Gensel with a date of death as December 29, 1941. According to the association, Private Leo Boles, Sergeant Cyril Provaznik, and Private Vernon Sutton also died in other locations around Corregidor in the December 29 bombings. http://31stinfantry-org.vps-vetventures-org.vps.ezhostingserver.com/World-War-2

143. **at least so it's thought.** The Allies' joint Army-Navy plan for defending the Philippines, completed eight months before Pearl Harbor, was called *War Plan Orange 3*, or WPO-3. In short, the plan called for the defense of central Luzon, the largest island. If lines could not be held, Allied forces would withdraw primarily to the Bataan peninsula for at least six months. By then, the US Navy could bring in reinforcements. Donald J. McNally, "What Price Surrender? The Court-Martial of General Edward P. King," US Department of State, US Army War College, 1996: 2–3. https://apps.dtic.mil/dtic/tr/fulltext/u2/a309256.pdf

144. **swiftlets and jungle fowl.** Dennis Lepage, "Bataan," Avibase: The World Bird Database, 2021. https://avibase.bsc-eoc.org/checklist.jsp?region=PHluba

145. *digging the ashes.* "Abucay, Bataan." https://www.bataan.gov.ph/government/city-municipalities/abucay/

146. **canned corned beef and hardtack biscuits.** So limited in variety were C rations early in the war that the troops often called them *C-Rats*. More varieties were introduced as the war progressed, including spaghetti, chopped ham, eggs and potatoes, noodles, pork and beans, ham and lima beans, and chicken and vegetables. David Vergun, "'C-Rats' Fueled Troops During and After World War II," US Department of Defense, August 13, 2019. https://www.defense.gov/Explore/Features/Story/Article/1933268/c-rats-fueled-troops-during-and-after-world-war-ii/

147. **"Did they tell you it's an easy job?"** Joe would later write about the position, "As a runner I saw a broader field. At first, I was naïve, not realizing how dangerous a job it was. But I learned quickly which areas were likely to have snipers in the trees and the snipers' favorite type of trees. I knew the safer routes, and also to be wary of both friend and foe. Quick on the trigger friendly fire can kill you." Estate archives.

148. **Private Rosbel Ybarra.** Joe relates this story twice in his writings, referring to the other runner as Private Jasso in one passage and as Private Ybarra in another. Rosters confirm that the C Company bugler was Private Rosbel S. Ybarra. "World War II Prisoners of the Japanese File, 2007 Update," National Archives. https://aad.archives.gov/aad/display-partial-records.jsp ?f=4512&mtch=2396&q=C&dt=2212&bc=&rpp=20&pg=70

149. **In a mix of dreams.** Describing his dreams in the Philippines, Joe mentioned how images would mingle: "My mind was full of wild dreams that kept racing and tripping over themselves." Estate archives.

Chapter 9: Ache from the Hacienda

150. **so he darts off the trail.** Joe notes, "For several weeks I lost all control of my bowels." Estate archives.

151. **Bamboo explosion.** Joe recounts this story several different ways at different times in his writings and interviews, but the main pieces all line up. He often downplays the severity of the wounds he received, but once lets on that the explosion could have easily taken his life. Estate archives.

152. **almost 78,000 Allied troops are now fighting on Bataan.** "April 9, 1942: Troops Surrender in Bataan, Philippines, in Largest-Ever U.S. Surrender," History.com, November 5, 2009. https://www.history.com/this-day-in-history/u-s-surrenders-in-bataan

153. **Jonathan Wainwright.** C. Peter Chen, World War II Database. https://ww2db.com/person_bio.php?person_id=78

154. **George Parker.** "The Generals of WWII," https://generals.dk/general/Parker/George_Marshall_Jr./USA.html

155. **Albert Jones.** Charles Underwood Jr., *Deadline: Captain Charlie's Bataan Diary*, Piscataqua Press, 2013: 72.

156. **Edward King.** American Defenders of Bataan and Corregidor Museum. https://philippinedefenders.pastperfectonline.com/archive/86CD8FC4-6D77-45D2-A008-167063116554

157. **"sixteenth move."** In *Undefeated* (117), Bill Sloan attributes this line to Captain Ralph Hibbs, medical officer of the 2nd Battalion.

158. **ration of horse.** Donald Knox, *Death March: The Survivors of Bataan*, Harcourt Brace Jovanovich, 1981: 86.

159. **the 31st sees almost constant combat.** For an extended description of the battle at Abucay and beyond, see the blog dedicated to Private First Class Denicio Macogay, 45th Infantry Regiment (Philippine Scouts), particularly "Along the Balantay: The 45th Infantry Regiment (PS) at the Abucay Line, Part 3." https://bataancampaign.wordpress.com/page/6/

160. **shrapnel seems to rain down.** Sloan, 118.

161. **26,000 civilian refugees were shifted.** "January 2, 1942: Manila Falls to Japan," World War Two Daily: World War II Day by Day. http://worldwart wodaily.filminspector.com/2019/04/january-2-1941-manila-falls-to -japan.html

162. **massive reinforcements.** Major John W. Whitman, *US Army Doctrinal Effectiveness on Bataan, 1942: The First Battle* (master's-degree thesis), US Army Command and General Staff College, 1984: 2. https://apps.dtic.mil /dtic/tr/fulltext/u2/a147751.pdf

163. **throwing me a party.** Joe relates his sixteenth birthday two different ways in his writings. In one he simply records, "No one cared." In the other he becomes more philosophical, almost wryly jocular, as presented in this book. Estate archives.

164. **bouts of fighting in Abucay.** Joe describes little of the actual fighting in his written narratives. But in his later years he typed a short poem, titled "Abu-cay Hacienda Remembered," about the action he had witnessed in January 1942:

    From out of the brush and fields of cane
    They staggered in, some helping the lame.
    With faces drawn, their eyes filled with hurt,
    Their tunics in shreds, and coated with dirt.
    For rest and water, a respite to revive.
    To stop this enemy, they need stay alive.
    They held their ground, through many a round.
    Artillery, mortars, and bullets did abound.
    "Pro Patria" for country, their motto said.
    They fought and died as many of them bled.
    The Nation's finest in this hour of need.
    Held back the enemy so others could succeed.

    Estate archives. (*Pro Patria*, or "For Country," is the motto of the 31st Infantry Regiment.)

165. **"Always check the trees, especially the tall ones."** This warning to the patrol is verbatim from Joe's notes. Estate archives.

166. **Too many bites can kill a man.** "Beware of the Bugs: Fire Ants Can Kill Americans," ABC News, July 2, 2006. https://abcnews.go.com/GMA /Health/story?id=2143091&page=1

167. **Joe stares at the lifeless face.** "RICO, Raymond, Private, 31st Infantry Regiment, US Army, Service #19051701, Enl. California. Walls of the Missing, World War II, Bronze Star, Purple Heart." http://www.interment.net/data /philippines/manila-american/surnames-r.html

Chapter 10: Final Days of Bataan

168. **the ubiquitous dust.** War correspondent Clark Lee spent several weeks hitchhiking around the back roads of the peninsula in February 1942. He described the constant, thick dust as one of the worst hardships of travel. Clark Lee, "'Bottomless' Dust Chokes Bataan Roads," *San Francisco Examiner,* February 9, 1942: 10.

169. **choking talcum waves.** Much of the soil on Bataan is volcanic, yet weathered and extremely fine, almost like talcum powder. Wilfredo B. Collado et al., *Simplified Keys to Soil Series: Bataan,* Philippine Rice Research Institute, 2013. https://www.philrice.gov.ph/wp-content/uploads/2015/08/Simplified -Keys-to-Soil-Series-Bataan.pdf

170. **nor does he care that much anymore.** "I was lost," Joe wrote. "I had lost my best friend. I had lost my desire to live, and I didn't know how to cope with it." Estate archives.

171. **expectation to survive each day.** Joe wrote: "You were expected to survive each day, and you were expected to survive the next day, and the next day, and on and on. Don't you dare not survive. You are needed. You must survive." Estate archives.

172. **a fraction of its former size.** Joe's observations, estate archives; Mack Dean, "WW2 Army Units and Sizes," June 6, 2021. http://www.worldwar2facts .org/ww2-army-units-and-sizes.html

173. **and flew to Australia.** Captain Robert Bulkley Jr., *At Close Quarters: PT Boats in the United States Navy,* Naval History Division, 1962: 13–19; James M. Scott, *Rampage: MacArthur, Yamashita, and the Battle of Manila,* W. W. Norton & Company, 2018: 1–3.

174. **No mail is . . . reaching the islands.** Edna Jerkins, Joe's mother, wrote at least three letters to her son between the events of Pearl Harbor (December 7, 1941) and the fall of Bataan (April 9, 1942) that are still found in the estate archives. All three letters are marked *Return to Sender: Service Suspended,* meaning they never reached Joe.

In the first, dated December 11, 1941, she writes, "My dear Little Boy. Just wonder how you are and what you are doing to-nite? I can imagine there must be quite a bit of excitement over there, but all we can do is just hope and pray that everything will come out alright, and you must be a brave Little American. I am proud of you. . . . Naturally I worry about you, but you just obey commands, and I believe we both will come out winners. . . . Remember that I love you lots."

In the second (December 18, 1941) she writes, "My Dear Little Joe. We are all sitting around listening to the radio. That's about all we do now. . . . Baby, please be careful. Mother prays all the time for you."

And in the third (December 29, 1941) she indicates that she received Joe's Christmas greeting to her (which Joe had sent in mid-November) and that she had mailed him a camera for Christmas (which Joe never received). She reaffirms her love for Joe, then ends with this postscript: "Son, write me just as often as possible, as you know what a strain I must live in."

On February 24, 1942, Edna received a letter from the War Department referencing a letter that she had written to the department on February 10, 1942, requesting information about her son. The department's letter reads, in part: "The records of this office show that Corporal Joseph Q. Johnson, Army serial number 19,056,236, is still serving in the Philippine Department. I regret to advise you that mail service to and from the Philippine Islands has been temporarily suspended. Due to the present situation existing in the Philippines, it is impossible to give the present status of enlisted men serving there. However, I am glad to advise you that the name of your son has not been shown on any casualty list." (Note also that the War Department mistakenly refers to Joe as a corporal. Joe was always a private.)

175. **lighting their cigarettes on the flaming bamboo.** Toland, *But Not in Shame,* 282–285.

176. **Description of aid station and field hospital.** "All the Angels of Bataan," March 7, 2014. https://bataancampaign.wordpress.com/2014/03/07/all-the-angels-of-bataan; Elizabeth M. Norman, *We Band of Angels: The Untold Story of American Nurses Trapped on Bataan by the Japanese,* Random House, 1999.

177. **"Late January, I turned sixteen."** Dale and Joe's dialogue with the doctor is verbatim from Joe's notes, estate archives.

178. **"He died a few hours after he was admitted."** A January 27, 1949, article in the *Amsterdam Recorder* [New York] recounts how the body of Captain Christopher J. Heffernan was brought home to the United States (archived at https://rgoing.livejournal.com/360139.html). Interestingly, the article reports Heffernan's date of death as April 9, 1942, which corresponds with Joe's notes and also the date published by the 31st Infantry Regiment Association. Yet the article contains two errors: The captain was not part of the Bataan Death March, nor did he die of malaria in a Japanese prison hospital on Bataan. Rather, Heffernan died the day Bataan surrendered (just before the march), and Mariveles was still an Allied field hospital at that point (not under Japanese control).

179. **in the hospital bombing.** Ten bombs fell. See also the account of Nurse Juanita Redmond in Norman, 80.

180. **He messes himself and keeps jogging.** Joe recounted this story to his relatives years later, saying he had uncontrollable diarrhea all the way across to Corregidor. Ultimately, he was glad to be dragged through the water. Interviews with the author.

181. **"and using us as bait."** This shark joke is verbatim from Joe's notes, estate archives.

Chapter 11: So Utterly Alone

182. **Features of wartime Corregidor.** "The Battle of Corregidor, the Battle That Forced MacArthur out of the Philippines," The Robinson Library, http://www.robinsonlibrary.com/history/history/worldwar2/corregidor.htm

183. **known as Monkey Point.** Timothy J. Mucklow, "The Navy Tunnel Station Cast: Tip of the Lance," *Federal History,* 2011. http://www.shfg.org/resources/Documents/FH%203%20(2011)%20Mucklow%20.pdf

184. **emaciated and sick.** War Department officials estimated that more than half of all troops left on Bataan by the time of its surrender were incapacitated from disease. Frank Hewlett, "Quinine Lack Blamed for Fall of Bataan," *Arizona Republic,* April 18, 1942: 1.

185. **but no longer able.** "U.S. Loses Bataan Under Jap Attack," *Tampa Morning Tribune,* April 10, 1942: 1, 11.

186. **largest surrender...against a foreign enemy.** Joseph A. Bors, "Bataan's Fall Traps 36,800—Worst U.S. Reversal," *Pittsburgh Sun-Telegraph,* April 9, 1942: 1. The figure 36,800 was only an estimate—and a low one at that; later reports, including those from Corregidor, pushed the number to nearly 80,000.

187. **3.9 million.** Eventually more than 36 million Americans would register for the draft, and 16 million troops total would serve in the US armed services during World War II. "Research Starters: US Military by the Numbers," The National WWII Museum, https://www.nationalww2museum.org/students-teachers/student-resources/research-starters/research-starters-us-military-numbers; "Take a Closer Look: America Goes to War," The National WWII Museum, https://www.nationalww2museum.org/students-teachers/student-resources/research-starters/america-goes-war-take-closer-look

188. **A massive effort is underway.** General Gordon Sullivan, *Mobilization: The U.S. Army in World War II,* US Center of Military History, 16–17. https://history.army.mil/documents/mobpam.htm

189. **the country will be avenged.** "Bataan Falls to Jap Horde," *Salt Lake Telegram,* April 9, 1942: 1.

190. **perishing along the way.** Many informative and graphic accounts have been written about the ordeal of the Bataan Death March. Manny Lawton's *Some Survived* (Algonquin Books, 2015) is a stirring first-person memoir, while *Tears in the Darkness* by Michael Norman and Elizabeth M. Norman, is an authoritative third-person treatment. The Normans write about survivor Ben Steele, who also sketched a number of pictures about his experiences.

191. **one of the ghastliest American experiences.** "Bataan Death March," November 9, 2009, updated June 7, 2019, History.com. https://www.history.com/topics/world-war-ii/bataan-death-march

192. **Many haven't eaten for days.** Dean Schedler, "Nurses, Soldiers Rest After Escape to Isle Fortress," *Sacramento Bee,* April 11, 1942: 6.

193. **and drop bombs.** "Official U.S. Communique, April 4, 1942," *Boston Globe,* April 14, 1942: 3.

194. **Corregidor can be held.** "Wainwright Due to Hold Corregidor," *Santa Cruz Sentinel-News* (evening edition), April 15, 1942: 1.

195. **drop bombs, one after another.** No exact tally exists of the number of bombs and artillery rounds that struck the island, but it has been estimated that Corregidor withstood more than 300 full-scale Japanese air raids and literally hundreds of thousands of heavy artillery rounds—up to 16,000 in a single day. Bill Sloan, "Corregidor: The Last Battle in the Fall of the Philippines," HistoryNet. https://www.historynet.com/corregidor-the-last-battle-in-the-fall-of-the-philippines.htm

196. **and black-naped orioles.** "Eco Corregidor," https://corregidor.org/eco/tee hankee/index_01.htm

197. **"I love you like a brother. I always will."** Spoken to Dale verbatim. Joe's notes, estate archives.

198. **seemingly able to drop rounds into any deep ravine.** This observation about high trajectories and narrow placement has been credited to General King. Sloan, "Corregidor."

199. **by order of General Wainwright.** Just before the surrender, General Wainwright transmitted a radio message to President Roosevelt: "There is a limit of human endurance, and that point has long been passed." Donnie Hudgens, "World War II Diary: Remembering Corregidor and the Battle of the Coral Sea...75 Years Later," *Rome New Tribune,* May 6, 2017. https://www.northwestgeorgianews.com/world-war-ii-diary/article_7dda2732-3341-5a95-a319-ffb88fd017e7.html

200. **a month since the fall of Bataan.** "The Battle of Corregidor," The Robinson Library.

201. **Corregidor...has fallen.** John M. McCullough, "10,000 Lost in Fall of Corregidor," *Philadelphia Inquirer,* May 7, 1942: 1.

202. **one small potato for each prisoner.** Joe's notes, estate archives.

203. **no idea when they will be freed—if ever.** I am grateful to Major General Robert Preston Taylor for the idea that a POW's experience differed from that of a regular prisoner because no concrete sentence had been imposed on the former. Chaplain Taylor was captured during the fall of Bataan, then survived the Death March and a series of prison camps including Bilibid, Cabanatuan, and several in Japan. Interview with Robert Preston Taylor,

World War II POW, University of North Texas Oral History Program; interview with Ronald Marcello, *Humanities Texas,* March 2015. https://www
.humanitiestexas.org/news/articles/interview-robert-preston-taylor-world
-war-ii-pow

204. **barracks after barracks.** The description of the Cabanatuan POW Camp is
from Taylor.

205. **Every fifteen yards...another man died.** Colonel John A. Adams, "75th
Anniversary of Battle of Bataan & Corregidor," March 7, 2017, The Dr.
Harold C. Deutsch World War II History Roundtable. https://www.youtube
.com/watch?v=x7qW0Z90bow

206. **"I am Commander Mori."** The wording of this speech is from Joe's notes,
estate archives. Joe identifies him as Captain Maita, but that is likely a pho-
netic remembrance, or something was initially lost in translation. The
speaker was most probably Lieutenant Colonel Shigeji Mori, commander of
Cabanatuan from May 1942 onward, who in 1947 was sentenced by a military commission to "confinement at hard labor for the term of his natural
life." *United States of America vs Shigeji Mori,* Headquarters Eighth Army,
United States Army, Office of the Staff Judge Advocate, Yokohama, Japan,
November 22, 1948. This trial is archived at http://www.mansell.com/pow
_resources/camplists/philippines/Cabanatuan/IMTFE_Case240_MORI
_Cabanatuan.pdf. In *Ghost Soldiers* (Anchor Books, 2001: 135), author
Hampton Sides describes Mori as "a calm, impenetrable man in his late fif-
ties who was said to have run a bicycle shop in Manila before the war."

207. **dig mass graves, and bury the dead.** Taylor.

208. **a man begins to recite the Lord's Prayer.** Specific to Joe's notes. Estate
archives.

209. **"Dale L. Snyder."** Cause of death: beheading. Date of death: May 30, 1942.
"The Birth of the 31st Infantry Regiment and Beyond," from *World War II,*
independently published: 36. Estate archives.

Part III

210. **That major.** Joe identifies him in three drafts of his manuscript as Major
Waltham, but this was a pseudonym. It's unclear from 31st Infantry records
who he was. Joe tells this story of meeting him again in Cabanatuan No. 1,
almost verbatim, in his notes. Estate archives.

211. **My mother...told him my real age.** Interestingly, Edna Jerkins gives no
hints in her letters to Joe in November–December of 1941 that she has written to the general—at least not in any letters found in the estate archives. It
may have been that she was trying to keep his spirits up, and didn't want him
to be disappointed if she was unable to get him out of the Army. Likewise,

Joe gives no indication that he has been informed of her request to the general until Joe meets the major in the POW hospital camp in spring 1942. The estate archives do show a letter from the War Department to Edna Jerkins dated May 20, 1942, indicating she was trying to track down Joe's whereabouts after the surrenders. The only information provided to her, with deep regrets, is that Joe "was serving in the Philippine Islands at the time of the final surrender," and that he—along with all American soldiers in that engagement—is currently considered "missing in action from the date of the surrender of Corregidor, May 7, 1942, until definite information to the contrary is received."

212. **if I wanted to escape with him.** Joe's notes, estate archives.

213. **Didn't think long about his offer.** Surviving in the jungle would have been difficult, yet not impossible. Indeed, a few hundred US soldiers managed to escape imprisonment or elude capture in the first place. See, for instance, Bob Welch, *Resolve,* Berkley Caliber, 2012.

214. **any Filipino who turned in an escaped American prisoner.** Cecilia Gaerlan, executive director of the Bataan Legacy Historical Society, offers some perspective on this inducement: "Although Japan granted the Philippines its 'independence' in 1943 as part of its Greater East Asia Co-Prosperity Sphere program, the Filipinos suffered greatly from atrocities inflicted not only on suspected guerrillas but on many innocent civilians. Torture, rape, pillage, and massacres, sometimes of entire villages, took place all over the country. The Kempei Tai (Japanese military police) used the method of 'Zonification,' rounding up suspected insurgents with the help of Filipino collaborators called Makapilis.... It was the same system that was used during the occupation of Manchuria and more frequently during the Second Sino-Japanese War. When liberation started on October 20, 1944, Zonification was used with more frequency and impunity." Gaerlan, "Liberating the Philippines: 75 Years After," The National WWII Museum, September 1, 2020. https://www.nationalww2museum.org/war/articles/liberation-of-phi lippines-cecilia-gaerlan

215. **they'd shoot five prisoners, sometimes ten.** Two of the numerous reports of this practice are to be found in Bob Reynolds, *Of Rice and Men,* Mindanao Books, 2019: 59–60, and in the testimony of PFC Harold G. Kurvers, archived at the Bataan Project, https://bataanproject.com/provisional-tank-group /kurvers-pfc-harold-g/

216. **That hell was mine, and mine alone.** The thoughts on the extreme loneliness that Joe felt are taken verbatim from his notes. Estate archives.

Chapter 12: Prerogative of Madness

217. **at the Pasay schoolhouse.** The Pasay Central School was closed by Japanese authorities when World War II broke out. It was reopened in March of 1945 with a new name, Epifanio Delos Santos Elementary School. Later it was renamed Padre Burgos Elementary School. Republic of the Philippines, Schools Division Office—Pasay City. https://www.depedpasay.ph/history/

218. **Thirty prisoners sleep in each classroom.** Joe recorded this number as thirty (three rows of ten), while former POW Al McGrew states the number was twenty (two rows of ten). See *Description by Al McGrew of His Arrival at Pasay,* http://www.mansell.com/pow_resources/camplists/philippines/nichols_pasay/mcgrew_arrives.html. In his *Conduct Under Fire: Four American Doctors and Their Fight for Life as Prisoners of the Japanese* (Penguin Books, 2005: 216), John A. Glusman notes that some "500 men were crowded into an eighteen-room schoolhouse" at Pasay. This would put the number at nearly twenty-eight per room, making Joe's recollection of thirty more likely.

219. **have been pried up and stacked.** Republic of the Philippines, Padre Burgos Elementary School. https://pbes.depedpasay.ph/about-us/

220. **oppressive temperatures have begun.** https://en.climate-data.org/asia/philippines/bataan-1846/

221. **On the straw hat was the number *176.*** Joe records this number as both 1176 and 1358 in different writings, but the story of the guard adding the *1* in front of the lower number is consistent. Estate archives.

222. **at Camp No. 1.** Joe describes No. 1 this way: "The Japanese let American officers run things up to a certain point." Estate archives.

223. **he's still alive.** The Johnson estate still has this card. The blank lines on the card are typewritten, so for security purposes the card was probably filled in by a Japanese clerk, with Joe dictating. Interestingly, the last line has a preprinted message with a blank that reads, *Please give my best regards to* _____. Somewhat cryptically, Joe's answer is *Memphis down in Dixie.* The front of the card is stamped in purple ink and reads, *U.S. Censorship. Examined by 479.* Estate archives. Veteran Bob Reynolds, a former POW of Cabanatuan, describes a similar postcard he was ordered to fill out on January 3, 1943 (*Of Rice and Men,* 66), which might have been in the same batch of mailings. Bob's parents received his card eight months later. It was their first word that he had survived the Death March.

224. **litter the horizon.** "Invaders Halted at Other Points in Philippines; Bases Attacked Again," *Ellensburg Daily Record,* December 13, 1941. https://news.google.com/newspapers?nid=860&dat=19411213&id=tbo0AAAAIBAJ&sjid=Q4MFAAAAIBAJ&pg=5129,4610386&hl=en

225. **longest runway in the Pacific.** See an illustration of the Nichols Field work detail by Al McGrew, H Company, 60th CAC, at http://www.mansell.com /pow_resources/camplists/philippines/nichols_pasay/nichols_plot.html

226. **PFC Norman "Hicks" Hinckley Jr.** Joe recounts the story of Hicks in his own writings. Hicks's age and date of birth are from the Find a Grave website, https://www.findagrave.com/memorial/152331012/norman-hicks -hinckley,%20accessed%202%20Feb%202019. Thanks to Anastasia Harman, granddaughter of former POW Alma Salm, for making available portions of her grandfather's unpublished wartime journals, which likewise recount Hinckley's story. https://webcache.googleusercontent.com/search?q=cache :E4BFOmyktusJ and https://www.luzonholiday.com/2019/02/01/norman -hicks-hinckley-jr/+&cd=1&hl=en&ct=clnk&gl=us&client=firefox-b-1-d

227. **"Cherry Blossom," "Pistol Pete," "El Lobo," and "the White Angel."** Joe's notes describe three of these four guards but never specify "Pistol Pete"— the nickname of the labor boss at Nichols Field, who may have been named Sergeant Major Mutsuo. Affidavits by several former POWs describe him as brutal and abusive, responsible for multiple beatings. A roster titled "Nichols Field Pasay Japanese Commanders Guards" is archived at http://www .mansell.com/pow_resources/camplists/philippines/nichols_pasay/nichols _pasay.html

228. **The body lies still in the grit and blood.** Joe describes observing the twinkling sunlight on the beheading blade as it fell, as if small particles of goodness were still left in his world of horror. Estate archives.

229. **"shall meet the same fate."** The exact wording of this speech is recorded in Joe's writings. Former POW Donald Bevier verified that "the White Angel" told the prisoners, "I'm going to kill every one of you." Brad Flory, *Donald Bevier's Three Years of Suffering and Unlikely Survival for His Nation,* Michigan Live, January 12, 2015. https://www.mlive.com/opinion/jack son/2015/01/brad_flory_column_donald_bevie.html

230. **the mix of ailments that steadily beat him down.** Joe's notes. Estate archives.

231. **Hinckley passes into eternity.** Norman H. Hinckley Jr. was buried in the Naval Hospital Unit of Bilibid Prison. A limited report of his death is archived at https://www.findagrave.com/memorial/152331012/norman-hicks -hinckley,%20accessed%202%20Feb%202019.#view-photo=172913135

232. *Crazy.* The Japanese term *kichigai* (meaning "crazy" or "insane") was occasionally used as an offensive word or insult. https://glosbe.com/ja/en/kic higai

233. *In your mercy, hear us.* https://www.methodistprayer.org/all/2019/7/29 /tuesday-evening-july-30

234. **"I'm Doctor Emmerson."** In other writings, Joe also refers to him as Dr. Immerman. Estate archives.

Chapter 13: The Bilibid Prison Respite

235. **and weighs 109 pounds.** Joe's notes, estate archives.
236. **the hospital unit.** Remnants of the Naval Hospital Canacao were relocated inside the prison after the bombings of Cavite and Sangley Point. The hospital workers were prisoners themselves. André Sobucinski, *The Saga of the Northcotts: Three Brothers at Bilibid Prison*, Navy Medicine Live. https://navymedicine.navylive.dodlive.mil/archives/12474
237. **"a chance of making it."** Verbatim, as remembered, from Joe's notes. Estate archives.
238. **the major turning point in the battle of the Pacific.** Tom Hone, "The Importance of the Battle of Midway," War on the Rocks (Texas National Security Review), September 12, 2013. https://warontherocks.com/2013/09/the-importance-of-the-battle-of-midway/
239. **"fought like hell for six months."** For a variety of helpful articles, see "The Battle of Guadalcanal," The National WWII Museum, August 6, 2019. https://www.nationalww2museum.org/war/articles/battle-guadalcanal
240. **an old bedsheet as a screen.** Joe's notes, estate archives.
241. **roll it into the truck bed.** Joe describes this method of lifting a heavy barrel in his notes. Estate archives.
242. **Joe has eaten the entire bag [of sugar].** Joe's notes, estate archives.
243. **thanking God that he's still alive.** Joe's notes, estate archives.
244. **"in the blood of our two peoples."** Associated Press, "Gen. MacArthur Returns," *Daily Current-Argus* [Carlsbad, New Mexico], October 20, 1944.
245. **a base of operations.** Dale Andrade, "Luzon 1944–1945," US Army Center of Military History. https://history.army.mil/brochures/luzon/72-28.htm
246. **two or three raids a day.** "Jap Freighters Bombed in Manila Bay," *San Bernardino Daily Sun*, December 8, 1944: 1; "Yanks Reach Outskirts of Ormoc Port," *Des Moines Register*, December 9, 1944: 2.
247. **moored at the docks.** During World War II, more than 150,000 Allied prisoners were transported in Japanese "hell ships." More than 21,000 of them died. As many as 19,000 of them were killed by friendly fire. Gregory Michno, *Death on the Hellships: Prisoners at Sea in the Pacific War,* Naval Institute Press, 2001.

Chapter 14: Three Ships from Hell

248. **the *Oryoku Maru*.** Aboard this 7,362-ton passenger-cargo ship were a total of about 3,200 people, including 1,619 POWs. "*Oryoku Maru*," POW Research Network Japan: http://www.powresearch.jp/en/archive/ship/oryoku.html and https://www.mol.co.jp/en/corporate/history/index.html

249. **packed with prisoners.** Joe reports that most of the men were standing; there was nowhere to sit, at least that he could see. Lieutenant Colonel O. O. Wilson described the situation in more detail: "The only way possible of crowding that number into such a small compartment was to have each man sit jammed into the crotch of the man behind him in four rows with five men to a row. When all the bays had been filled in this fashion, all remaining space in the hold was filled by men in a standing position packed one against the other, cutting off all air for men in the bay." Account of Lt. Col. O. O. Wilson, "Trip to Japan," Darnell W. Kadolph Papers, COLL/689, box 1, folder 3, Naval History and Heritage Command, Washington, DC. https://www.history.navy.mil/browse-by-topic/wars-conflicts-and-operations/world-war-ii/1944/oryoku-maru.html

250. **1,620 Allied prisoners are on board.** Numbers for various hell ships are given in Norm Haskette, "U.S. Navy Hellcats Bomb Hellship *Enoura Maru*," The Daily Chronicles of World War II. https://ww2days.com/u-s-navy-hellcats-bomb-hellship-enoura-maru-1.html

251. **his tongue is swelling in his throat.** Recounted by hell-ship survivor Navy ensign George Petritz in Anne Stanton, "He Thought He Would Die," *Detroit Free Press,* February 11, 2004: 1B–2B.

252. **With dawn's first light.** Joe recalls that tugs moved the ship at first light. Technically, she was moved by tugs to an anchorage outside the harbor on the night of December 13, then weighed anchor and headed for Japan the next morning. POW Research Network Japan.

253. **a pail of rice and eggplant sauce.** Joe reports this meal as lunch (occurring "mid-afternoon"), but it was probably breakfast—which makes sense, given that he hadn't slept the night before and was up from the hold so early in the morning. The ship was attacked at about 8 a.m. POW Research Network Japan.

254. **unaware there are POWs aboard.** Initially, the *Oryoku Maru* sustained six rocket hits and a 250-kilogram-bomb blast, causing a fire to break out. POW Research Network Japan; Robert Nott, "Scores of Bataan POWs Died on Japanese 'Hell Ships,'" *Santa Fe New Mexican,* April 9, 2020. https://bit.ly/3sDtMxp

255. **forgiveness for the pain he's caused.** Joe's notes, estate archives.

256. **Smoke billows from its stern.** Recounted by POW George L. Curtis, watching from below the deck cover. "Nightmare of the Hellship," World War II Today. https://ww2today.com/15-december-1944-nightmare-of-the-hellship-oryoku-maru-continues

257. **on the western coast of Luzon.** Associated Press, "Survivor Tells of Japanese Inhumanity," *Windsor* [Ontario] *Daily Star,* March 23, 1946: 1.

258. **in the yellowish haze of smoke.** Most likely from burning coal reserves in the ship. George Weller, "Death Cruise: Yanks Bomb Yanks—G.I.s on Jap Hell

Ship Victims of Strafing," *Chicago Daily News*, November 13, 1945. http://www.mansell.com/pow_resources/newspaper/newsfrompast-cruiseofdeath.html

259. **a machine gun and snipers, looking for escapees.** Ibid.

260. **The ship is nearly submerged.** The *Oryoku Maru* sank soon after this. Fuller details are in Weller, "Death Cruise," Part V, and in "89 of 1,619 Americans Survived; 7 Japs Face Trial for Slaughter," *Shreveport Times*, March 20, 1947: 44.

261. **tennis courts...topped with barbed wire.** This particular ordeal was widely documented in trials at war's end. See, for instance, John Grover, "Series of Hells," *Kansas City Star*, September 9, 1945: 5A.

262. **driven to a cemetery and decapitated.** "Eight Japs to Face Trial for Deaths of 1,300 Prisoners Aboard Troopships," *Harrisburg Telegraph*, February 27, 1947: 35.

263. **The corporal passes out but stays alive.** Weller, Part V.

264. **the corporal with the amputated arm dies.** Ibid.

265. **It's Christmas morning 1944.** Weller, Part VII.

266. **fed bran and dried fish while they wait again.** Ibid.

267. **heads for the open sea.** Dr. Gregory Kupsky, "*Enoura Maru* Leaves on December 27, 1944; Is Attacked on January 9, 1945," the *Enoura Maru* Project, US Department of Defense: 5, 6. https://www.dpaa.mil/Portals/85/WWII%20Hellship%20Losses.pdf

268. **The capital is only 110 miles away.** Scott, *Rampage*, 9–10.

269. **rice is mixed with steamed fish.** Joe's notes, estate archives.

270. **tossed overboard.** Kupsky, 7.

271. **torsos protrude through the netting.** According to Kupsky (7), a total of 300 were killed. See also Lee A. Gladwin, "American POWs on Japanese Ships Take a Voyage into Hell" (Part 2), *Prologue*, Winter 2003, https://www.archives.gov/publications/prologue/2003/winter/hell-ships-2.html

272. **the ship stops moving.** By the time the *Brazil Maru* reached the port of Moji on January 30, 1945, some 440 POWs had died aboard the vessel. Bob Hackett, "BRAZIL MARU: Tabular Record of Movement," Revision 3. http://www.combinedfleet.com/Brazil_t.htm

273. **still living by the time they reached their destination.** Norm Haskette, "U.S. Navy Hellcats Bomb Hellship *Enoura Maru*," The Daily Chronicles of World War II. https://ww2days.com/u-s-navy-hellcats-bomb-hellship-enoura-maru-1.html; "2 'Hellship' Defendants to Die," *Honolulu Advertiser*, May 9, 1947: 1.

Chapter 15: *Under the Cold Ground*

274. **looking them over as if they were beef at a cattle show.** The civilians were either contractors or middlemen tasked with evaluating and then distributing men to various prisoner camps in Japan. Lawton, *Some Survived*, 214.

275. **his veins stand out like knotted cords.** POW Norman Tant, who was later incarcerated at the Omine-machi coal mine with Joe, recorded these observations of fellow prisoners. Norman Tant, "Hero of Bataan 'Death March' Recalls the Joys of Liberation Day," *Atlanta Constitution,* September 15, 1946: 1.

276. **but he keeps his smile to himself.** Joe's notes, estate archives.

277. **Then he eats the peel.** Joe's notes, estate archives.

278. **Omine-machi coal-mining camp.** Roger Mansell, "Hiroshima POW Camp #6-B: Omine, Yamaguchi," POW Resources, http://mansell.com/pow _resources/camplists/hiroshima/hiro-6-omine-yamaguchi/hiro_6_sanyo .html. In 1996, a memorial was erected at the camp entrance reading *We record the fact here, wishing eternal peace never to repeat such a tragedy as this.* Tadashi Sano, "Silent Storyteller: Former POW Camp 'Shinwa Ryo' in Mine," *Mainichi Shimbun,* August 12, 2011 (translated by Kinue Toku-dome), US-Japan Dialogue on POWs, https://www.us-japandialogueon pows.org/Ominememorial.htm

279. **care for her and her child.** Specific to the first night inside the mining camp. Joe's notes, estate archives.

280. **president for the last twelve years.** Interestingly, FDR had just attended a conference with President Sergio Osmeña of the Philippine Commonwealth during which the former reaffirmed his intention to keep Japan under Allied control and policing for an indefinite period after the war ended. "Roosevelt Dies," *La Grande* [Oregon] *Observer,* April 12, 1945: 1, 7.

281. **the ranking American officer.** This was probably Captain Jerome McDavitt. When the war was finally declared over, McDavitt was still in Omine-machi, and food and supplies were air-dropped into the camp. Fashioning an American flag from the recovered parachute silk, McDavitt and others proudly flew the Stars and Stripes over the prison camp. Bob Monk, "Ex-POW Saves His Prison Flag," *Star-Herald,* September 6, 1973: 1; Susan Owen, "Association Displays Flag Sewn by GIs in WWII Prison Camp," Association of Former Students, Texas A&M University, July 3, 2018. https://www.aggienet work.com/news/148962/association-displays-flag-sewn-by-gis-in-wwii -prison-camp/

282. **Goldie, Three Fingers, and Bill Crowley.** Emily Bavar, "Bataan Death March Survivor Knows War Scars Are Deep," *Orlando Sentinel,* April 25, 1955: 11.

283. **A likable Texan named Bob Mainer.** Joe spells this name two different ways in his notes—Mainier and Manier—and writes simply that he came from

Rusk, Texas. Most likely this was Robert Virgil Mainer of Rusk, Texas, born January 18, 1916. Mainer is listed as a sergeant in the Chemical Warfare Service. "World War II Draft Cards of Young Men, 1940–1947," National Archives, Washington, DC; Record Group Title: Records of the Office of the Provost Marshal General, 1920–1975; Record Group Number: 389; "World War II American and Allied Prisoners of War, 1941–1946" [online database], Ancestry.com, 2005.

284. **radish, and a small sardine.** The precise contents of these bento boxes are detailed in Joe's notes, estate archives.

285. **This camp's rough.** Joe describes the perplexing incident of the four prisoners arbitrarily beaten. Estate archives.

286. **sent to yet another camp.** Joe's name is found on camp rosters at Fukuoka, but only his name and rank are listed; other prisoners, by contrast, have their name, rank, next of kin, home address, and age all detailed. *Fukuoka P.O.W. Camp Names List,* National Archives and Records Administration, Declassification Review Project NND 883078, Record Group 407, Box 104, February 16, 1946. http://www.mansell.com/pow_resources/camplists/fukuoka/fuku_17/FUK-17_Rosters_1946-02-16.pdf

287. **Fukuoka POW Camp No. 17.** A few photos still exist of the camp. One of the best collections, curated by Linda Dahl, is at http://www.mansell.com/pow_resources/camppics/fukuoka/fuku-17/fuku17-pics.html

288. **some forty miles across the bay from…Nagasaki.** https://www.distancefromto.net/distance-from-nagasaki-to-omuta-jp

289. **A wooden fence…encloses the compound.** John M. Gibbs, "Fukuoka Camp No. 17 on the Island of Kyushu, Japan," July 31, 1946, American Defenders of Bataan and Corregidor Museum, https://philippinedefenders.pastperfectonline.com/archive/5433C564-4CAC-4D75-BC40-994245440878

290. **three cars of coal a day by shovel.** Testimony of PFC Harold G. Kurvers, archived at the Bataan Project, https://bataanproject.com/provisional-tank-group/kurvers-pfc-harold-g/

291. **"lung infection. Weak heart."** Joe's notes, estate archives.

292. **citizens were dying of starvation.** Scott, *Rampage,* 55–56.

293. **the Americans are hitting the port.** "Planes in Again: Fighters and Bombers Gang Up on Tokyo Airfields and City of Nagasaki," *Kansas City Star,* July 5, 1945: 2.

294. **dropping their deadly loads on…Omuta.** "Japan Seared in Fire Raid by Big Ships: Three Cities Burning After Superforts Drop Incendiaries," *Lexington Leader,* July 26, 1945: 1.

295. **He hears no sound.** Joe reported that he felt the force of the blast, but heard nothing. Estate archives.

296. **a toothbrush but no anesthesia.** Specific to Joe's notes. He described the pain, simply, as "excruciating." Estate archives.

297. **The mat is vacant.** Joe notes that Bob Mainer died in the camp hospital at Fukuoka right after the bombing of Nagasaki and the airdrops into the camp, most likely on August 9 or 10 of 1945. Other records, however, indicate that while Bob did indeed die in the Fukuoka camp hospital (of croup pneumonia), his death occurred on March 20, 1945—more than four months before the bombing. Undoubtedly the death of his friend and the end of the war were so closely intertwined in Joe's memory that he conflated the two events when describing them five decades later. "Fukuoka POW Camp #17 Omuta," Camp Rosters, Americans: http://www.mansell.com/pow_res ources/camplists/fukuoka/fuku_17/fukuoka17.htm. Robert V. Mainer's headstone can be viewed at https://www.findagrave.com/memorial/83945479 /robert-v-mainer.

298. **Joe tries to pray.** Joe's notes, estate archives.

Chapter 16: Emancipation

299. **mushroom cloud hangs over Nagasaki.** Joe recorded that prisoners in the camp reported seeing the cloud across the bay. The atom bomb was used for the second time against Japan in the bombing of Nagasaki at noon, Tokyo time, on August 9, 1945. Associated Press, "Nagasaki Hit by 2nd Atom Bomb," *Paducah Sun-Democrat*, August 9, 1945: 1.

300. **capabilities that stagger the mind.** Testimony of POW Mick Hummerston, "Fukuoka #17 Branch Prisoner of War Camp," 2/4th Machine Gun Battalion. http://2nd4thmgb.com.au/camp/omuta-miike-fukuoka-17-b-japan/

301. **reduced to wastelands.** Robert G. Nixon, "Japan's Last 30 Days," *Pittsburgh Sun-Telegraph,* August 9, 1945. Perhaps as many as 214,000 people—military personnel and civilians, men, women, and children—died from both blasts. Precise estimates were difficult to obtain because of the bombs' overwhelming destruction. Reports range from 39,000 to 74,000 dead in Nagasaki and from 66,000 to 140,000 dead in Hiroshima. Seren Morris, "How Many People Died in Hiroshima and Nagasaki?," *Newsweek,* August 3, 2020, https://www.newsweek.com/how-many-people-died-hiroshima -nagasaki-japan-second-world-war-1522276; "The Atomic Bombings of Hiroshima and Nagasaki," Atomic Archive, https://www.atomicarchive .com/resources/documents/med/med_chp10.html; Alex Wellerstein, "Counting the Dead at Hiroshima and Nagasaki," *Bulletin of the Atomic Scientists,* August 4, 2020, https://thebulletin.org/2020/08/counting-the-dead-at-hiro shima-and-nagasaki/.

302. **a full surrender without conditions.** Earnest Barcella, "Japan Surrenders Unconditionally; Hostilities Cease," *Greenville Daily Advocate,* August 15, 1945: 1.

303. **mix of melancholy and hope.** Joe described his feelings in those last few days in the camp in an August 6, 2013, email to his friend Bruce Merrihew. Estate archives.

304. **another half billion.** Associated Press, "War Ends, Japan Accepts. Truman's Announcement," *St. Louis Globe-Democrat,* August 15, 1945: 1.

305. **from three million to ten million people.** R. J. Rummel, *Statistics of Demo-cide: Genocide and Mass Murder Since 1900,* Center for National Security Law, School of Law, University of Virginia, 1997. https://www.hawaii.edu /powerkills/SOD.CHAP3.HTM

306. **by the camp's Japanese commander.** Fukuoka No. 17 was commanded by Asao Fukukara, later executed for war crimes. Martin Elvery, "VJ Day: Tribute for Brother Who Died in Prisoner of War Camp," *Oxford Mail,* August 16, 2015. https://www.oxfordmail.co.uk/news/13600458.vj-day-tri bute-brother-died-prisoner-war-camp/

307. **"and taking care of your health."** Attributed to Fukohara Tai Dona. Knox, *Death March,* 442–443.

308. **the POWs are able to leave.** Fukuoka Camp No. 17 ended up being fully liberated on September 2, 1945. John M. Gibbs, "Gibbs Report: Fukuoka #17," July 31, 1946. http://www.mansell.com/pow_resources/camplists/fu kuoka/Fuku_17/fuku_17_gibbs_report.html

309. **POW camps throughout Japan.** Some 5,000 of the estimated 34,000 Allied prisoners in Japan were ill and needed immediate medical attention; about 8,000 of these 34,000 were Americans. "Allied War Prisoners in Japan Ill, in Need of Attention," *Freeport Journal-Standard,* August 29, 1945: 1.

310. **medical kits, and canned beer.** Joe reports that the "mercy planes" first flew over the camp within days of the Nagasaki bombing. A second mercy drop of 125 Superforts dropped more than 875,000 pounds of food, clothing, and medical supplies into sixty Allied prisoner-of-war camps on Honshu and Kyushu. Twelve of these camps were near Fukuoka, where Joe was interned in Camp No. 17. United Press, "Mercy Planes 'Bomb Camps," *Abilene Reporter-News,* August 28, 1945: 1.

311. **finds its way to Joe at Fukuoka.** This letter from Edna Jerkins was addressed to Pvt. Joseph Q. Johnson, Address 19 056 236 POW, Camp Fukuoka, Hon-shu, Japan. Civilian Message Form, International Red Cross Committee, Geneva, Switzerland. Estate archives.

312. **Raymond Ward Shipley.** Shipley, born March 10, 1920, was twenty-five by the time he met Joe. His draft-registration card lists his home address as Baltimore. He died in 1995 in Riverside, California. "U.S., Social Security Applications and Claims Index, 1936–2007" [online database], Ancestry.com; "Casualties and Missing Personnel, 1939–1945" (Reference No. WO 361/1978), The National Archives, Kew, London, England; "U.S.,

World War II Prisoners of the Japanese, 1941–1945" [online database], Ancestry.com.

313. **September 12, 1945.** In Joe's first letter home to his mother, dated September 16, 1945, he writes, "I had to escape on crutches from my camp on Sept. 12. Your birthday." Estate archives.

314. **ordered to kill any remaining POWs.** The rumor of this kill order was verified after the war. Indeed, the Japanese War Ministry had issued such an order in 1944—a year before war's end: "To annihilate them all, and not to leave any traces." Civilian internees, including women and children, were also to be killed. "Primary Sources: Kill-All Policy," *Bataan Rescue,* PBS, http://www.shoppbs.pbs.org/wgbh/amex/bataan/filmmore/ps_order.html; "Order to Kill All POWs," http://www.mansell.com/pow_resources/Formosa/doc2701-trans.html and http://www.mansell.com/pow_resources/Formosa/taiwandocs.html. Laura Hillenbrand discusses this order at length in her biography of POW Louis Zamperini: "All captives were to be 'liquidated' on September 15 [1945]. Women and children would be poisoned; civilian men would be shot; the sick and disabled would be bayonetted." *Unbroken,* Random House, 2010: 291–292.

315. **glaring as the train speeds by.** Surrender came slowly for many Imperial Japanese soldiers, who had been taught to prefer death to surrender. Additionally, Imperial troops were deployed throughout the Pacific Theater, and General MacArthur estimated it would take at least twelve days for the emperor's cease-fire order to reach scattered remnants of Japan's armed forces. United Press, "Japs Tell U.S. Raid on Transports Preceded 'Cease Fire' Command," *Lancaster Intelligencer Journal:* 1, 12; "The Fate of Japanese POWs in Soviet Captivity," The National WWII Museum, August 28, 2020: https://www.nationalww2museum.org/war/articles/japanese-pows-in-soviet-captivity

316. **an American soldier wearing an M.P. armband.** Occupation troops were scheduled to arrive in Japan on Sunday, August 26, 1945, but were postponed two days by typhoons, which means Joe would have spent at least thirteen days in the POW camp after the war was declared over. "Occupation of Japan Near," *Binghamton Press,* August 21, 1945: 6; "U.S. Occupation of Japan Waits 48 Hours More," *Pittsburgh Sun-Telegraph,* August 25, 1945: 1; Leonard Milliman, "Japan Is Occupied Thursday," *Corsicana Semi-Weekly Light,* August 31, 1945: 1.

317. **"Nichols Field."** The worksite and airport were retaken by the Allies in February 1945. Today the facility is known as Manila Ninoy Aquino International Airport, commonly referred to as Manila International Airport. "Nichols Field," Pacific Wrecks, https://pacificwrecks.com/airfields/philippines/nichols/; "History of Manila Ninoy Aquino International Airport," https://www.mnl-airport.com/history

Chapter 17: A Time to Heal

318. **the morning light nearly blinds the young man.** Joe recounted this detail specifically. Estate archives.

319. **he will never see Shipley again.** Joe tried to locate Shipley several times after the war, without success. Estate archives.

320. **"so we can see what we've got here."** The hospital-staff dialogue is verbatim from Joe's notes. Estate archives.

321. **"your recovery will take time."** In Joe's first letter home to his mother (September 16, 1945), he mentioned he'd been told it would probably be "three or four months" until he could walk again. Estate archives.

322. **"Lots of [bad] stuff happened to the civilians."** For a horrific and in-depth treatment of the unrestrained and indiscriminate atrocities that occurred during the battle for Manila, see Scott, *Rampage*. Military Legal Resources has archived the full postwar trial of General Tomoyuki Yamashita, who was responsible for the Japanese army in the Philippines toward the end of the war; found guilty of his troops' atrocities, he was sentenced to death, and hanged in 1946. https://www.loc.gov/rr/frd/Military_Law/Yamashita _trial.html

323. **"I have no one to be happy *with*."** Verbatim from Joe's notes, estate archives.

324. **his first letter since being released.** All letters home are verbatim. Estate archives.

325. **"about 26 men left in my company out of 183."** All material in Joe's letters is quoted verbatim. Presumably Joe is referring to D Company, 1st Battalion, 31st Infantry, although he had been separated from his company for some time and it's uncertain where he might have received this information so early after the war's end. According to 31st Infantry records, 23 D Company men were killed in action or died of wounds during WWII, and another 71 died in captivity (*Lowe, 31st Infantry Regiment*, 436–446), equaling 94 dead out of 183 men in the company. Joe may be counting those wounded in action as well.

326. **the questions he asks of Providence.** I am grateful to writer John Eldredge for articulating the core of the *reversal concept*, and I've included the idea here because it feels indicative of the overall tone of Joe's later years, as articulated by himself and by the people I interviewed about him. Joe wrote about his surprise meeting with Perpetua at Nichols Field haltingly and even paradoxically: "A true love story that is both warm yet heartbreaking.... It still haunts yet warms me to this day.... I lived each and every one of these events.... This was my education, my introduction to the ways of the world." The actions and dialogue in this chapter are as Joe described them in his notes. Estate archives.

327. **"You have always been in my heart."** Joe writes, "For the next few days, [Perpetua] came every morning. We would talk and hold hands. She told me how she had prayed every day for my safety, and how her prayers had been answered. She talked of her job, and about her young boy, and how handsome and sweet he was. She was excited about going to nursing school. I would lay back and listen and gaze into her lovely brown eyes. Just having her so close gave my soul a cleansing. It suddenly dawned on me: I was wanted. She said as soon as I got on my feet, we could start doing things together and planning our future. She was always smiling and happy.... Each time she had to leave it was a tearful goodbye on her part." Estate archives.

328. **time will change everything.** The details about Joe's travel itinerary and his feelings during the trip home come from a manuscript that Joe had promised to write about his postwar years. He wrote seven pages of a rough draft before he died, and many of his new stories are told more than once therein with slight variations, as if he was trying out various ways of beginning the manuscript. Estate archives.

329. **soldiers arriving from the Pacific Theater.** Some 73,000 patients from the Pacific Theater alone were treated at Letterman Army Hospital in 1945. "Letterman General Hospital," National Park Service. https://www.nps.gov /places/000/letterman-general-hospital.htm

330. **a Western Union telegram.** Joe sent this message to his mother from Letterman, saying he was home. Estate archives.

331. **exhausted and emotionally drained.** From the partial manuscript Joe wrote about his postwar experiences. Estate archives.

Joe, age ninety

332. **Hobbling off the train on my crutches.** Joe recalls that he did not want to be carried off the train on a stretcher, so he "hobbled down the platform using [his] crutches." Estate archives.

333. **marry Perpetua.** Joe vowed that he would someday write an entire book about Perpetua, once observing that her story "is now a work in progress. Hers is a heartbreaking yet warm and loving story. It has me doing a lot of soul searching and is emotionally hard for me to write. I hope to have it completed soon." Before his death in 2017, he ended up writing just seven pages about her, mostly about his thoughts on his way home from the Philippines in 1945. Her last name was never revealed, nor was any further information about her ever divulged beyond what is included in this book.

334. **with many conflicted thoughts.** In private writings, Joe describes his feelings on the hospital plane home: "My morale had hit bottom. I never dreamed

that going home would hit me this way. My heart and mind was still back in Manila. I remember running scenarios through my brain on what I should've done, or what I could do, or I would do concerning Perpetua. I am wracked with guilt. I lay on my stretcher with my face turned toward the window, and my eyes again well with tears." Estate archives.

335. **that only keeps hurting you.** I am grateful to Holocaust survivor Dr. Edith Eva Eger for expounding upon this idea. When Dr. Eger was sixteen, her parents were killed by the Nazis and she was sent to Auschwitz. Upon her liberation, she came to the United States and became a psychologist. In her book *The Choice,* she describes her decision late in life to return to Germany, visit Auschwitz, and forgive her former tormentors. While staying at Berchtesgaden, Hitler's hideout in the Alps, she wrote: "I stood on the site of Hitler's former home and forgave him. This had nothing to do with Hitler. It was something I did for me. I was letting go, releasing the part of myself that had spent most of my life exerting the mental and spiritual energy to keep Hitler in chains. As long as I was holding on to that rage, I was in chains with him, locked in the damaging past, locked in my grief. To forgive is to grieve—for what happened, for what didn't happen—and to give up the need for a different past. To accept life as it was and as it is. I do not of course mean that it was acceptable for Hitler to murder six million people. Just that it happened, and I do not want that fact to destroy the life that I clung to and fought for against all odds." Dr. Edith Eva Eger, *The Choice,* Scribner, 2017: 212.

336. **It is so much easier to be forgiving than to harbor a gutful of hate.** This line is verbatim from a 2006 email sent by Joe to his friend Frank Aldridge.

337. **worked my brain over and straightened my butt out.** This phrase is verbatim from Joe's notes relating his experiences in the psych ward. Everybody who knew Joe in his later years describes his remarkable ability to forgive. He had truly put the past behind him. Author interviews with family members and neighbors, estate archives.

338. **pilgrimage back to the Philippines.** Joe described this trip, very briefly, to several family members. Little is known about the trip or his response except that he found Perpetua's grave marker, inquired about their son, and found out he too was deceased. Joe's close friend Tom Zmugg said that Joe mentioned Perpetua only once or twice to him, and that he had simply said, "She was the first meaningful relationship I ever had." Zmugg said Joe learned about his son's passing from a priest in Manila; describing Perpetua as "upstanding and stellar," the priest confirmed that she had indeed become a nurse. Interview with the author, 2020. Joe's friends Richard and Michele Shirley said that Perpetua "was the love of his life." They confirmed that Marilyn was understanding of Joe's trip back to the Philippines—and that

Joe said of Marilyn's response to the trip, "She's an understanding person." Interviews with the author, 2020.

339. **Schow-Donnelly Award.** The wording on the September 26, 2006, notice of Joe's Schow-Donnelly Award for Service Before Self reads, "You were selected…because of your selfless devotion to duty and tireless work in bringing to the public forefront the plight of all POW/MIA servicemen and women." The award was named for Lieutenant Colonel K. C. Schow Jr., USAF (Ret.), and Major Michael Connelly, USAF (Ret.). Past recipients include Arizona Cardinal and Army Ranger Pat Tillman (who died fighting in Afghanistan in 2004), Ross Perot, and baseball legend Curt Schilling. Estate archives.

340. **feeling so down with Marilyn gone.** A number of Joe's friends in Sun City described how Joe spiraled downward in his last year. He and Marilyn had been married for fifty-nine years (1956–2015).

341. **I had tears in my eyes.** Joe's close friends, Richard and Michele Shirley, reported this. Interview with the author, 2020.

342. **The guy who was supposed to have died…my ankle was crushed.** This section comes verbatim from Joe's interview with Tom Zmugg, Sun City Grand Armed Forces Group, 2016.

343. **I searched and struggled.** Joe's spiritual transformation is as he described it to Steve Graig. Interview with the author, 2020.

344. **laid things out plain and simple.** The preacher was Dr. Charles Stanley — senior pastor of First Baptist Church, Atlanta, Georgia — and his TV show was *In Touch with Dr. Charles Stanley.* https://web.archive.org/web/201 00819145457/http://www.intouch.org/about/about-dr.-charles-stanley

345. **Only God keeps you going.** Line is verbatim from a postwar poem of Joe's. Estate archives.

346. **Once I was bitter and untrusting….** Section is verbatim from an email of Joe's to his friend Frank Aldridge, 2006. Estate archives.

347. **Several years ago….** Entire section verbatim. Ibid., estate archives.

348. **change for the better.** Joe's seven bulleted "new values" are verbatim from a poem of his. Estate archives.

349. **came back with a stack of letters.** Joe apparently disposed of Perpetua's letters, regrettably, because none of them exist in his files. The only known correspondence that exists between them is a copy of the final note that Joe wrote in the Nichols Field hospital. It reads, in part: "My dear, sweet Perpetua. My hand is trembling as I write this. My heart is so full of love for you and always will be. These last few days with you have brought me back to life. You are so loved…. My heart says stay here with you, but it is being overruled by my conscience…. Please forgive me if you can, but I must go home to my loved ones. They have prayed, like you, for my safe return….

When I am well and able, I'll come back to you, and we'll share our lifetime together." Estate archives.

350. **You'll only hurt yourself....** Section is verbatim from an essay of Joe's, 2007. Estate archives.

351. **I've lived a charmed life. I have no complaints.** Verbatim. Estate archives. Joe elaborates on this in an interview with John General ("Shore Talk," October 25, 2000) archived at https://www.youtube.com/watch?v=wOcg4 Ufh39g&feature=youtu.be

352. **the supreme sacrifice.** Of the thirty-one men in Joe's recruit platoon who fought in the war, twenty-one had perished by war's end, most as prisoners of the Japanese. Schow-Donnelly Award press release, "Voices Take Flight." Estate archives.

353. **I'm looking toward my burial ground with no fear.** Verbatim from Joe's notes, 2002. Estate archives.

354. **we don't get this world for long.** Joe died on June 24, 2017, at the age of ninety-one. He is buried at Arlington National Cemetery.

About the Author

Marcus Brotherton is a *New York Times* bestselling author and coauthor dedicated to writing books that inspire heroics, promote empathy, and encourage noble living. Among his commendations is the Christopher Award, given for literature that "affirms the highest values of the human spirit."

Notable solo projects include *Shifty's War, A Company of Heroes, We Who Are Alive and Remain,* and *Blaze of Light,* the authorized biography of Medal of Honor recipient Gary Beikirch.

Notable collaborations include books with the elite WWII paratroopers featured in HBO's *Band of Brothers* miniseries, the elite WWII Marines featured in HBO's *The Pacific,* quadruple amputee and Afghan combat veteran SSG Travis Mills, Oscar-nominated actor and foundation CEO Gary Sinise, and the legendary Lt. Buck Compton, who prosecuted Sirhan Sirhan for the murder of Bobby Kennedy.

Born in 1968 in Canada, Marcus earned a bachelor's degree from Multnomah University in Portland, Oregon, and a master's degree from Biola University in Los Angeles, where he graduated with high honors.

He and his wife have three children and live in the Pacific Northwest.

MarcusBrotherton.com